Issues in the Social Sciences: 11

Series Editor: Katherine Harrison

Pornographies:
Critical Positions

Issues in the Social Sciences

Titles in the Issues in the Social Sciences series are published periodically. The peer-reviewed series presents current academic research into contemporary social issues in an accessible and engaging style that is designed to immerse researchers and students alike in active debates in the Social Sciences.

Editorial Advisory Board
Eric Allison, *The Guardian*, UK
Lisa Blackman, Goldsmiths, University of London, UK
Stephen Edgell, University of Salford, UK
Rosalind Gill, City, University of London, UK
Graeme Gilloch, Lancaster University, UK
Dan Goodley, University of Sheffield, UK
Jane Kilby, University of Salford, UK
Clement Macintyre, University of Adelaide, Australia
Ross McGarry, University of Liverpool, UK
Catherine McGlynn, University of Huddersfield, UK
Caroline Miles, University of Manchester, UK
Andrew Mycock, University of Huddersfield, UK
Sophia Price, Leeds Beckett University, UK
Jayne Raisborough, Leeds Beckett University, UK
Stuart Shields, University of Manchester, UK
Jonathan Tonge, University of Liverpool, UK
Imogen Tyler, Lancaster University, UK

Pornographies:
Critical Positions

Edited by
**Katherine Harrison
and Cassandra A. Ogden**

University of Chester Press

First published 2018
by University of Chester Press
University of Chester
Parkgate Road
Chester CH1 4BJ

Printed and bound in the UK by the
LIS Print Unit
University of Chester
Cover designed by the
LIS Graphics Team
University of Chester

Editorial material
© University of Chester, 2018
Foreword, introduction and individual chapters
© the respective authors, 2018

All Rights Reserved
No part of this publication may be reproduced, stored in a retrieval system or transmitted in any form or by any means without the prior permission of the copyright owner, other than as permitted by current UK copyright legislation or under the terms and conditions of a recognised copyright licensing scheme

A catalogue record for this book is available
from the British Library

ISBN 978-1-908258-32-8

CONTENTS

Series Editor's Preface   vii

Acknowledgements   ix

Contributors   x

Introduction   1
Katherine Harrison and Cassandra A. Ogden

Chapter One   23
Politics and Ethical Conflict in a Social Movement:
Pornography and the 'Sex Wars' in (Lesbian) Feminism
Christian Klesse

Chapter Two   49
Women's Pornography
Feona Attwood

Chapter Three   70
Postfeminist Sexpertise on the 'Porn and Men Issue':
A Transnational Perspective
Laura Favaro

Chapter Four   96
Revolting Women: Performing the 'New Explicit'
Emma L. E. Rees

Chapter Five   116
'*Slutty & Sluttier*, Starring …': The Rise of the
Postfeminist Porn Star in Contemporary Celebrity
Culture
Camilla A. Sears

Pornographies

Chapter Six — 141
Sexing Up Post-War Japanese Cinema: Looking at 1960s/1970s 'Pinky Violence' Films
Laura Treglia

Chapter Seven — 167
'Slutburgers' and Sexual Subjects? The Re-Sexualisation of Women in Fast-Food Advertising and Culinary Culture
Natalie Jovanovski

Chapter Eight — 193
The Aestheticisation of the Real Body in Politics and Pornography
Tim Gregory

Chapter Nine — 220
Gay Porn, Ink
Joseph Brennan

Chapter Ten — 242
Barebacking and Historical Time
Ricky Varghese

Chapter Eleven — 264
Pricked, Probed and Possessed: Medical Pornography and the Birth of the Fetish Clinic
Brenda S. Gardenour Walter

Chapter Twelve — 287
"I'm Going to Stump You": Fetish, Confession and the Transformative Potential of the Erotic Crip Body
Krista K. Miranda

Index — 308

SERIES EDITOR'S PREFACE

Pornographies: Critical Positions – the eleventh volume in the *Issues in the Social Sciences* (*ISS*) series – constitutes an important opportunity to explore an area that, despite being well established territory for Social Sciences researchers, is still considered risky business for undergraduate teaching. The chapters in the volume investigate both debates about pornography and pornographic media texts themselves, providing readers with insightful context for, and well-chosen examples of, the sexually explicit and the critical tools with which to make sense of it. The collection will thus be of great interest and utility to readers encountering the study of pornography for the first time, and to lecturers and researchers committed to establishing porn studies as a vital area of inquiry for scholars at all levels.

This volume is my final contribution to *ISS* as Series Editor, having left the University of Chester after nearly ten years in autumn 2017 for a new position at Leeds Beckett University. During my tenure as Series Editor, I relied on departmental colleagues to act as editors and, in some cases, contributors to the *ISS* volumes. I would like to take this opportunity to express my particular and heartfelt thanks to former colleagues in the Department of Social and Political Science at the University of Chester for their assistance: Karen Corteen, Jonathon Louth, Ross McGarry, Sharon Morley, Cassie Ogden, Alessandro Pratesi, Ben Revi, Paul Taylor, Steve Wakeman and Paul Wagg, all of whom undertook editing duties or wrote individual chapters between 2013 and 2018, and, together, produced four excellent, well received volumes: *Corporeality: The Body and Society* (2013); *Work and Society: Spaces, Places and Identities* (2014); *Edges of Identity: The Production of Neoliberal Subjectivities* (2017); and *Pornographies: Critical Positions* (2018). I would also like to thank the external colleagues who have provided detailed, anonymous feedback during the preparation of this and other volumes in the *ISS* series since I re-launched it as a peer-reviewed enterprise in 2013. Their thoughtful and instructive comments have helped to ensure the high quality of each of the books. Similarly, the seventeen members of the Editorial Advisory Board have given their time to support the series and, when called upon, have assisted generously with calls for papers, editorial advice, feedback and ordering copies of the books for their universities' libraries. As I have observed before in the pages of the ISS books, the series would not be possible without the hard work and professionalism of Sarah Griffiths, Managing Editor of the University of Chester Press. Thanks to her for hours of copy-editing, formatting, liaising with editors and contributors, organising publicity and sales and, no doubt, many other tasks essential to the production of the books. Finally, it is necessary to recognise and thank the Department of Social and Political Science and the University of Chester Press for continuing to support, staff and finance the *ISS*. It is rare for an academic department to maintain its own book series, and rarer still for a so-called 'new' university to sustain an in-house independent, not-for-profit academic press, especially one that functions with such professionalism, inclusivity and commitment to high standards. Viva *Issues in the Social Sciences*! Viva the University of Chester Press!

Katherine Harrison
Series Editor
March 2018

ACKNOWLEDGEMENTS

Katherine Harrison and Cassandra A. Ogden would like to thank and acknowledge the support of a number of people and organisations. Our gratitude is due to colleagues and students in the Department of Social and Political Science at the University of Chester, particularly Alessandro Pratesi, Joe Rigby and others who were integral to the organisation of the conference 'Pornography' in March 2013, which first generated the idea for this volume of essays. We would also like to sincerely thank all of the contributors to this volume, who bore with us patiently during the extended period of its preparation for publication. Special thanks are due to Ben Sears, who kindly provided assistance in relation to Camilla A. Sears's chapter. Finally, and as usual, many thanks are directed to Sarah Griffiths, Managing Editor of the University of Chester Press, who, with dedication and expertise, helped steer this book to publication.

CONTRIBUTORS

Feona Attwood is Professor of Cultural Studies, Communication and Media at Middlesex University, UK. She is the author of *Sex Media* (2017), Editor of *porn.com: Making Sense of Online Pornography* (2010) and *Mainstreaming Sex: The Sexualization of Western Culture* (2009), and Co-Editor of *The Routledge Companion to Media, Sex and Sexuality* (2017) and *Controversial Images* (2012). She is Founding Co-Editor of the *Porn Studies* journal and Co-Editor of the *Sexualities* journal.

Joseph Brennan is Lecturer of Media and Communications at the University of Sydney, Australia, where he was awarded his PhD. He has published extensively on gay pornography in leading scholarly journals, including: *European Journal of Cultural Studies*, *Journal of Homosexuality*, *Porn Studies*, *Sexuality & Culture* and *Psychology & Sexuality*, where he also serves as editorial board member. In addition to his work on gay pornography, he is active across the fields of fan and celebrity studies, having published in such venues as: *Arthuriana*, *Celebrity Studies*, *Continuum*, *Disability & Society*, *Discourse, Context & Media*, *International Journal of Cultural Studies*, *M/C Journal*, *Media International Australia*, *Popular Communication* and *Sexualities*. He is Guest Editor of the *Journal of Fandom Studies'* thematic issue on 'queerbaiting' – to be released in 2018 – and is also compiling an edited book collection on the topic for a university press.

Laura Favaro is a sociologist and teacher. Her PhD thesis (City, University of London) examined women's online magazines, drawing on interviews with producers, editorial and user-generated content. Currently she is a Research Fellow for the Spanish National Research Plan Project of Excellence entitled 'The resignification of the woman victim on social network sites'. Her interests include feminist theory and methodology, gender and sexuality, and media, communication and culture. She has published in English and Spanish, and her work has appeared in books such as *Aesthetic Labour: Rethinking Beauty Politics in Neoliberalism* (eds. Elias, Gill, & Scharff, 2017) and journals including *Feminist Media Studies*, *Australian Feminist Studies* and the *Journal of Gender Studies*.

Brenda S. Gardenour Walter holds a PhD in Medieval History from Boston University, USA. Her research examines the role of Aristotelian discourse, learned medicine and scholastic theology in the construction of alterity and the continued influence of medieval otherness on the horror genre. Her most recent publications examine the multivalent relationships between cultural constructions of the body, architectural theory and the natural world. She is Associate Professor of History at the Saint Louis College of Pharmacy.

Tim Gregory is a practitioner, theorist and Lecturer in Art at UNSW Sydney, Australia. He has published on the intersection of pornography with politics, colonisation and technology. His current research project is on the role of pornography in 'authenticating' white futurity in settler colonies. He has exhibited at the Art Gallery of New South Wales, the Perth Institute for Contemporary Art and the Arsenale in Venice. He is the Founding Co-Editor of *ON Journal* and recipient of the UNSW Vice-Chancellor's teaching award.

Katherine Harrison is Senior Lecturer in Media and Cultural Studies at Leeds Beckett University, UK. Between 2008 and 2017, she was Senior Lecturer in Sociology at the University of Chester, UK, and Series Editor of the *Issues in the Social Sciences* book series, published by the University of Chester Press. Her research interests lie in visual cultures, particularly iconic twentieth-century photographs. She is also collaborating on research projects concerning knitting, postfeminism and domestic cultures (with Cassandra A. Ogden) and 'poverty porn' television.

Natalie Jovanovski is a Postdoctoral Research Fellow in Sociology at Swinburne University of Technology, Australia. Her research areas include feminist politics, theory and activism, the gendering of food culture, and food insecurity. Her most recent publication is *Digesting Femininities: The Feminist Politics of Contemporary Food Culture*, published by Palgrave Macmillan in 2017.

Christian Klesse is Reader in the Department of Sociology at Manchester Metropolitan University, UK. Christian studied Social and Economic History, Anthropology, Politics, Contemporary German Literature and Gender and Ethnicity Studies in Germany and the UK and holds a PhD in Sociology from the University of Essex. His research interests lie in the fields of gender and sexual politics. He has conducted research into non-monogamy and polyamory, transnational LGBTQ activism and Queer Film Festivals in Europe. His work is interdisciplinary and – often – collaborative. He is author of *The Spectre of Promiscuity. Gay Male and Bisexual Non-monogamies and Polyamories* (Routledge, 2007).

Krista K. Miranda, a US-based interdisciplinary scholar in Gender, Sexuality, Disability and Performance, received her PhD in Performance Studies at New York University in 2015. From 2016–2017, she was a Visiting Lecturer in Dance at Middlebury College. She joins the Women's, Gender and Sexuality Studies programme at Northeastern University as their 2017–2018 Visiting Scholar in Disability and Performance, where she will complete her manuscript, *Playing with Your*

Contributors

Parts: Dismantling Bodily Wholeness through Queer and Crip Performance. Her work can be found in *The Oxford Handbook on Dance and Theater* and *Women & Performance: A Journal of Feminist Theory*.

Cassandra A. Ogden is Senior Lecturer in Sociology at Liverpool John Moores University. Her PhD thesis explored the experiences of children with Inflammatory Bowel Disease, which fuelled her interest in exploring the social disgust of particular bodies and the stigma people face due to perceived differences of the body. Much of Cassandra's current work utilises a critical disability studies perspective but she has also published and co-published on disability hate crime, childhood illness experiences, the social and legal responses to smoking in public and its impact upon the incarcerated, quality of life research, the narrative inquiry technique and the use of food banks in Cheshire.

Emma L. E. Rees is Professor of Literature and Gender Studies at the University of Chester, UK, where she is Director of the Institute of Gender Studies. In 2013 her second book, *The Vagina: A Literary and Cultural History* was published, and a revised, paperback edition came out in 2015. She has published widely in the field of gender and representation, was the inaugural Political Writer in Residence at Gladstone's Library, and is currently working on a monograph that looks at feminism's fractures. She runs the biennial international, interdisciplinary Talking Bodies conference, and is Editor of *Talking Bodies: Interdisciplinary Perspectives on Embodiment, Gender, and Identity* (Palgrave, 2017).

Camilla A. Sears was awarded her PhD in Criminology at Simon Fraser University, Canada, in 2011. Between 2012 and 2017 she was Assistant Professor in the Faculty of Arts at Thompson Rivers University, Canada, where she taught courses in Criminology and Sociology. Camilla's research focusses on the impact of neoliberal policies on the regulation of sex and the body, as well as Reality TV and postfeminist media cultures. Her articles have been published in *Feminist Media Studies* and *Genders*.

Laura Treglia is currently an independent researcher in Gender Studies and Film with a special focus on Japanese society and culture. She holds a PhD in Gender Studies (SOAS, University of London) and has previously worked as a lecturer at the University of Chester (UK). Her main research interests include Japanese popular culture, (feminist) film theory, genre and cult cinema, girl studies, the construction of class, gender, sexuality and violence in films and television worldwide. Forthcoming chapters in edited volumes and journal articles address issues of representation of sex, gender and bodies on screen, the dynamics of power and the gaze, revenge and violence in Japanese grindhouse films from the early 1970s.

Ricky Varghese received his PhD in Sociology of Education from the University of Toronto in 2014. He serves as an Advisory Editor for *Drain: A Journal of Contemporary Art and Culture* and has been the Lead Editor for two of its issues, "Ruin" (2014) and "AIDS and Memory" (2016). He is presently preparing an edited collection of essays for the University of Regina Press, *Sex at the Limit: Essays on Barebacking* with an afterword by Tim Dean and has been invited to edit a special issue of the journal *Porn Studies*, "Porn on the Couch: Sex, Psychoanalysis, and Screen Cultures/Memories." In addition, he is trained professionally as a social worker, with Bachelor's and Master's degrees in Social Work, and runs a private practice as a psychotherapist in downtown Toronto. He is also a candidate in training at the Toronto Institute of Psychoanalysis.

INTRODUCTION

Katherine Harrison and *Cassandra A. Ogden*

Pornography has long been at the centre of passionate debates surrounding the limits of sexual freedom, as well as at the heart of moral panics concerning its potential to corrupt individuals and society. For every argument that highlights the degrading, oppressive or harmful effects of pornography (particularly for women, though there is currently increasing public concern about online porn addiction for men and the effects of pornography on children and young people) (Dworkin, 1981; Dines, 2011), there is another that contends that pornography is merely a representation of sex with which people can choose freely whether or not to engage, and which may even provide improvements in sexual rights, intimate relationships or for individual health (see, for example, Arrowsmith, 2011; *Men's Health*, 2012; *Telegraph* Men, 2015). Likewise, while many observers understand pornography to be an intrinsically patriarchal medium, produced by a voracious sex industry that exploits women's bodies routinely for heterosexual male gratification and profit (Boyle, 2010), there are supplementary arguments which insist that pornography does not necessarily always reproduce this conventional gender/power dynamic and can instead function as a radical site where heterosexual female and minority sexual and gender identities, non-normative bodies and queer sexual practices can be played out, with the perfomers' agency, for the pleasure of audiences that are otherwise ignored by or subsumed within mainstream, heteronormative discursive constructions of sex (see McNair, 2002; McNair, 2012; Taormino, Parreñas Shimizu, Penley, & Miller-Young, 2013; Mowlabocus, 2016). To complicate the picture further, with the exception of pornography that evidences criminal acts (such as child sex abuse or 'revenge porn'), porn today is understood less as something prurient that happens out of sight in the shadows and more as a highly visible aspect of mainstream contemporary social life, with pornographic imagery and tropes permeating the everyday as they migrate from specifically designated adult entertainment to commonplace visual culture and routine intimate practices that constitute embodied gender norms and relations (McNair, 2002; Levy, 2005; Paasonen, Nikunen, & Saarenmaa, 2007; Attwood, 2009; Boyle, 2010). Pornography is, therefore, a site of perpetual, sometimes vehement, debate and is a subject ripe for academic inquiry. It is for this reason that *Pornographies: Critical Positions* draws together a range of perspectives on porn, including those of established porn scholars and new voices, to provide a snap-shot of current critical work in porn studies. This volume raises questions and provides insights into both what porn does and what we, as scholars, can do productively with porn.

As outlined above, debates about pornography are predicated on differing conceptualisations of what porn is – smut versus representation, oppression versus empowerment, harm versus pleasure, furtive private activity versus public cultural norm – and where it is located – specialist subscription websites versus what McNair (2002) has described as an everyday, mainstream "pornosphere" (p. 38). As such, a singular definition of porn risks reproducing a misleading and reductive "pornonormativity" (Attwood, 2010a, p. 237) that fails to account for the expansive, nuanced reality of pornography and porn cultures today. Instead of attempting to define pornography, then, this volume reflects and recognises the variety of types of pornography in circulation and the manifold interpretations of these by referring to pornograph*ies* in the plural: a diverse, polysemic assemblage of pornographic texts and sites that are produced in different material and

Introduction

cultural contexts with distinctive authorial intentions and variable effects, and consumed by heterogeneous audiences within particular interpretive frameworks and with mixed subjective responses. The study of pornographies understood thus provides valuable opportunities for critical engagement to illuminate what they tell us about a range of important areas of concern within the parameters of the Social Sciences, Arts and Humanities: sex, sexualities, gender, bodies, identities, cultures, intimate relationships, propriety, health, representations, normativity, queerness, discrimination, agency, memory, consumption practices and more.

This book aims to introduce readers to the academic study of, and debates about and within, pornographies in a number of their most interesting and varied instantiations. The volume cannot claim to be a comprehensive examination of pornography because – just as other collections of academic work on the same subject before it (e.g. Church Gibson, 2004; Williams, 2004; Paasonen et al., 2007; Attwood, 2010b; Boyle, 2010) – such an aspiration is inevitably thwarted by the sheer variety and scope and the fast changing nature of the pornographies that exist. The chapters contained here each engage with an interesting debate about, or debate posed by, pornography, and the volume includes analyses of many specific examples of pornography, predominantly in visual form but also textual discourses that frame and construct our understandings of pornography. The volume takes in mainstream heteronormative and queer porns (the 'gay for pay' scene and amputee porn are objects of analysis, for example), niche fetish cultures (such as 'barebacking', or condomless sex, and medical pornography), video porn, online porn, explicit art (including the work of performance artist Casey Jenkins and experimental documentary maker Vincent Chevalier), and the broader "pornification" of mass culture in sites such as cookery shows and advice given to women via online discussion boards by 'sexpert' agony aunts (Paasonen et al., 2007, p. 1). It is intended that this diversity both reflects (to the extent that it is possible) a range of extant pornographies which readers may not have hitherto encountered, and furnishes readers with carefully explicated knowledge of the significances of these cultural products. In so doing, the volume follows the advice of Henry Jenkins (2004) who writes that "it is irresponsible to discuss pornography in the abstract, in the absence of concrete images. Without specifics, the debate becomes too easy" (p. 3). In other words, an academic book about porn that does not include detailed descriptions of the material under scrutiny (sometimes in the form of visual images), as well as intelligent analysis, risks divesting the arguments of specific meaning and, at worse, prompting readers to "imagine what they want to see" and thus reinforcing, rather than challenging or extending, pre-existing assumptions (Jenkins, 2004, p. 3).

For readers new to porn studies, it is useful to provide a very brief overview of the main trends in scholarship in this area over the last twenty or so years. There is not space in this Introduction to rehearse the entire history of intellectual responses to pornographies, which began in earnest during the mid-twentieth century as second-wave feminist activists and scholars identified the porn industry as a powerful node in the apparatus of the patriarchal oppression of women (see, for example, Dworkin, 1981; MacKinnon, 1993). The academic debate about pornography in the contemporary period is as enduring as it is multifaceted and scholarly considerations of porn today are correspondingly reflective of a variety of foci and positions, some of which remain deeply polarised. For example, following in the radical tradition of second-wave feminist stances towards pornography in the twentieth century, the US American feminist writer Gail Dines (2011) argues

Introduction

strongly in her book *Pornland: How Porn Has Hijacked Our Sexuality* that hard-core pornography is a social harm and "serious public health issue" (p. xiii) with dangerous effects that are "played out on people who never agreed to participate" (p. ix). For Dines (2011) – recalling the work of the most famous twentieth-century anti-porn feminist, Andrea Dworkin (1981) – pornography represents and encourages "A kind of sex that is debased, dehumanized, formulaic, and generic ... the result of an industrial product created by those who get excited not by bodily contact but by market penetration and profits" (p. x). So influential is porn on our sexual behaviours and attitudes, according to Dines (2011) that pornographers have effectively "set up camp in [our] sexual identity" (p. xi). Dines sees this as a particularly dangerous state of affairs for women and young people and is critical of scholars whom she considers engage with pornographic materials as regular cultural texts without always acknowledging their special harms (as cited in Cadwalladr, 2013).

Contrasted with this perspective, the editors of *The Feminist Porn Book* (Taormino et al., 2013) set out to examine what they describe as "a thriving feminist porn movement" powered by feminist porn directors, performers, educators and academics (p. 9) and dedicated to producing and/or interrogating the potential for porn to generate pleasure for women, both straight and queer. Explicitly inclusive of the voices of female pornographers and porn performers, Taormino et al. (2013) challenge the view that pornography can be generalised as a medium that exploits and harms women. Similarly, Clarissa Smith (2007) has examined women as consumers of pornography and provides rich empirical data to support the understanding of porn as a medium with which some women engage pleasurably.

Pornographies

To complicate this latter perspective of pornographic female empowerment, influential critiques of "sexual subjectification" (Gill, 2009), which highlight the equation of individual and consumer choice with emancipation under patriarchal neoliberal capitalism, have cast doubt on porn's status as a route to free and equal sexual citizenship for women, gay people and other non-normative sexual subjects. According to Rosalind Gill (2009), the contemporary tendency to conceptualise women as knowing and enthusiastic sexual subjects is part of a neoliberal reconstruction of femininity in the figure of "the sexually autonomous heterosexual young woman who plays with her sexual power and is for ever 'up for it'". Far from being real sexual emancipation, individual women's embrace of pornography (as either producers or consumers) might be better understood as a retrograde step for feminism; an ideological manifestation of postfeminism that misleads women into identifying continued sexual subjugation as empowerment in ways that benefit patriarchal neoliberal capitalism, not least in terms of women's participation as producers and consumers in the sex-entertainment market. As Stephen Maddison (2010) puts it, "neoliberalism offers us subjectivities and choices that propose new sexual freedoms, yet these foreclose sexuality to the sphere of economic enfranchisement" (p. 25). Nevertheless, recognising the expansion of the repertoire of porn beyond the heteronormative mainstream and beyond the paradigm of patriarchal oppression has allowed theorists such as Richard Dyer (2004) and Sharif Mowlabocus (2007; 2016) to provide valuable insights into queer pornographies and the sexual cultures that surround them. For theorists such as these, queer porn is a space of visibility and identity for sexual minorities that have traditionally been marginalised. Recent studies of porn have opened up the arena to subcultural and queer pornographies,

Introduction

amateur and gonzo porn, netporn, and porn in many of its seemingly infinite varieties (see, for example, Biasin, Maina, & Zecca, 2014). Such studies set out to consider the new forms of pornography that have appeared since pornography stopped being understood by scholars as a singular, monolithic 'thing'. While this has opened up a terrain that, as acknowledged above, is impossible to traverse comprehensively, it has subjected pornographies to sustained critical attention from a range of disciplinary and theoretical perspectives and invited consideration of porn's many competing meanings and utilities.

In light of these recent intellectual directions and despite some continuing dissent about studying pornographies, it appears that the most vehement years of what the film scholar Linda Williams (1989) has described as the "anti-anti" debate (p. 23) – the reductive *anti*-pornography versus *anti*-censorship-of-pornography argument – may now be behind us, at least in academic circles (as discussed by Christian Klesse in Chapter 1 of this volume). Indeed, the establishment of the interdisciplinary journal *Porn Studies* (Routledge) by Feona Attwood (who also contributes to this book in Chapter 2) and Clarissa Smith in 2014, suggests that pornography is now widely considered to be an important focus of critical attention and attracts enough new research to sustain a dedicated forum for debate. In contemporary scholarly life, it is generally accepted that the study of pornographies has ceased to be a controversial intellectual pursuit, although it still comes with special challenges, pitfalls and highly vocal critics (see, for example, Cadwalladr's (2013) news report on the criticisms and petition levelled against Attwood and Smith on news of the launch of *Porn Studies*). This collection of essays contributes to the tradition of studying and teaching pornography as a site of scholarly interest, rather than as a problem to be resisted or kept out of the curriculum. However, in compiling this volume, we, as editors, are keenly aware of the special status that pornography still has within the Academy and in the minds of the public at large. Despite the continuing existence of pornography, the enduring moral panic about it, and a plethora of careful and insightful academic analyses of sexually explicit material (some of which are cited above), there is still reluctance in universities to teach porn studies as part of undergraduate degree curricula. The analysis of pornography has not fully filtered down into the teaching syllabi of British universities, beyond a few specialist modules. This continuing reticence about actively studying porn as a core component of disciplines like Sociology and Media and Cultural Studies at undergraduate level is due, perhaps, to a combination of practical considerations (how many lecturers and students would feel comfortable watching pornographic films together in class, for example?) and institutional wariness about the reputational damage – dubbed "'porn prof' scandals" by the British tabloid press (Jones & Carlin, 2010, p. 181) – likely to be incurred by seeming to condone the exposure of young people to hard-core sexual material and fetish cultures. As Mark Jones and Gerry Carlin (2010) found when their classes on pornography became an object of scrutiny by the news media, teaching and researching pornography in the context of a modern university is a salient reminder that "the alleged ubiquity of pornography in the contemporary environment is in fact continually and vigorously resisted by multiple administrative, legal, moral and technological constraints" (p. 177). Likewise, film scholar Linda Williams (1989) and media theorist Henry Jenkins (2004) have written instructive accounts of their experiences of the practicalities and pitfalls of teaching porn within formal university settings. Notwithstanding all these cautionary tales, it is our aim with this volume to open up porn studies to new, young scholars in order to show how pornography might be

Introduction

encountered through an academic lens and considered in relation to the new insights it offers into very many of the key areas that constitute the daily intellectual diet of the undergraduate Social Sciences and Humanities student. While scholarly studies of pornography have certainly proliferated in the first years of the twenty-first century, the majority of these works have been published as advanced journal articles or as full-length monographs. There have been relatively few recent edited collections of informative, engaging, entry-level writing on pornography designed with a student readership in mind. Linda Williams's (2004) edited collection, *Porn Studies*, is perhaps the exception, though the case studies included in this book may now be less accessible to undergraduate readers who do not remember, for example, the leaking of the infamous Tommy Lee and Pamela Anderson sex tape in 1997. As Williams (2004) argued about her own volume, accessible edited collections of essays like this one reflect and engage with what undergraduate students are no doubt fully aware of: that there has been "a veritable explosion of sexually explicit materials" in recent times and that pornographies have become "fully recognizable fixtures of popular culture" (p. 1), that cannot and should not be ignored at any level of adult social scientific or humanities education.

To open this volume of twelve essays and to contextualise the present-day reconsideration of porn as a source of potential pleasure and empowerment for women and sexual minority groups, Christian Klesse provides an overview of the 'sex wars' (also known as the 'porn wars') that took place within feminist intellectual and activist circles in the UK, USA and elsewhere from the late 1970s until the early 1990s. The sex wars produced strongly polarised positions, which pitted 'anti-porn' feminists (such as Andrea Dworkin) against 'sex-positive' feminists in a battle for making claims to the very meaning of pornography for straight and queer women. Klesse's chapter unpicks the 'for or against' paradigm for debating porn that endured throughout the late twentieth century and mired feminists and others in a stalemate of irreconcilable 'anti-porn' versus 'anti-censorship' views. As Klesse's account shows, this had the result of silencing 'sexually deviant' groups and reinforced dualistic gender divisions. Klesse calls for an understanding of pornography as a diverse arena where gazes are shifting and new possibilities for sexual fulfilment are explored. Pornography for Klesse has fuelled problematic debate that conflates issues regarding males, females and representations of sexual practices and sexualities. He argues that what is needed is a critical debate about pornography that avoids the inflation of pornographic sexual oppression across the whole gender system.

Having provided the historical context underpinning the contentions of pornography within the Academy, particularly within feminist thought, the volume continues with Feona Attwood's essay 'Porn for Women' (Chapter Two). This chapter lays the groundwork for understanding women's complex relationships with pornography. Attwood directs our interest towards the diversity of pornography and the manifold ways in which women and men consume it. The reader is challenged to think about how pornography has the potential to queer sexual desire whilst avoiding dictating what women should do and how to do it. Attwood argues that while many women find pornography degrading, others use it to elicit their own sexual satisfaction. Through her exploration of the diverse consumption of porn, Attwood raises the possibility that pornography – without necessarily being 'feminist' – helps to challenge heteronormative assumptions about sex and about women's sexual desires and behaviours.

Introduction

Gender and the consumption of pornography are the main foci of Laura Favaro's work in Chapter Three, which explores peer responses to women who feel distressed after discovering their male partners' use of pornography. Based on a close analysis of online chat forums linked to women's magazines published in the UK and Spain (but also attracting users from other countries, including the USA, India and several Latin American nations), the chapter examines both peer-to-peer chat and the advice offered by editorial 'sexperts'. The chapter shifts the emphasis away from men's consumption of pornography to women's discussions about it, and how women are taught to cope in relation to pornography. Favaro reveals that, although women's predominant emotion when thinking about male partners' use of porn is distress, the advice that they are offered by online communities of peers and sexperts teaches them to 'resign' themselves to their male partner's porn habits, to consider their negative emotional responses to be a consequence of their own low self-esteem, and/or to transform themselves into 'better' lovers via the incorporation of pornographic costumes and activities into their sexual repertoires. In this chapter, Favaro, therefore, takes a critical approach to postfeminist ideas about female openness to pornography and considers the kinds of gendered sexual pleasures and intimate relational possibilities that are brought to the fore in public chat rooms where pornography is constructed as a problem for women.

Continuing the theme of consumption, with a title taken from porn performer and performance artist Annie Sprinkle's art work, 'Public Cervix Announcement', Emma L. E. Rees in Chapter Four examines representations of the female body and how these are received in instances where women control the production of the images of themselves. Through an exploration of feminist performance artist Casey Jenkins – the so-called 'vaginal knitter' – Rees discusses how her artwork was deemed inappropriately 'explicit', which is of particular interest as the representation is owned by and is the product of the agency of the feminist artist and conveys a woman taking control of her own body to convey meaning and purpose against the conventional 'pornified' representations of women's genitals that are more conventionally produced in patriarchal mainstream pornography. The accusations of pornography levelled at Casey Jenkins are, according to Rees, based on patriarchal conceptions of the vagina as lacking, dirty and perverse. In this chapter, Rees coins the concept of the 'New Explicit' to describe the process of recuperating the sexual objectification of the female body by creating representations that refuse to fit in with patriarchal conceptions of it. This entails women regaining control of and re-possessing their own sexual organs. Crucially, 'New Explicit' self-representation is different to the neoliberal "sexual subjectification" described by Gill (2009) as a way of convincing women to perform their own objectification along conventional pornographic lines. While Jenkins's 'vaginal knitting' and other female performance artists' utilisations of their vaginas in art (e.g. Annie Sprinkle, Carolee Schneemann) might be seen as obscene, they also embody women's autonomy and female-centred sexual explicitness. The lack of acceptance of these representations in a society where male-dominated pornography is tolerated demonstrates the extent to which vaginas have been owned by patriarchy and thus how the concept of the 'explicit' has been constructed to both permit and deny representations of women's bodies depending on authorial gendering.

Explicit female performance is further explored by Camilla A. Sears who reveals the voices of 'postfeminist porn stars' in Chapter Five. These voices are made audible through Sears' analysis of interviews conducted with female porn performers

Introduction

and published in a variety of online public fora. Sears utilises these interviews to understand what female porn performers say about their work and how this ties in with current media discourses that represent the female 'porn star' as empowered and agentic. Sears finds that the interviews tend to reinforce this discourse with many performers discussing repeatedly their enjoyment of their work with reference to 'dream jobs' and work satisfaction, as opposed to engaging in sex work out of desperation or lack of other opportunities for similar remuneration. Mindful that it is wrong to doubt the personal enthusiasm of the interviewees without knowing them personally, Sears instead questions the role that such interviews play in (re)constructing gendered norms and identities in the context of neoliberal sexual subjectification, which has arguably replaced older notions of sexual objectification. Furthermore, Sears demonstrates that, throughout the interviews, the performers simplify the roles of power, gender and sexuality within the heteronormative world of pornography. The chapter argues that current understandings of women's work in pornography lack diversity and that there must be acknowledgement of and spaces for the voices of female performers who do not have the positive experiences that the producers and consumers of porn recognise and approve.

In Chapter Six, Laura Treglia explores a little documented but culturally rich pulp genre of mid-twentieth-century Japanese cinema, 'pinky violence' that featured female nudity and sexual suggestion at a time when women on the Japanese screen were largely represented in traditional passive and domestic terms. Questions regarding possibilities of empowerment and agency amongst women in pornography are therefore paramount as Treglia shows that while some of the soft-core pornographic tropes in the films doubtlessly depend on an objectivising male gaze (Mulvey, 1989), the films also negotiate the changing social, political and sexual positions of women in post-war Japanese society, and may therefore be understood as nascent feminist texts. The action heroines of soft-core 'pinky violence' are understood by Treglia to be far more progressive and empowered than the women represented in more recent Japanese pornographic texts that have been consumed on a global scale. In analysing the 'pinky violence' genre, Treglia critiques claims that Japan has a pornographic culture that depends on the spectacle of passive female bodies and the eroticisation of violence against women, and argues that a better understanding of Japanese pornography requires a fuller knowledge of the post-war socio-political conditions in which the Japanese porn cinema and contemporary Japanese understandings of gender arose.

Chapter Seven recognises the expansion of the "pornosphere" to take account of the mainstreaming of porn that has occupied recent work in porn studies (see McNair, 2002; Paasonen et al., 2007; Attwood, 2009). Focussing on the television and billboard advertising campaigns of the US fast-food giant Carl's Jr., Natalie Jovanovski shows how pornographic motifs have migrated from hard-core pornography into everyday mass culture. Jovanovski argues that the Carl's Jr. emphasis on high calorie, indulgent, so-called 'dirty' food is legitimised via the utilisation of female models and celebrities who seem to derive 'gustatory pleasure' from eating in its advertising. The pornographic motifs of 'hot lesbians', the 'cougar', the 'girl-next-door' and the 'spicy other' are employed by Carl's Jr. to construct sexualised understandings of its food products that arguably challenge the restrictive idea that women should not have hearty appetites but also reproduce unsettling patriarchal, heterosexist and Orientalist assumptions. The chapter exposes the representations of women throughout mainstream culinary

Introduction

culture, such as the British TV cook Nigella Lawson and the Indian-American *Food Network* celebrity Padma Lakshmi, that replicate these same tropes in order to distance women from the traditional understanding of the kitchen as a site of female subordination and instead construct it as a place of female empowerment. Jovanovski argues that while representing women as enjoying food is potentially an empowering alternative to discourses that construct any form of appetite as a masculine characteristic, contemporary food advertising and culinary culture pornifies women's bodies and their relationships with food in unhelpful and reductive ways.

Following the shift in emphasis in the volume to the expanded pornosphere, Chapter Eight turns to an examination of a specific pornographic text that demonstrates considerable political significance, thus illustrating how pornography and the seemingly discrete sphere of women in public life coincide. Tim Gregory examines the pornographic productions that accompanied the rise to prominence of the Alaskan politician Sarah Palin during the Republican Presidential campaign in the USA in 2008. The hard-core pornographic film, *Who's Nailin' Paylin?* (2008), produced by Hustler Video, plays out issues of gender and authenticity in image politics. While the film itself is an unsubtle patriarchal response to a powerful woman's upward political trajectory, Gregory shows that it also sheds light on the tactics used by politicians to present themselves as authentic, while simultaneously performing a contrived political identity to make themselves desirable to the electorate. Gregory conceptualises this political performance in terms of the modernist concept of 'zero design', which enables a suspension of disbelief in obvious artifice. It is this zero design that enables the consumers of pornography to believe that they are viewing 'real' sex while simultaneously understanding it to be a representative performance. Just as *Who's Nailin' Paylin?*

depends on the conceit that the 'real' Sarah Palin is a sexually voracious dominatrix, Sarah Palin's own political performance was characterised by staged 'transgressions' in which she seemingly revealed to the electorate her 'authentic' self. These 'transgressions', which included folksy slips of the tongue to reveal her (inauthentic) working-class origins, and also her infamous euphemistic exhortation to 'drill baby, drill' in a Vice Presidential debate regarding the energy crisis, were part of a strategy to construct Palin's political persona as part 'hockey mom' and part 'MILF' ('Mother I'd Like to Fuck'). Thus, Gregory shows that US American politics – and perhaps global politics in the age of spectacle – depends on the same performative zero design strategies as *Who's Nailin' Paylin?* and that pornography can thus be understood as an important source of critique of contemporary image politics.

In Chapter Nine, Joseph Brennan builds on the volume's theme of authenticity in pornography but also shifts the focus away from heteronormative to queer porn, concentrating on 'gay for pay' pornography made in the USA. Brennan analyses the significances of performers' tattoos in this hard-core queer porn scene. As Brennan recounts, a number of 'gay for pay' performers are known for their body art and use it to communicate their true sexual identities in a complex world where male porn actors are understood by straight male audiences to be acting out gay sex while really being straight in real life. Brennan shows how the tattoos on display in the 'gay for pay' genre negotiate ideas about masculinity and sexuality and engage with the discrimination faced by openly gay male porn performers in the porn industry. The chapter focusses on case studies of two well-known tattooed 'gay for pay' performers, Brice (from the US porn studio Sean Cody) and Axl (from the porn website Active Duty). Brice's textual tattoo declaring 'Born This Way' expresses his authentic gay sexuality

Introduction

even as the genre he works in depends on the conceit that the actors are heterosexual in real life, while Axl's neo-Nazi white supremacist tattoos challenge the 'gay for pay' genre's ostensible tolerance of gay sex. Counterintuitively, as Brennan shows, it is Brice who is stigmatised and forced to leave the 'gay for pay' pornography industry, while – despite viewers' complaints – Axl remains a star. The chapter concludes that even within 'gay for pay' pornography, homophobia restricts what declarations of self-identity the performers are allowed to make.

The next essay by Ricky Varghese (Chapter Ten) maintains the volume's attention to queer pornography by examining the controversial practice of 'barebacking' (condomless sex) in gay male porn. Varghese invites us to think of bareback porn as a valuable historical site: a sexual archive for understanding queer male sex, sexual identity and sexual subjectivity in the aftermath of the AIDS crisis, a time in which gay male sexuality and the virus became inextricably intertwined, both literally at a physical level for some men, and metaphorically in the public consciousness for gay men in general. Varghese engages specifically with an example of pre-condom porn, *Cruisin' the Castro* (1981), and the more recent work of queer Canadian video artist Vincent Chevalier, which incorporates images from contemporary bareback pornography. Chevalier's experimental documentary film *Breeden* (2014) utilises techniques such as collage, representations of part-bodies, an emphasis on point of view and other intertextual staging and casting references to bareback porn, which, taken together, have the effect of establishing the original porn as a productive site of temporal rupture in historical understandings of queer sex. In the historical context of the post-AIDS crisis world, pre-condom porn and bareback sex at once signify pleasure and risk, a moment of both (potentially) becoming the virus and self-dissolution. Far from being conceived of as an entirely negative, dangerous act indicative of the historical trauma of the AIDS crisis, Varghese shows how bareback sex in pornography may signify an active embrace of the virus (or its imaginary spectre) to indicate the sexual symbiosis of human and viral DNA and to disrupt or 'queer' normative understandings of sex as situated within a linear temporal narrative of heteronormative reproduction. Drawing on the work of philosopher Rebecca Comay, critical theorist Walter Benjamin and queer theorist Leo Bersani, Varghese conceptualises bareback pornography as an inventive pedagogic space that allows audiences to rethink sex as a historical category and to reconceptualise AIDS and queer sexual subjectivity in radical ways.

In Chapter Eleven, Brenda S. Gardenour Walter explores the extreme and little documented world of medical pornography and fetish clinics. The chapter tracks some of the defining features of medical pornography, such as doctor-patient roles, treatments and elective surgical procedures. In so doing, Gardenour Walter interrogates the hegemony of Western biomedical discourse by juxtaposing the 'normal' clinic with the fetish clinic and exposing the true horrors and hypocrisies of clinical 'detachment'. Gardenour Walter notes that – surprisingly – the fetish clinic is better stocked with equipment than most hospitals and provides the 'patient' with respect, truly informed consent and a sense of fulfilment that a regular clinic led by standard biomedical practice does not. Ultimately the chapter shows how virtual and physical BDSM (Bondage and Discipline, Sadism and Masochism) in medical fetish clinics illuminate the ways in which Western biomedical culture has pervaded everyday life and medicalised sexual desires and practices. BDSM clinics highlight how cold and disorientating medical clinics are and how patients are treated as objective entities, whilst interactions in the BDSM clinic are

Introduction

based on qualities which are commonplace in BDSM communities such as mutual respect, negotiated consensuality and communication.

Finally, Chapter Twelve takes the form of a close analysis of the banned hard-core pornographic film, *Long Jeanne Silver* (1977). Krista K. Miranda explores the role of the sexualised impaired body in pornography. Arguing that amputee porn performer Jeanne Silver's 'stump', and amputee fetishism in general, is both an unconventional source of erotic pleasure and a locus of potential liberation from normative assumptions about sex and desire, Miranda demonstrates how Silver's body cannot be straightforwardly regarded as 'other'. Jeanne Silver's erotic body and erotic life (which is played out in the autobiographical porn film *Long Jeanne Silver* (1977) and also narrated in her memoir and interviews) are threats to normative taxonomies of bodily wholeness that underpin intelligible categories of sex, gender, sexuality and compulsory able-bodiedness. Thus, while Silver's oeuvre has been regarded as freakish and obscene, and consequently censored by authorities that seemingly remain unperturbed by the most excessive contortions of normative bodies in pornography, it can also be understood as a queer challenge to the limitations of how bodies and sex intersect.

The twelve chapters that comprise this volume thus provide readers with an intriguing overview of pornograph*ies* in some of their heterogeneous range. In this diverse theoretical interrogation we hope to encourage readers to resist understanding pornographies as texts or sites that should be *either* celebrated *or* berated and instead to consider them as rich cultural objects within and around which important questions may be asked about sex and representations of sex today. Just as importantly, the volume may be considered as a case in point of the value of boldly opening up pornographies to critical interpretations that are intentionally accessible to scholars at undergraduate level and beyond.

References

Arrowsmith, A. (2011, 12 October). Porn is good for society. *The Guardian*. Retrieved from https://www.theguardian.com/commentisfree/2011/oct/12/porn-society-government-opt-in

Attwood, F. (2010a). Toward the study of online porn cultures and practices. In F. Attwood (Ed.), *porn.com: Making sense of online pornography* (pp. 236–243). Digital Formations, Vol. 48. New York, NY: Peter Lang.

Attwood, F. (Ed.). (2010b). Conclusion: Toward the study of online porn cultures and practices. In F. Attwood (Ed.), *porn.com: Making sense of online pornography* (pp. 236–243). Digital Formations, Vol. 48. New York, NY: Peter Lang.

Attwood, F. (Ed.). (2009). *Mainstreaming sex: The sexualisation of Western culture*. London, United Kingdom: I. B. Tauris.

Biasin, E., Maina, G., & Zecca, F. (Eds.). (2014). *Porn after porn: Contemporary alternative pornographies. (Mapping pornographies: Histories, geographies, cultures)*. Milan, Italy: Mimesis International.

Boyle, K. (Ed.). (2010). *Everyday pornography*. Oxford, United Kingdom; New York, NY: Routledge.

Cadwalladr, C. (2013, 16 June). Editors of sex studies journal attacked for promoting porn. *The Observer*. Retrieved from https://www.theguardian.com/culture/2013/jun/16/journal-editors-attacked-promoting-porn

Church Gibson, P. (Ed.) (2004). *More dirty looks: Gender, pornography and power* (2nd ed.). London, United Kingdom: British Film Institute.

Dines, G. (2011). *Pornland: How porn has hijacked our sexuality*. Boston, MA: Beacon Press.

Dworkin, A. (1981). *Pornography: Men possessing women*. London, United Kingdom: Women's Press.

Introduction

Dyer, R. (2004). Idol thoughts: Orgasm and self-reflexivity in gay pornography. In P. Church Gibson (Ed.), *More dirty looks: Gender, pornography and power* (2nd ed.) (pp. 102–109). London, United Kingdom: British Film Institute.

Gill, R. (2009, 23 May). From sexual objectification to sexual subjectification: The resexualisation of women's bodies in the media. *Monthly Review*. Retrieved from https://mronline.org/2009/05/23/from-sexual-objectification-to-sexual-subjectification-the-resexualisation-of-womens-bodies-in-the-media/

Jenkins, H. (2004). So you want to teach pornography? In P. Church Gibson (Ed.), *More dirty looks: Gender, pornography and power* (2nd ed.) (pp. 1–7). London, United Kingdom: British Film Institute.

Jones, M. & Carlin, G. (2010). "Students study hard porn": Pornography and the popular press. In K. Boyle (Ed.), *Everyday pornography* (pp. 179–189). London, United Kingdom & New York, NY: Routledge.

Levy, A. (2005). *Female chauvinist pigs: Women and the rise of raunch culture*. London, United Kingdom: Simon & Schuster.

MacKinnon, C. A. (1993). *Only words*. Cambridge, MA: Harvard University Press.

Maddison, S. (2000). *Fags, hags and queer sisters: Gender dissent and heterosocial bonds in gay culture*. Basingstoke; London, United Kingdom: Macmillan.

Maddison, S. (2010). Online obscenity and myths of freedom: Dangerous images, child porn, and neoliberalism. In F. Attwood (Ed.), *porn.com: Making sense of online pornography* (pp. 17–33). Digital Formations, Vol. 48. New York, NY: Peter Lang.

McNair, B. (2002). *Striptease culture: Sex, media and the democratization of desire*. London, United Kingdom; New York: Routledge.

McNair, B. (2012). *Porno? Chic! How pornography changed the world and made it a better place*. London, United Kingdom; New York: Routledge.

Men's Health. (2012, 16 October). Is porn harmful? Retrieved from http://www.menshealth.com/sex-women/porn-debate

Mowlabocus, S. (2007). Gay men and the pornification of everyday life. In S. Paasonen, K. Nikunen, & L. Saarenmaa (Eds.), *Pornification: Sex and sexuality in media culture* (pp. 61–71). Oxford, United Kingdom; New York, NY: Berg.

Mowlabocus, S. (2016). *Gaydar culture: Gay men, technology and embodiment in the digital age*. Oxford, United Kingdom; New York, NY: Routledge.

Mulvey, L. (1989). Visual pleasure and narrative cinema. In L. Mulvey (Ed.), *Visual and other pleasures* (pp. 14–26). Basingstoke, United Kingdom: Macmillan.

Paasonen, S., Nikunen, K., & Saarenmaa, L. (Eds.). (2007). *Pornification: Sex and sexuality in media culture*. Oxford, United Kingdom; New York, NY: Berg.

Smith, C. (2007). *One for the girls: The pleasures and practices of reading women's porn*. Bristol, United Kingdom; Chicago, IL: Intellect.

Taormino, T., Parreñas Shimizu, C., Penley, C., & Miller-Young, M. (Eds.). (2013). *The feminist porn book*. New York, NY: Feminist Press at the City University of New York.

Telegraph Men. (2015, 17 March). Why porn might actually be good for you, *The Telegraph*. Retrieved from http://www.telegraph.co.uk/men/relationships/11477028/Why-porn-might-actually-be-good-for-you.html

Williams, L. (1989). *Hard core: Power, pleasure, and the "frenzy of the visible"*. Berkeley, CA: University of California Press.

Williams, L. (Ed.). (2004). *Porn studies*. Durham, NC; London, United Kingdom: Duke University Press.

CHAPTER ONE

POLITICS AND ETHICAL CONFLICT IN A SOCIAL MOVEMENT: PORNOGRAPHY AND THE 'SEX WARS' IN (LESBIAN) FEMINISM

Christian Klesse

> We have the right to be furious and to direct our pain into
> attacking the porn merchants, the porn apologists
> (and they include, unfortunately, S/M dykes),
> the porn buyers and consumers.
> Sheila Jeffreys (1993, p. 222)

> Antiporn gender is a rigid binary of potentially violent, dominant
> men and subordinated, silenced women. This is not a reflective
> description, but itself a production of gender that tells a
> story that [...] depends for its coherence on
> the porn narrative it attacks.
> Lisa Duggan (1995, p. 8)

The term 'sex wars' designates a period of heated debate and intense conflicts on sexuality and sexual politics within the feminist and lesbian feminist movements in a range of countries, including the USA and the UK, from the late 1970s into the early 1990s. In the sex wars, radical feminists with an anti-porn agenda clashed on a range of issues with libertarian or 'sex-positive' feminists who took an anti-censorship stance and promoted women's sexual agency and erotic experimentation. The debate produced strongly polarised positions, although none of the camps was homogeneous in terms of composition and political outlook. Controversies related to a wide range of sexual practices and phenomena, including heterosexuality, bisexuality, BDSM, sex work, the use of sex toys, transsexuality, butch and femme, etc. Yet diverging views about pornography played the most significant role in a dynamic that escalated and resulted in a polarisation of views on sexuality among feminists. The sex wars left many activists scarred and had a long lasting impact on feminist theorising of sexuality (Vance, 1992a; Duggan & Hunter, 1995; Bronstein, 2011; Walters, 2016).

This chapter turns to the historical example of the sex wars for a number of reasons. The sex wars illustrate that conflicts around sexuality have the capacity to cause serious rifts even within social movements that think of themselves as "progressive" or liberal. The sex wars further demonstrate the existence of a multiplicity of positions on sexuality within feminism. They are a prime example for the ongoing skirmishes around 'difference' within feminism. And last, but not least, they gave rise to a distinctive 'sex-radical' (or 'sex-positive') streak within feminist politics and a critical theory of sexuality, which can be seen as a precursor of queer theory and politics (Jacobs & Klesse, 2014).

The chapter is structured as follows: I will briefly sketch some of the historical events, which have been dubbed the sex wars; I will concentrate on events in the USA and, to a lesser extent, the UK, limiting the discussion to conflicts that relate to pornography in a more narrow sense; I will then explain the dynamics of the conflict by analysing important shifts in the theorisation of sexuality within feminism and lesbian feminism and show how they shaped anti-porn positions; I will then turn to the critique of anti-pornography ideas and argue that libertarian feminism stimulated the formation of a sophisticated vision of queer sexual politics. This sex-positive queer feminism has sustained an ongoing creative endeavour to create alternative, non-heteronormative erotic and sexually explicit texts and images.

The sex wars in the USA and the UK

In the 1970s, feminist anti-pornography groups sprang up across the USA. While most group members were initially still sceptical regarding censorship as an adequate tool, many groups quickly adopted more restrictive strategies (Duggan, 1995). According to Vance and Snitow (1984), the sex wars erupted after several years of anti-porn activism, which had unfolded largely unchallenged until libertarian and anti-censorship feminists raised concerns about what they considered to be misguided and dangerous political and legal demands. In the face of clashing agendas and values, the exchange quickly escalated into an aggressive interchange shaped by mutual hostility.

The Barnard Conference

The extent of the controversy can be exemplified with the confrontations at the 1982 Scholar and Feminist IX Conference 'Towards a Politics of Sexuality' held at the Barnard Center for Research on Women at Barnard College in New York in 1982. In the face of growing anti-porn activism during a period of right-wing political hegemony, the organisers felt the need to make a creative space for refocussing the agenda "on what seemed to be a central question, even paradox: how could feminism at the time reduce the sexual danger women faced and expand their sexual pleasure, without sacrificing women's accounts of either one?"(Vance, 1992b, p. xx). Adopting the couplet pleasure/danger as a core theme shows that the organisers were centrally concerned with questions of power and violence and did not adhere to an uncritical or naive brand of sexual liberationism.

The agenda presented under the pleasure/danger theme was not accepted by other feminists. Anti-pornography feminists started to mobilise against the event. This included a concerted campaign of phone calls and letters by anti-porn feminists to College officials and trustees – including the President of Barnard College, Ellen V. Futter – which denounced the conference as "non-feminist" and claimed that the organisation was taken over by "sexual perverts" (Vance, 1992b, xxi). This campaign by Women Against Pornography (WAP) and some other groups resulted in College officials confiscating copies of the conference booklet. Anti-porn feminists picketed the conference. Protesters wore T-shirts with the slogans "For Feminist Sexuality" on the one side and "Against S/M" on the other (Hunter, 1995; Vance, 1992b). Some participants were insulted at the conference, while others were named and denounced in leaflets distributed during the protest for their political beliefs or alleged non-normative sexual practices. In some cases, anonymous calls were made to employers and some individuals were ostracised in certain environments as a result of the smear campaign (Vance, 1992c, pp. 433–434, Nestle, 1998; Echols, 2016). Even if anti-censorship feminists managed to take control of the Barnard Feminist Conference and effectively banned WAP women from speaking, this came at a high price. The Conference diaries had been confiscated and the major sponsor, the Helena Rubinstein Foundation, withdrew funding for any future events (for further discussion of the events, see Pally, 1982; Schulman, 1994; Nestle, 1998). For many libertarian, 'sex-positive' or 'sex-radical' feminists, anti-porn feminism had revealed its most oppressive features in these events. They now realised that they had to do something about it. For them, the Barnard Conference marked the beginning of the sex wars, i.e. "the impassioned, contentious, and, to many, disturbing debates, discussions, conferences, and arguments that continued unabated at least until 1986" (Vance, 1992b, p. xxii).

Politics and Ethical Conflict in a Social Movement

The Minneapolis Ordinance

As expressed in the names of some anti-porn organisations such as Women Against Violence Against Women (WAVAW, Los Angeles) or Women Against Violence in Pornography and Media (WAVPM, San Francisco), anti-porn feminists saw pornography first of all as a problem of violence against women. This aspect of anti-porn analysis is most explicitly expressed in the writing of Andrea Dworkin, a relentless anti-porn activist and author of several books, including *Pornography: Men Possessing Women* (1981). Dworkin's definition of pornography as violence went far beyond the common charge that pornography would depersonalise and objectify women (Kappeler, 1986). As quotations from Dworkin's early articles demonstrate, she saw pornography as the eroticisation of murder, the terroristic destruction of women or the propaganda of "sexual fascism" (Dworkin, 1988, p. 200). "The pornographers, modern and ancient, visual and literary, vulgar and aristocratic, put forth one consistent proposition: erotic pleasure for men is derived from and predicated on the savage destruction of women" (Dworkin, 1988, p. 21). Dworkin (1988) continues: "The eroticization of murder is the essence of pornography" (p. 22). In a different text she states: "Pornography is the propaganda of sexual fascism. Pornography is the propaganda of sexual terrorism" (Dworkin, 1988, p. 200).

Even if many anti-porn feminists acknowledged the existence of so-called soft porn, for most, the essence of porn was revealed in its most violent excesses. This is also evidenced in the nature of the slide shows that were used by many anti-porn organisations throughout the 1970s and 1980s and depicted examples of the most gruesome hard-core films available on the market (Vance, 1992b). For Dworkin (1988), pornography is a feminist issue, because "pornography says that women want to be hurt, forced, and abused; pornography says women want to be raped, battered, kidnapped, maimed, pornography says women want to be humiliated, shamed, defamed; pornography says that women say No but mean Yes – yes to violence, Yes to pain" (p. 200). Anti-porn ideology assumed that the objectification of women and the representation of sexualised violent acts towards women in pornography caused real-life violent acts against women. In fact, the production and screening of such material was seen as nothing other than an accumulation of violent acts, firstly against the actress, secondly against women who may be exposed to the images, and thirdly against the collective of women (who are the potential victims of the excessive violence that will follow the consumption of porn by men). "Women as a gender-class are in the anti-pornography lobby on the basis of their recognition that they and the particular victim are one", argues Kappeler (1986) to challenge the individualism that underpins the rationality of obscenity law. Anti-porn feminists believed that they had to look for stronger legal remedies than the ones that had been provided by censorship and obscenity legislation. They campaigned for the rights of women to take civil action against pornographers, because as a violent act pornography infringed upon their civil and human rights.

On 30 December 1983, Minneapolis City Council narrowly approved a new ordinance, which gave individual women the right to take legal action against people involved in the production and distribution of pornography. The ordinance had been drafted and propagated by the leading feminist anti-pornography activists Andrea Dworkin and Catherine MacKinnon, who considered pornography to be a discriminatory and harmful practice with implications on women's position in the public sphere (Bracewell, 2016). The first version was vetoed by the Minneapolis city mayor Donald Fraser in 1984. A revised version was soon after introduced in the Indianapolis City

Council. The Indianapolis Ordinance was struck down only in 1986 and declared to be unconstitutional, since it infringed on the right of "free speech" certified in the First Amendment of the US Constitution. Versions of the ordinance were introduced and debated in several locations across the USA in the 1980s (Duggan, 1995). Whereas in Minnesota the ordinance had been primarily a project of feminist activists, the New Right and Christian forces took the lead in most of the other venues, often in alliance with feminist organisations (Vance, 1992b). These coalitions, their broad definition of pornography and their move towards censorship worried libertarian feminists who set up The Feminist Anticensorship Task Force (FACT) in New York and Madison, Wisconsin to counter the threat of governments using the new powers to suppress sexually explicit materials. It was mainly due to the campaign of FACT and their alliance with concerned media groups that the Indianapolis Ordinance was struck down in 1986 in the Appeals Court (Khan, 2014).

The Meese Commission
In the years 1985–1986, the Attorney General's Commission on Pornography, also known as the Meese Commission, provided yet another arena for right-wing politicians to appropriate feminist anti-pornography arguments. Implemented during the second term of the presidency of Ronald Reagan, the commission's task was defined as finding "new ways to control the problem of pornography" (as cited in Vance, 1992b, p. xxvii). Although the commission backed the Supreme Court's decision on the ordinance and agreed that its implementation in Indianapolis (or any other place) would have breached the First Amendment in its final report of 1986, it condemned so-called "violent pornography" (a category that included both rape and sadomasochism). Its final report was split on the question whether to condemn any explicit depiction

of sex outside of marriage (Hunter, 1995, p. 26). Andrea Dworkin and Catherine MacKinnon spoke as experts before the commission on the harms of pornography to women (Dworkin, 1988). According to Vance (1992b), the moral right capitalised on this kind of feminist anti-pornography activism and strengthened later attacks by the Federal Government on the National Endowment for the Arts (NEA) for its financial support for museums, which exhibited or planned to purchase art work of a sexually explicit kind. This included the scandalising of NEA's endorsement of the artist Robert Mapplethorpe's controversial photographic documentation of gay male BDSM and leather culture. Feminist and lesbian feminist artists had funding by the NEA blocked in these culture wars (Duggan, 1995). In 1991, The US Congress forced the NEA to ask funding applicants for a declaration that they would refrain from producing art that "might be considered obscene". The US Supreme Court upheld the requirements that artists receiving funding from the NEA needed to meet "general standards of decency" (Meyer, 1993; Khan, 2014, p. 63).

Key events in the UK
In the UK similar debates were taking place throughout the 1980s, only on a much more limited scale. In the UK the lesbian feminist organisations that sustained the "anti-pornography" agenda were the Leeds Revolutionary Feminists (founded in 1978), Lesbians Against Sadomasochism (LASM), Women Against Violence Against Women (WAVAW), and – in the late 1980s – CPC (Campaign Against Pornography and Censorship) (Smyth, 1992; Smith, 1993). The group Feminists against Censorship started to challenge anti-porn campaigns in the late 1980s (Rodgerson & Wilson, 1991). At the same time, the queer feminist OutRage! affinity groups LABIA (Lesbians Answer Back in Anger) and PUSSY (Perverts Undermining State Security)

(a mixed gender group) took up the fight against censorship and for sex education (Smith, 1994).

Like in the USA, conflicts around BDSM were prominent in the UK debates (Healey, 1996). Throughout the 1980s, women's participation in BDSM in feminist groups, spaces, events and demonstrations was repeatedly challenged. The radical feminist anti-BDSM campaign culminated in the publication of the book *Against Sadomasochism* (Linden, Pagano, Russell, & Star, 1982). Contributors to the book condemned BDSM (inclusive of lesbian variations) as the fetishisation and eroticisation of an implicitly heterosexual gender/power dynamic resting on male supremacy and class rule (Jeffreys, 1993). In 1985, London feminist and lesbian feminist circles engaged in a six month long battle on BDSM, fetishism and dress codes around the question of whether a lesbian SM group should be expelled from the London Lesbian and Gay Centre (LLGC) (Ardill & O'Sullivan, 1987). As scholar, artist and activist Sue Golding remembers, "The feminist movement was divided into the good, the bad and the ugly. The bad women who fucked around but had serial monogamy and a sense of sex that had to do with love. The ugly were the women who were seen as male and had a sense of sex that had to do with consent" (as quoted in Smyth, 1992, p. 26). The 'bad' women also used porn and sex toys.

With anti-porn feminism gaining hegemony, feminist culture became increasingly censorious with regard to sexually explicit material for women. Spaces where certain sexual practices could be discussed were shrinking. For example, London's lesbian and gay bookshops refused to sell openly publications such as the BDSM anthology *Coming to Power*, edited by the San Francisco lesbian BDSM group Samois (1981). Pat Califia's (1988) lesbian sex book *Sapphistry* and the lesbian feminist sex-radical magazine *On Our Backs* were shunned in a similar way.

Pornographies

The London bookshops Gay's the Word, Silvermoon and Sisterwrite also refused to stock or sell Della Grace's photographic documentation of lesbian BDSM entitled *Love Bites* (1991). The increasingly repressive climate provided the context for the formation of the early OutRage! affinity groups, LABIA and PUSSY, to fight against censorship and to promote "queer sex" (Smith, 1993). Cherry Smyth (1992, p. 38) refers to the summer of 1988 as the "Summer of Sex" of British lesbian feminist politics. Sheba Feminist Publishers organised a mixed conference called 'Putting the Sex Back into Politics' and published Joan Nestle's (1996) socio/autobiography *A Restricted Country* and the Sheba Collective's (1989) collection of lesbian erotic texts entitled *Serious Pleasure*. The first issue of the lesbian sex magazine *Quim* appeared in summer 1988 and the first lesbian sex toy and magazine mail order company, Thrilling Bits, started its services. The first ever UK Lesbian Summer School provided space for a discussion of the controversial issues raised in the 1985 BDSM-related membership row at the London Lesbian and Gay Centre, described above. In the following year anti-censorship feminists organised a series of workshops under the title 'Making it Public' which explored issues such as butch/femme, monogamy/ non-monogamy, inter-racial relationships, sexual taboos, sex and disability, safer sex and the usage of sex toys. According to Smyth (1992), these activities were inspired by the Barnard Conference in the USA, discussed above, and "aimed to secure an atmosphere that would be non-judgemental and would avoid the SM/vanilla chasm" (p. 40).

Ideological currents within radical feminism and political lesbianism

How can we explain the salience of the anti-pornography agenda within the sexual politics of the late 1970s to the early 1990s? And why did it turn out to be so divisive *within* feminism? In the following section, I show how the sex wars were fuelled by wider ideological shifts within feminism and lesbian feminism. The critique of sexual relations has always been an aspect of feminist politics, for example in work contesting violence against women (Jacobs & Klesse, 2014). Yet the intensity of the controversy among feminists during the sex wars can only be explained by the confluence of strong ideological currents in the wider terrain of feminist politics. Firstly, radical feminism defined sexuality as *the* foundation of patriarchal gender relations. Secondly, the opening up of lesbian identity to all women by the project of 'political lesbianism' (described below) had paradoxical effects. It *played down* the significance of sexuality (as a source for lesbian identity) and at the same time *inflated* its role as a projection screen for idealised scripts of egalitarian lesbian intimacy. Eroticism between women was thus burdened with the discursive task of representing a revolutionary alternative to patriarchal domination (Stein, 1997).

Some strands within radical feminism posited sexuality as the key relation in the constitution of hierarchical gender relations via the institutionalisation of oppressive heterosexuality. For example, Catherine MacKinnon takes sexuality as the core ingredient and starting point to produce "a feminist political theory exclusively from an analysis of sexuality" (Diamond & Quinby, 1984, p. 5). For MacKinnon (1989), sexuality creates gender and establishes gender as a hierarchy: "How are the qualities we know as male and female socially created and enforced on an everyday level? Sexual objectification of women – first in the world, then in the head, first in visual appropriation, then in forced sex, finally in sexual murder – provides answers. Male dominance is sexual: men in particular, if not men alone, sexualized hierarchy; gender is one" (p. 127). This view implies a rigid characterisation of heterosexual relations as oppressive: "Heterosexual sexual relations ... are characterized by an ideology of sexual objectification (men as subjects/masters; women as objects/slaves) that supports male sexual violence against women" (Ferguson, 1984, p. 108). The critique of objectification led to a rejection of all sexual practices that were alleged to normalise male sexual violence. Feminists were urged to take control of their bodies and build a truly feminist erotic culture based on mutual intimacy and egalitarianism.

Heterosexual penetrative intercourse was defined as an oppressive act of male 'conquest' in which men take 'possession' of women's bodies. These metaphors are used frequently in Andrea Dworkin's book *Intercourse* (1987). A similar position was taken by the Leeds *Revolutionary Feminists* who pronounced in their manifesto "Political Lesbianism: The Case against Heterosexuality": "Giving up fucking for a feminist is about taking your politics seriously" (Leeds Revolutionary Feminists, 1981a, p. 8). The manifesto culminates in the demand on all women to follow this advice and become political lesbians. In an afterword to publication of the original paper the Leeds Revolutionary Feminists state: "We defined Political Lesbianism as woman-identified-woman who did not fuck men. We now think its rubbish to say that women fuck men; what happens is that men fuck women, or women get fucked by men" (1981b, p. 67). This statement recalls a formulation in the "The Woman-Identified Woman" by the US group Radicalesbians (1970/1997), according to which "the essence of 'woman' is to get fucked by men" (p. 397). It may not seem surprising that this statement outraged many women who considered "penetration" (of whatever kind) to be part of their repertoire of sexual practices (Segal, 1994).

Not all political lesbians made their case in such a divisive manner, but many saw sexuality and intimacy with men as a critical issue. "It is the primacy of women relating to women, of women creating new consciousness of and with each other which is at the heart of women's liberation, and the basis of the cultural revolution" conclude the Radicalesbians from their analysis (1970/1997, p. 399). The philosophy of political lesbianism was also fuelled by Adrienne Rich's (1983) influential "Compulsory Heterosexuality and Lesbian Existence" which conceives of a lesbian continuum and welcomes all women into the lesbian community. Political lesbianism dissolved the boundaries between feminism and lesbianism. Its discourse proposed lesbianism to be the ultimate icon of feminist commitment.

These ideological shifts had various effects with regard to the representation of lesbian sexuality. Lesbian sexuality was de-emphasised for the sake of strengthening a commonality based on affection, intimacy and a shared commitment to the anti-porn struggle. Moreover, as Gayle Rubin argues, conflating lesbianism (an erotic experience) and feminism (a political ideology) undermined any justification of lesbian sexuality beyond or outside of the feminist struggle (English, Hollibaugh, & Rubin, 1987). This created a fertile ground for restrictive community standards to blossom. A further problem emerged from the fact that cultural lesbianism offered lesbian reality as an absolute – quasi utopian – alternative. The representation of lesbian identity as a vanguard stance created a fruitful soil for self-righteous attitudes. It may not be too surprising, therefore, that "political lesbians" who had a strong investment in these images were irritated by the erotically charged bar culture of working-class butches and femmes, the erotic practices of BDSM dykes or women in the sex industry (Hollibaugh, 2000; Nestle, 1996). "Maybe some of the confusion about lesbianism and sexuality occurred when lesbianism began to be the model for describing good sex. Everybody, heterosexual or homosexual, used it to describe not-genitally organised sexual experience", remembers Amber Hollibaugh (English et al., 1987, p. 69).

Critiquing anti-pornography feminism

The true significance of the sex wars cannot be grasped if they are simply understood as clashes between so-called 'pro-sex' or 'anti-sex' factions. A more thorough analysis reveals that the controversy was fuelled by profoundly "different views about women's sexual agency, the theory of social construction, the connections between sex and gender, and the nature of representation" (Vance & Snitow, 1984, p. 127). From the point of view of libertarian feminists the following assumptions of anti-pornography feminists were highly problematic. In the following, I discuss the assumptions that strike me as the most salient and significant ones.

Against the conflation of categories

Some critics were frustrated with the conflation of categories and layers of analysis within many feminist critiques of pornography. Many arguments of the anti-porn movement worked to play down the significance of distinctions in terms of genre (such as for example hard-core/soft-core). All pornography was considered to be violent, with the most extreme forms revealing the essence of what pornography really was about (Dworkin, 1988). For libertarian feminists, anti-porn feminism operates on the common assumption that an analysis of pornography can describe 'real' women's actual sexual experiences and situations. In brief, there was a common conflation of the levels of representation, experience and actual behaviour. According to a 'slippery slope' type of argument, pornography was said to *depict* violence, *be* violent, *legitimise* violence and *cause* future acts of violence, such as rape and harassment. Leaving aside the notoriously difficult question of media effects here, there are divided opinions on this matter within the social sciences (Segal, 1998; McNair, 2014). Anna-Marie Smith (1993) points to the significance not only of the position and identification of viewers, but also of the wider social and symbolic framework to understand what is really going on in acts of consuming pornography. The denial of these issues by anti-porn feminists means that "[t]he possibility that the meaning of sexually explicit material could be profoundly shaped by their wider context in non-sexist feminist works is simply ruled out" (1993, p. 79).

The critique of representation
Anna-Marie Smith (1993) rejects simplistic objectification arguments by highlighting the complexities of representation. In a critical discussion of the policy statement of the Campaign against Pornography and Censorship (CPC), a British anti-porn group, Smith (1993) contests the claim that pornography objectifies women's bodies, because it does not tell the "whole truth" about them. "This ... is true about any representation. 'Truthful' and 'complete' representations are impossible. To represent something is to take it out of one context – such as the everyday world – and to put it into another context – such as sexual fantasies", she argues (Smith, 1993, p. 84). We further need to take account of the specific social context that shapes fantasies. BDSM scenarios, for example, are embedded in a particular set of cultural codes and values, which ritualise power while aiming to maintain consensus (Taylor & Ussher, 2001; Bauer, 2014). Smith (1993) complains about the frequent slippage "between representations of violent imagery, in which the model is actually not subjected to violence, and actual violent acts against the model" (p. 81) and "from representation of sexual practices to actual sexual practices" (p. 81). The conflation of representation and real acts of violence may add moral weight to the arguments of anti-pornography feminists,

but also deflect from the task of generating a sound critique of sexist representations in pornography.

Classical objectification arguments have rested on a critique of the "male gaze" (Mulvey, 1975). Yet critics suggest that it matters who gazes and with what intention. The gaze is inherently unstable and susceptive to a shifting pornographic imagination. Ann McClintock (1992) argues that "Identification in porn can be multiple and shifting, bisexual and transsexual, alternately or simultaneously" (p. 125). This means that it is impossible to make any meaningful generalisations about "men" or "women" and their respective relation to pornography (Duggan, 1995).

The critique of censorship
Libertarian feminists often argued that if the state gets more powers for censorship and criminalisation, the primary targets will be sexual minority cultures (lesbians, gay men, BDSMers, etc.) and not the industry that is responsible for producing the bulk of the undoubtedly sexist and heteronormative pornographic mainstream. It may also encourage practices for internal community censorship (Duggan, 1995). For example, critics in the UK refer to the refusal of community bookshops to stock *Love Bites,* Della Grace's 1991 photography book on lesbian BDSM communities, among others, because of fear of prosecution (Smith, 1993; Smyth, 1992). *Quim,* a British lesbian sex magazine, too, was hit hard by community censorship. As Smith (1993) concludes insightfully, anti-pornography feminism "ignores the existence of alternative sexually explicit texts, and fails to recognise the fact that they are already the main targets of attack for the customs officials, the judiciary and the Obscene Publications Squad" (p. 80).

Politics and Ethical Conflict in a Social Movement

The critique of gender reinforcement and victimisation

"Antipornography organizing dramatizes the differentiation between male and female desire" by demonising male sexuality (or masculine styles of sexuality) and idealising female sexuality (or feminine orientations to sexuality), argue Vance and Snitow (1984, p. 130). These authors prefer a feminist critique which goes beyond a defence of women (or femininity) towards a political critique of gender: "The paradox of feminism is that the object of protection and defence ('women') is also the object of scrutiny and criticism – that which we hope to eliminate" (Vance & Snitow, 1984, p. 131). Radical feminism risks reinforcing dualistic gender epistemologies by repeating the master/slave analysis over and over again. This has the effect of making it impossible to talk about women's erotic agency. "In the end, two sexual silences are created: silence about what women actually do and silence about what images women find arousing" (Vance & Snitow, 1984, p. 132).

Closely linked to this problem is the common victimisation of women who work in the sex industry. They are said to be victimised by brutal pornographers, objectified by the male gaze or duped by false consciousness stemming from accumulated experiences of abuse (Jeffreys, 1993). For example, Andrea Dworkin made the following statement in front of the Attorney General's Commission on Pornography on 22 January 1986:

> The women in the pornography, sixty-five or seventy percent of them we believe are victims of incest or child sexual abuse. They are poor women; they are not women who have opportunities in this society. They are frequently runaways who are picked up by pimps and exploited. They are frequently raped, the rapes are filmed, they are kept in prostitution by blackmail. (1988, p. 278)

While acts of violence in the workplace certainly take place in the sex industry, Dworkin's generalisation here is incapable of conceiving of motivations to work in the porn industry other than violence and mental health problems. This is at odds with research that documents women's motivations, which include the wish to earn money, have flexible working conditions, gain fame or transgress sexual norms. Women who work in alternative porn often further wish to educate or create alternative images (Abbott, 2010; Bakehorn, 2010).

Critique of mono-causal analysis
Many libertarian and anti-censorship feminists criticised the mono-causal analysis and the single-issue focus at the heart of anti-pornography feminism. Anti-pornography feminism inflates the dimension of sexual oppression at the expense of other forms of oppression, which in turn nurtures unrealistic hopes that transformations in the sexual field have major effects in dismantling the whole gender system. As Vance and Snitow (1984) argue:

> The political task of feminism is to work for concrete and material changes that enable women and men to experience sexuality less attached and formed by gender. These changes include social and economic equality; the end of compulsive heterosexuality; access to birth control, abortion, and sex education; recognition of children as sexual; a reconsideration of public/private distinctions; and the protection of mothers and children outside of marriage and nuclear families. (p. 131)

In the context of the more specific debate about pornography, some critics consider a concern with sex workers' working conditions as the most significant issue for feminists (Smith, 1993).

Politics and Ethical Conflict in a Social Movement

Towards a reflexive theory of difference
Some read the sex wars as "a logical continuation of feminists' attempts to deal with difference – in this case sexual – among women" (Vance & Snitow, 1984, p. 133). Black feminists had politicised questions of "difference" in their critique of the refusal or reluctance of white mainstream feminists to address questions of racism (Lorde, 1984; hooks, 1981). Sexuality, too, had caused social divisions within the feminist movement since its inception. A salient problem was the strong homophobia of mainstream feminist organisations. Yet in the 1970s and 1980s, other forms of sexual difference were politicised and started to unsettle many in the movement. In the course of the sex wars, controversies erupted around BDSM, bisexuality, sex work, the usage of sex toys, etc. (Healey, 1996). In this context, Gayle Rubin (1992, p. 15) proposed her theory of power as sexual stratification and made an argument for "benign sexual variation". Jana Sawicki (1991) sees a solution in embracing Audre Lorde's (1984) call for a reflexive politics of difference, i.e. a politics that acknowledges power relations around different positions and counters oppression and privilege (p. 18). Within black feminism 'difference' is described as both relational and intersectional. This leads to the insight that "sexuality may be thought about, experienced, and acted on differently according to age, class, ethnicity, physical ability, sexual orientation and preference, religion, and region – indeed, according to the multiple intersection of these factors" (Vance & Snitow, 1984, p. 133).

Towards a queer analysis of sexuality/power
Many libertarian-minded feminists were horrified by the ways in which anti-pornography feminists posed as the guards of feminist sexual morality. When they found themselves (or their friends and allies) construed as perverts, cop-outs or dupes of patriarchy, many disidentified with the feminist project

(Califia, 1994). Others continued to consider themselves as "feminists", but rejected feminism's claim to represent the only valid critique of sexuality. As Gayle Rubin (1992) argued, "I want to challenge the assumption that feminism is or should be the privileged site of a theory of sexuality. Feminism is the theory of gender oppression. To assume automatically that this makes it the theory of sexual oppression is to fail to distinguish between gender, on the one hand, and erotic desire, on the other" (p. 307). This strategic call for a critical theory of sexuality which is not coextensive with feminism was later also taken up by queer theorists such as, for example, Eve Kosofsky Sedgwick (1990). Rubin has always been adamant that she considers this separation to be strategic and of temporary nature and should not be understood as an anti-feminist statement (Butler & Rubin, 1994). For Rubin and for many others, queer and feminist approaches designate complementary and not mutually exclusive political projects. "Many women adopt 'queer' as a mark of a particular historical relation to, not a repudiation of, feminism", argues Lisa Duggan (1995, p. 14). My reading of the sex wars suggests that feminism played a central "core" role in the genealogy of queer theory. Through their theorisation of the sex wars, anti-censorship and 'sex-radical' feminists paved the way for the emergence of novel theories of gender and sexuality under the lose designation of "queer".

Conclusion

Why is it important to talk about the sex wars today? The critique of feminist anti-pornography ideology by anti-censorship feminists has contributed to a more sophisticated understanding of representation, people's engagement with different forms of media, the potential role and significance of sexually explicit texts and imagery for different groups of users, the enhanced vulnerability of stigmatised sexual communities by generalised censorship practices, the non-heterogenous nature of social movements and the significance of coalition politics. It has fed into novel theorisation of gender, sexuality, fantasy, subjectivity and power. The debates of the sex wars have created a rich archive of critical theories on pornography. I suggest that this archive can be as a source for critical engagement with the current battles around sexuality, representation and media practices. We are currently experiencing a revival of anti-pornography feminism, largely fuelled by novel concerns about uncontrolled access or exposure to pornography via the Internet and new social media (Smith & Attwood, 2013). Under the catchphrases of an alleged 'sexualisation' or 'pornification' of society, calls for censorship, criminalisation and regulation have gained a firm hegemony (Paul, 2005; Long, 2012; Boyle, 2010). Anti-porn campaigns in the UK have led to the introduction of new repressive laws regarding so-called 'extreme pornography' (depicting rape, violent sex or sex with corpses or animals), for example the Criminal Justice and Immigration Act 2008 and the Criminal Justice Courts Bill 2015 (applying to England, Wales and Northern Ireland) and the Criminal Justice and Licensing (Scotland) Act 2010 (applying to Scotland) (Wilkinson, 2009; Woodhouse, 2016). The declared aim to protect children and adolescents legitimises and sustains contemporary campaigns for further control, regulation and censorship.

The work of previous generations of anti-censorship feminism provides complex analysis to think through the relationship between sexual fantasy, representation and what potential harms or pleasures pornography may bring about for women. It is rich in examples of how to construct effective campaigns and may give clues to those who wish to add alternative voices to contemporary debates. Remembering the sex wars serves as a reminder that the work of 'sex-radical' libertarian feminists of the 1970s and 1980s is at the heart of the genealogy of queer theory and politics. It may stimulate an ongoing endeavour to create alternative – queer feminist and transfeminist – sexually explicit images and stories beyond and against the pornographic mainstream.

References

Abbott, S. A. (2010). Motivations for pursuing a career in pornography. In R. Weitzer (Ed.), *Sex for sale* (pp. 47–66). London, United Kingdom: Routledge.

Ardill, S., & O'Sullivan, S. (1987). Upsetting the applecart: Difference, desire and lesbian sadomasochism. In Feminist Review (Eds.), *Sexuality: A reader* (pp. 277–304). London, United Kingdom: Virago.

Bakehorn, J. A. (2010). Women made pornography. In R. Weitzer (Ed.), *Sex for sale* (pp. 91–114). London, United Kingdom: Routledge.

Bauer, R. (2014). *Queer BDSM intimacies.* Basingstoke, United Kingdom: Palgrave.

Boyle, K. (Ed.). (2010). *Everyday pornography.* London, United Kingdom: Routledge.

Bracewell, L. N. (2016). Beyond Barnard: Liberalism, antipornography feminism, and the sex wars. *Signs: Journal of Women in Culture and Society 42*(1), 23–48.

Bronstein, C. (2011). *Battling pornography: The American Feminist Anti-Pornography Movement, 1976–1986.* Cambridge, United Kingdom: Cambridge University Press.

Butler, J., & Rubin, G. (1994). Sexual traffic (Judith Butler interviews Gayle Rubin). *Differences, 6*(2–3), 62–99.

Califia, P. (1988). *Sapphistry.* Tallahassee, FL: The Naiad Press.

Califia, P. (1994). *Public sex.* San Francisco, CA: Cleis Press.

Diamond, I., & Quinby, L. (1984). American feminism in the age of the body. *Signs, 10*(1), 119–125.

Duggan, L. (1995). Introduction. In L. Duggan & N. D. Hunter (Eds.), *Sex wars* (pp. 1–14). London, United Kingdom: Routledge.

Duggan, L., & Hunter, N. D. (1995). *Sex wars*. London, United Kingdom: Routledge.

Dworkin, A. (1981). *Pornography: Men possessing women*. London, United Kingdom: The Women's Press.

Dworkin, A. (1987). *Intercourse*. London, United Kingdom: Arrow.

Dworkin, A. (1988). *Letters from the war zone*. London, United Kingdom: Secker & Warburg.

Echols, A. (2016). Retrospective: Tangled up in pleasure and danger. *Signs: Journal of Women in Culture and Society, 42*(1), 11–22.

English, D., Hollibaugh, A., & Rubin, G. (1987). Talking sex: A conversation on sexuality and feminism. In Feminist Review (Eds), *Sexuality: A Reader* (pp. 63–81). London, United Kingdom: Virago.

Epstein, D., & Renold, E. (Eds.). (2005). Special Issue: Pleasure and danger revisited: Sexual identities in the 21st century'. *Sexualities, 8*(4), October.

Ferguson, A. (1984). Sex war: The debate between radical and libertarian feminism. *Signs: Journal of Women in Culture and Society, 10*(1), 106–112.

Grace, V. (1991). *Love bites*. London, United Kingdom: GMP.

Healey, E. (1996). *Lesbian sex wars*. London, United Kingdom: Virago.

Hollibaugh, A. (2000). *My dangerous desires*. London, United Kingdom: Duke University Press.

hooks, B. (1981). *Ain't I a woman*. Boston, MA: Southend.

Hunter, N. D. (1995). Contextualizing the sexuality debates. A chronology. In L. Duggan & N. D. Hunter, *Sex wars* (pp. 16–29). London, United Kingdom: Routledge.

Hutchins, L., & Kaahumanu, L. (1990). Bicoastal introduction. In L. Hutchins & L. Kaahumanu (Eds.), *By any other name* (pp. xx–xxvi). San Francisco, CA: Alyson.

Jacobs, S., & Klesse, C. (2014). Introduction. *International Journal of Politics, Culture and Society, 27*(2), 129–152.

Jeffreys, S. (1993). *The lesbian heresy*. London, United Kingdom: The Women's Press.

Kappeler, S. (1986). *The pornography of representation*. London, United Kingdom: Polity.

Khan, U. (2014). *Vicarious kinks*. Toronto, Canada: University of Toronto Press.

Leeds Revolutionary Feminists. (1981a). Political lesbians: The case against heterosexuality. In Onlywomen Press (Eds.), *Love your enemy* (pp. 5-10). London, United Kingdom: Onlywomen Press.

Leeds Revolutionary Feminists. (1981b). Afterword from Leeds Revolutionary Feminists. In Onlywomen Press (Eds.), *Love your enemy* (pp. 66-68). London, United Kingdom: Onlywomen Press.

Linden, R. R., Pagano, D. R., Russell, D. E. H., & Star, S. L. (Eds.). (1982). *Against sadomasochism*. San Francisco, CA: Frog in the Well.

Long, J. (2012). *Anti-porn*. London, United Kingdom: Zed.

Lorde, A. (1984). *Sister outsider*. New York, NY: Crossing Press.

MacKinnon, C. (1989). *Toward a feminist theory of the state*. London, United Kingdom: Cambridge University Press.

McClintock, A. (1992). Gonad the barbarian and the Venus flytrap: Portraying the female and male orgasm. In L. Segal, & M. McIntosh (Eds.), *Sex exposed* (pp. 111-131). London, United Kingdom: Virago.

McNair, B. (2014). Rethinking the effects paradigm in porn studies. *Porn Studies, 1*(1-2), 161-171.

Meyer, R. (1993). Robert Mapplethorpe and the discipline of photography. In H. Abelove, M. A. Barale, & D. Halperin (Eds.), *The lesbian and gay studies reader* (pp. 360-380). London, United Kingdom: Routledge.

Mulvey, L. (1975). Visual pleasure and narrative cinema. *Screen, 16*(3), 6-18.

Nestle, J. (1996). *A restricted country*. London, United Kingdom: Pandora.

Nestle, J. (1998). *A fragile union*. San Francisco, CA: Cleis Press.

Pally, M. (1982, 24 May-6 June). The fireworks at the Sexuality Conference: Whom should feminists fuck? *New York Native*, 14-16.

Paul, P. (2005). *Pornified. How pornography is damaging our lives, our relationships, and our families*. New York, NY: Owl Books.

Radicalesbians. (1970/1997). The women-identified woman. In M. Blasius & S. Phelan (Eds.), *We are everywhere: A historical sourcebook of gay and lesbian politics* (pp. 396–399). London, United Kingdom: Routledge.

Rich, A. (1983). Compulsory heterosexuality and lesbian existence. In A. Snitow, C. Stansell, & S. Thompson (Eds.), *Desire* (pp. 212–241). London, United Kingdom: Virago.

Rodgerson, G., & Wilson, E. (Eds.). (1991). *Pornography and feminism*. London, United Kingdom: Lawrence & Wishart.

Rubin, G. (1992). Thinking sex: Notes for a radical theory of the politics of sexuality. In C. S. Vance (Ed.), *Pleasure and danger* (pp. 267–319). London, United Kingdom: Pandora.

Samois (Eds.). (1981). *Coming to power*. Boston, MA: Alyson Press.

Sawicki, J. (1991). *Disciplining Foucault*. London, United Kingdom: Routledge.

Schulman, S. (1994). *My American history*. London, United Kingdom: Cassell.

Sedgwick, E. K. (1990). *The epistemology of the closet*. Berkeley, CA: University of California Press.

Segal, L. (1994). *Straight sex*. London, United Kingdom: Virago.

Segal, L. (1998). Does pornography cause violence? The search for evidence. In P. C. Gibson & R. Gibson (Eds.), *Dirty looks* (pp. 5–21). London, United Kingdom: British Film Institute.

Sheba Collective. (Eds.). (1989). *Serious pleasure*. London, United Kingdom: Sheba.

Smith, A.-M. (1993). "What is pornography?": An analysis of the policy statement of the Campaign Against Pornography and Censorship. *Feminist Review, 43*, 71–87.

Smith, A.-M. (1994). Outlaws as legislators: Feminist anti-censorship politics and queer activism. In V. Harwood, D. Oswell, K. Parikson, & A. Ward (Eds.), *Pleasure principles* (pp. 20–40). London, United Kingdom: Lawrence and Wishart.

Smith, C., & Attwood, F. (2013). Emotional truths and thrilling slide shows: The resurgence of antiporn feminism. In T. Taormino, C. Parreñas Shimizu, C. Penley, & M. Miller-Young (Eds.), *The feminist porn book* (pp. 41–57). New York, NY: The Feminist Press.

Smyth, C. (1992). *Lesbians talk queer notions*. London, United Kingdom: Scarlet Press.

Stein, A. (1997). *Sex and sensibility. Stories of a lesbian generation.* London, United Kingdom: University of California Press.

Taylor, G. W., & Ussher, J. M. (2001). Making sense of S&M: A discourse analytic account. *Sexualities, 4*(3), 293–314.

Vance, C., & Snitow, A. B. (1984). Towards a conversation about sex in feminism. A modest proposal. *Signs: Journal of Women in Culture and Society, 10*(1), 126–135.

Vance, C. S. (Ed.). (1992a). *Pleasure and danger*. London, United Kingdom: Pandora.

Vance, C. S. (1992b). More danger, more pleasure: A decade after the Barnard Sexuality Conference. In C. S. Vance (Ed.), *Pleasure and danger* (pp. xvi–xxxix). London, United Kingdom: Pandora.

Vance, C. S. (1992c). Epilogue. In C. S. Vance (Ed.), *Pleasure and danger*. (pp. 431–440). London, United Kingdom: Pandora.

Walters, D. S. (Ed.). (2016). Special issue: Pleasure and danger: Sexual freedom and feminism in the twenty-first century. *Signs: Journal of Women in Culture and Society, 42*(1), Autumn. Retrieved from http://signsjournal.org/pleasure-and-danger-sexual-freedom-and-feminism-in-the-twenty-first-century-a-special-issue-of-signs-available-with-open-access/

Wilkinson, E. (2009). Perverting visual pleasure: Representing sadomasochism. *Sexualities, 12*(2), 181–198.

Woodhouse, J. (2016). Extreme pornography: UK law, Briefing Paper 5078, 7 January 2016, House of Commons Library. Retrieved from http://researchbriefings.files.parliament.uk/documents/SN05078/SN05078.pdf

CHAPTER TWO

WOMEN'S PORNOGRAPHY

Feona Attwood

Pornography has often been presented as a form of violence against women or an expression of patriarchy, and more recently, as the source of the sexualisation of mainstream culture with significant negative impacts on women. At the same time the development of feminist porn studies (see for example, Penley, Parreñas Shimizu, Miller-Young, & Taormino, 2013; Maina, 2014) and "The *Fifty Shades* phenomenon" in which E. L. James's book trilogy (2011–2013) became a worldwide bestseller, followed by a widely publicised film (2015), has made women more visible than ever as producers and consumers of pornography.

In this chapter, I provide an introduction and brief overview of some of the developments in pornographies that are produced and consumed by women. This is necessarily highly partial given both the timescale in which I am interested (1970s to the present day), the wide range of pornographies and other varieties of sexually explicit material that are available, and the relative scarcity of academic work on the production, content and reception of pornographies for women. My aim here is to introduce some of the key contributions to academic literature in the area, chart some of the most well-known areas of production and consumption during the period, and consider three key themes – characterising women's porn, authenticity and participation.

Domesticating pornography
The relationship between women and pornography has often been described as fraught. An expectation that both men and

women will pass judgement on images of women in terms of their desirability has been evident in women's lack of ease with sexual imagery in some studies (Boynton, 1999; Eck, 2003). As partners of men who engage with porn, women have expressed dislike of their partners' consumption (Shaw, 1999), and a tendency to associate porn with men's tastes (Wilson-Kovacs, 2004, p. 8). A perception that porn is disapproved of both as anti-feminine and anti-feminist, and a concern about the treatment of women as porn labourers, have also been factors in women's responses to porn (Ciclitira, 2004; see also Parvez, 2006). As Clarissa Smith has noted "female consumers of pornography are constantly dogged by questions of harm, subordination, objectification and authenticity and the need to consider women's well-being before their own pleasures in watching or reading porn" (2013, p. 167).

Yet there is a reasonably long documented history of women's engagement with pornography. A growing academic literature traces this, noting pornographies such as slash (amateur productions that take fictional characters as a starting point for creating narratives of desire, sex and romance) and *yaoi* (media produced by professionals and amateurs depicting boys and men in a range of sexual scenarios), the 'domesticated' forms of porn that women have been able to access most easily (Juffer, 1998), the more recent visible engagements with a variety of pornographies, new forms of production and consumption, and the growth of 'female-friendly', feminist, lesbian and queer pornographies.

As Jane Juffer (1998) has argued, "women have had a longer, more productive history writing and reading erotica than they have in producing or watching visual porn" (p. 5); a finding borne out in Wilson-Kovacs's (2004) study of women's employment of sexually explicit materials "in everyday passionate encounters" where she found that women perceived erotica to be "informative", "inspiring" and a source of solitary pleasure (pp. 14–15). Alongside erotica, the "domesticated pornographies" that Juffer describes, such as sexual self-help books and videos, lingerie catalogues and adult cable programmes, have been much more accessible for women than other kinds of pornography. The success of these has often depended on emphasising their difference from (and downplaying their similarities to) other kinds of sexually explicit material, for example, through a focus on "finding the truth of one's identity" in some erotica, in the aspiration to "better partnership" in sexual self-help materials (Juffer, 1998, p. 7), or in the claim to possess aesthetic value. This has allowed domestic pornographies to circulate more widely than other kinds of pornography and to become more visible in mainstream venues (Juffer, 1998, p. 122).

Another avenue for women's involvement in pornography has been in the amateur production and consumption of forms such as slash and femslash fiction. Becoming popular in the 1970s with the pairing of *Star Trek* characters Spock and Kirk (Penley, 1992; Jenkins, 1995), amateur communities developed more extensively online (Busse & Lothian, 2017).

Porn comics have also been a popular site for women's pornography. Little academic attention has been paid to Anglophone porn comics for women produced within the US market (Roberts, 2015) but the development of a Japanese tradition has been quite widely researched. Originating in *shojo-manga* (girls' comics), originally dominated by male *mangaka*, *shonen-ai* (boys' love) – a genre of male-male romance – was developed by female *mangaka* during the 1970s, focussing on intense, eroticised relationships between *bishonen* or "beautiful boys" (Madill, 2017; see also McLelland, 2000; Levi, McHarry, & Pagliassotti, 2010; Nagaike & Suganuma, 2013). A related genre – "ladies' comics" (see Shamoon, 2004, p. 82) – portrayed "real (or at least realistic) women actively pursuing their own sexual pleasure" and "taking the initiative in sexual experimentation" (Shamoon, 2004, p. 79; see also Jones, 2005), the comic format allowing for the portrayal of female pleasure and orgasm in a way that is not possible on film. Whereas ladies' comics virtually excluded the male body, putting the female body on display (Shamoon, 2004, p. 83) – as Anglophone comics for women have also tended to do (Roberts, 2015) – *shonen-ai* (boys' love) manga focussed on men's bodies and sex between men.

Based on the *shonen-ai* of the 1970s a wider range of Boys' Love (BL) media, often focussing on *uke* ("bottom") and *seme* ("top") pairings (see Sihombing, 2011), featuring a range of sexual themes including rape, non-consensual sex, BDSM (bondage, discipline, sadism and masochism), incest and underage sex, with a mainly female fan base and mostly created by women (Mizoguchi, 2003), has gained increasingly wide circulation. Through the mid- to late-1990s, Boys' Love (often called *yaoi* outside Japan and with a corresponding genre in China called *danmei*, see Chao, 2016) developed a global market and transnational fandom (Nagaike & Suganuma, 2013; Wood, 2006; Wood, 2013), becoming the site of many amateur online productions.

A focus on men's bodies has continued to be a popular one for many female consumers of porn. As Alexandra Hambleton (2016) notes, the female-friendly porn films produced by Silk Labo draw on aspects of popular Japanese media culture such as TV dramas with their focus on "stressed career women, lonely women who have given up on men, university students looking for love, young couples dating in fashionable or exotic locations" and J-pop 'idols' who provide the style template for Silk Labo's *"eromen"* performers. Lucy Neville (2015) suggests that women's pleasures in m/m (male/male) porn are partly explained by the lack of pressure to identify with any of the performers. Participants in her research reported feeling less anxious about the enjoyment of watching male performers, and appreciating what they viewed as the better production values and acting, more experimental and interesting performances, and wider range of body types in m/m porn.

A third area of development has been in female-friendly and feminist visual porn in the USA, Australia and Europe. Notable in the 1980s in this respect was the founding of Femme Productions dedicated to making porn from a woman's point of view and the launches of lesbian porn magazine, *On Our Backs*, and lesbian porn company, Fatale Video. As Lynn Comella (2013) notes, the advent of the VCR, video technology and desktop publishing in the early 1980s provided feminists with access to affordable means of porn production. New means of distribution were provided by entrepreneurs, creating a "sex-positive synergy" (Comella, 2013, p. 82) that linked together a range of enterprises. For example, Susie Bright, a founder of *On Our Backs* magazine and creator of the widely toured lecture/show "How to Read a Dirty Movie", curated a selection of porn videos for the feminist sex shop Good Vibrations in the 1980s, as well as developing *Herotica*, a book of erotica by women, with Good Vibrations owner, Joani Blank. Similarly, the work of Tristan Taormino, the feminist porn director and sex educator, was strongly influenced by her contact with customers at the sex shop Babeland (Comella, 2013).

Carly Milne has described the 1990s development of women's involvement in porn as a "cultural revolution ... when younger women took inspiration from the sex pioneers of the 1970s and 80s, thereby setting off a new wave of women pornographers" (2005, p. xiv). Women steadily became more visible within well-known porn businesses – for example, the performer Belladonna became the first female director for Evil Angel in 2003, and took on a wider variety of roles within porn work – as journalists, editors, photographers, producers, marketers, curators, retailers, product developers, promoters and sales workers (see Milne, 2005), and later still, as online sexperts, cultural intermediaries and sexbloggers (see Attwood, 2010a). A series of discussions by feminist writers challenging the conventions of pornography and exploring its possibilities for women were also published (see for example, Tisdale, 1995; Palac, 1998; Sprinkle, 1998). The rise of feminist porn critics and reviewers such as Susie Bright and later Violet Blue, also amplified this process. Blue described her experiences of searching for porn that might appeal to women:

> I saw authentic female orgasms that had me gripping my thighs together in stunned erotic empathy. I saw riveting blow jobs that made my mouth water with envy. I found websites where pairs of women and men tore each other's clothes off with passion that startled me. I watched films with gorgeous cinematography, natural lighting, beautiful real people as performers. And I saw a whole host of independent porn that blew my mind." (2006, p. xi)

The emergence of women-owned porn sites has been cited as "a significant trend in the industry" since the mid-1990s (Lane, 2001, p. 113), with women's involvement often seen as "helping shape and change society's views on sexuality" (Milne, 2005, p. xiii). The launch of The Feminist Porn Awards in 2006, books such as Violet Blue's *The Smart Girl's Guide to Porn* (2006) which "tells women how to find porn they'll like" and porn websites for women such as Hot Movies for Her, Porn Movies for Women, Porn for Women and For the Girls have all worked to make porn for women more visible and accessible. More filmmakers have identified themselves or their work as feminist including Shine Louise Houston and Madison Young in the

USA, Ms Naughty in Australia and Erika Lust, Anna Span, Petra Joy and Mia Engberg in Europe.

Consuming porn

Little research has been carried out with actual porn consumers but I draw on a handful of studies here to introduce some of the evidence we have about women's experiences with pornography, beginning with an outline of differences and similarities in the accounts of women and men. Maika Böhm, Philipp Franz, Arne Dekker, and Silja Matthiesen's (2014) study of pornography consumption by German students aged 20-30 found a higher incidence of male students who consume pornography, and that those male students who do so consume pornography considerably more frequently. Male students had also been familiar with porn since their adolescent years, while female participants were more likely to become pornography consumers at a later age. For both, porn consumption and masturbation were closely linked. Women experienced pornography as sexually arousing but were concerned with ethical practices around pornography while men worried about addiction (though none matched the criteria for this). In relationships, pornography was accepted as a part of the partner's solo sexuality. While both male and female students drew inspiration from their consumption of porn, this was mainly to enrich their own sexual fantasies – ideas from pornography were only occasionally introduced into partner sex. Porn consumption as a couple appeared to be more problematic; participants – especially men – seemed to find it harder admitting in a relationship context the kind of pornographic material they preferred. Generally speaking though, the study found that both male and female participants showed a high degree of competence in choosing and employing pornography and in integrating it into their lives.

The pornresearch.org project (see Smith, Barker, & Attwood, 2015) also found some differences in the responses of male and female participants. Men rated their engagement with pornography more highly than women and reported more frequent engagement. In terms of sources of porn, downloads were important for men, as were amateur sites and specialist sites catering to specific sexual interests, while women were more interested in fiction sites and sex blogs. Men seem more inclined to use porn to *express* arousal, whereas women are more likely to use pornography as a *means to arousal*. Women also reported that they were more likely to engage with porn as a means to reconnect with their bodies, and to use with partners. Men reported that they were more likely to choose to turn to pornography when feeling bored or having nothing better to do.

Yet there were also a number of similarities in participants' responses. Very few men or women reported that they were attracted by Internet pop-ups, suggesting that both groups actively searched for porn. In terms of sources of porn for men *and* women, the most popular by far were tube sites, while roughly equal numbers consumed porn in DVD and magazine form. In addition differences were apparent *within* groups that identified by gender and by sexual orientation. For example, younger women (aged 18–25 years) engaged with pornography much more than older women, indicating a possible generational shift. Although "When I feel horny" came out as a top answer across the survey, queer respondents were more likely to cite "to feel involved in a world of sex out there" (26.1%), "to reconnect with my body" (16.2%), "for recognition of my sexual interests" (52.5%), "to see things I wouldn't do" (11.2%) than other respondents. These choices suggest that for queer viewers pornography is significant in coming to terms with their sexualities.

Looking at the detailed responses of participants is an important way forward in understanding women's engagement with pornography. A set of interviews with women carried out by Clarissa Smith (2013) suggested that porn provides an important space for engaging imagination, the body and sexuality. For example, it could serve the purpose of engendering "a sense of preparing and planning for being part of a couple" (Smith, 2013, p. 159). It could be about recovering something that was experienced as lost – for example, a former self which was "sexy, spontaneous, responsive", be "a means of keeping alive a sense of excitement in the midst of the domestic" (Smith, 2013, p. 160) that might involve a "heightened perception" of the body (Smith, 2013, p. 161), or open up "the possibilities of play and … agreeing to explore fantasy" (Smith, 2013, p. 163).

In the pornresearch.org project, while young female participants described their engagements with porn as linked to arousal, there were also indications that porn played a role in terms of relieving stress, building mood and contributing to an overall feeling of well-being. Participants also described engagements with porn that they perceived as part of their sex lives, regardless of – and sometimes quite separately to – others:

> Solo sex is really important to me, whether or not I'm in a relationship, and porn is one of the components of that, for me.

For some participants it was an important part of their relationships with others:

> It provides stimulation, and inspiration for sexual fantasies. It also provides ideas for trying new things with my partner. It also provides a way to turn us both on when watching it together, and give us a different kind of sexual experience.

This took on a particular importance when women were separated from their partners:

Pornographies

> Being from different countries, my partner and I must now and then spend extended periods of time apart. To keep intimacy alive and to connect sexually with each other during this time (and sometimes when we're together!) we share pornographic videos and images we find online.

In addition, porn played a particular role in relation to the development of sexual interests, desires, fantasies and energies. One participant described porn as "a safe and fun way of exploring", another remarked that engaging with porn "taught me what I like and what I don't like", while a third noted that it was significant "because i constantly meditate about my desires and my sexuality, i like to be confronted by my desires, even the ones i would never admit in public" and another told us "I'm a submissive girl currently without a Dominant, so I have to channel my submissive energy and the best way I've found is through Dominant/submissive porn".

What is notable here, even in this small group of participants, is the range of roles that porn engagement can play. Even if we consider the broad theme of "learning from porn", it is clear that this can take a number of different forms; it can be used for ideas of things to do with a partner, it can be a way of exploring sexuality safely, it can work as part of a process of figuring out what a person's fantasies are and it can play a role in helping someone confront their own – possibly un-nameable – desires. Porn can also have varied significance and function for the same person. As one participant noted, "I've used it 'casually' in terms of laughing over parody porn and a few drinks with friends, more traditionally as a tool for arousal before or during masturbation or partnered sex, as a sort of adult sex education (to be taken with a grain of salt), to help keep my sex life active during long distance relationships, and as a course of study during my undergraduate career."

Developing women's porn studies

In this final section I want to take up three issues – characterising women's porn, authenticity and participation – and to relate these to the work I have outlined here.

One of the interesting questions that arises from the public developments in porn production and the more private accounts revealed through audience research is how we might disentangle what we count as "women's" porn from "porn for women", "female-friendly", "feminist", "lesbian" and "queer" pornographies (Maina, 2014). Clearly, not all porn produced or consumed by women is feminist. Neither need one be a woman to make, perform in or consume feminist porn. There is no clear-cut model of where and how feminist pornographers work. Some are independent while others work for or with more 'mainstream' companies. Others identify as feminists but do not label the films they perform in as feminist (Taormino in Voss, 2014, p. 204). Anne Sabo has characterised women's "re-visioned" porn as that which features "women who confront culturally imposed sanctions regulating their behavior", "who reject the speed limits of desire enforced upon women" and "who refuse to be labeled" (2012, p. 5). The authors of *The Feminist Porn Book* describe feminist porn as a movement that "promotes aesthetic and ethical practices that intervene in dominant sexual representation and mobilize a collective vision for change" (Penley et al. 2013, p. 15). Those interventions include contesting and complicating "dominant representations of gender, sexuality, race, ethnicity, class, ability, age, body type, and other identity markers", exploring "concepts of desire, agency, power, beauty, and pleasure", and seeking to "unsettle conventional definitions of sex, and expand the language of sex" (Penley et al. 2013 , pp. 9–10). Another common theme in both feminist and queer pornographies is the way they focus on performers' agency and consent (Penley et al. 2013, p. 12), on notions of fair-trade and sustainable modes of production (Maina, 2014), on ethical labour, and on the provision of a safe and consensual work environment (Penley et al., 2013).

Debates about what counts as 'feminist' porn continue (see for example, Stryker, 2015), as do attempts to quantify 'women's porn'. The Australian feminist pornographer Ms Naughty notes that "Women's erotic tastes are just as expansive and diverse as men's" (Naughty, 2013, p. 76), yet she also suggests that in her own experience what has been most likely to sell to women is "Heterosexual couples porn, both romantic and 'tasteful hardcore' … good-looking naked men and erotic fiction" (2013, p. 76). A key issue has become which women are being referred to in discussions about "women's" porn. As Ms Naughty argues, these discussions often rest on an assumption that the "women" in question are "heterosexual, cisgender, white, and middle class" (Naughty, 2013, p. 76) and as she notes, the term "porn for women" can be "stereotypical, assumptive, problematic, and just plain wrong" (Naughty, 2013, p. 76; see also Hill-Meyer, 2013).

As Giovanna Maina has argued (2014), a pivotal concept in the development of pornographies for women and for feminism has been 'authenticity', though what counts as authentic and real often varies dramatically (see Attwood, 2010b). Female-friendly porn and erotica has sometimes been regarded as "soft, tender, non-explicit" (Williams, 1990, p. 231), in line with notions of an authentically feminine taste and expression of sexuality. Femme Productions, founded in the 1980s by Candida Royalle, privileges storylines, high production values and romance to this end. A prominent lesbian porn aesthetic however, has focussed instead on appropriating "sex acts once considered definitive of heterosexual and gay male pornography, such as penetration, dirty talk, rough sex, and role-playing" (Butler, 2004, pp. 181–182, 169).

Authenticity has also been claimed in terms of the social context of production and reception (Levin Russo, 2007, pp. 239–240). For example, the Cyber-Dyke online porn network claimed its porn as "aimed at real women and lesbians" as part of a broader political project to "redeem porn" (in Moorman, 2009, p. 158).

In contrast, queer approaches may not "take the gender binary or the pursuit of genuineness so seriously" (Ward, 2013, p. 135). Indeed in some queer porn authenticity is linked less to an idea that the authentic can be characterised and more to the representation of diversity and the refusal of the "politically correct". While some feminist producers such as Petra Joy exclude practices such as "extreme anal sex" and "cum shots into the woman's face" as "degrading" (quoted in Mondin, 2014, p. 191), Barbara DeGenevieve (2014) the artist and pornographer has maintained that the fetishisation and objectification of (queer) bodies and practices is necessary for generating the dynamics of authentic pornographic desire. Her site, Ssspread.com, which operated from 2001 to 2004, featured everything "from vanilla sex, to masculinity, to blood sports, to violence" (2007, p. 234), providing a place where "power dynamics are subverted, inverted and perverted" (2007, p. 236). This queer approach can be seen as part of a broader mission to challenge the distinctions between categories such as art, porn, erotica, sex, education and spirituality, found also in the work of Annie Sprinkle and of "post-porn" producers (see Stüttgen, 2009; Biasin, Maina, & Zecca, 2014).

Authenticity may also mean different things for individual porn consumers. In Böhm's (2014) study worries about authenticity seem to underpin women's concerns about the pleasure performed by female porn stars and how "real" it is, while men worried about how porn might impact on the "real" of their bodies, sex lives, well-being and relationships. At the same time porn clearly played an important role in the participants' sense of sexual self, one that was often rather separate to partner sex. Smith (2013) notes that for one participant in her study authenticity seemed to refer to "a sense of the performative exceeding its own scripting where the performers appear to go beyond the call of duty to a spontaneous loss of their professional control in unguarded pleasure" (p. 164), while for another, the pleasure of the porn she liked lay partly in its ordinariness, recognisability, and "the seeming genuineness of the various performances", though another still appreciated the "professional" polish of porn performance (2013, p. 165).

A number of researchers have pointed to community and connection as being particularly important in the development of women's and of feminist pornography. Ingrid Ryberg (2013) describes queer, feminist and lesbian pornography as constituting a kind of interpretive community "characterized by a politics of constructing safe space" (p. 190). Slash and other fan cultures can also be understood as communities that may be separate and sometimes rather hidden forms of culture, though they are clearly related to other developments both in media culture and in political activity. For example, Busse and Lothian (2017) argue that gay and lesbian television representations of the 1990s and 2000s, gay and lesbian political movements and the shared pleasures of slash fan fiction are connected as part of the same landscape. Other kinds of online communities congregate around particular porn styles and preferences as taste cultures (Attwood, 2007). In the fan cultures of Silk Labo and m/m porn community-making is also important. Hambleton (2016) has argued that the parties held for Silk Labo fans create a space in which pornography loses its taboo quality for women and becomes something to celebrate. Neville (2015) shows that m/m porn represents a kind of queer space for some of its female consumers, one which allows them to explore nonconformist, non-reproductive and non-familial sexuality, push boundaries and engage with taboo and unknowable sexual experiences. Julie Levin Russo (2007, p. 243) argues that in fact it is the development of community based around shared cultural and political values that is the most significant way in which porn can really be said to represent something 'authentic'. But connection need not take the form of tight-knit networks. According to Deller and Smith (2013) reading *Fifty Shades of Grey* is, in part, "a declaration of participation" for its readers, participation in the phenomenon of the book and its huge success, and in taking up a position in the public debates about female sexuality, erotica and BDSM practices that the book occasioned, thereby becoming "part of the conversation" about the significance of these topics.

As Jane Juffer predicted, women's increased involvement in the production and consumption of sexually explicit texts has led to "an expansion of access for more, different groups of women" (1998, p. 236). And these texts are extremely diverse – there is no monolith of porn or erotica, but a range of forms. Neither are these cordoned off from 'the mainstream' as is often argued, nor does porn flow into mainstream media, changing and corrupting it. Indeed pornographies may well draw on existing forms and genres from the mainstream and elsewhere. Ladies' comics and *yaoi* derive from an earlier tradition of *shojo-manga*. The domesticated pornographies that Juffer describes draw on sex advice, fashion, self-care, adult cable shows. Some of the pornographies that women enjoy are appropriated from other markets – hence the appeal of m/m pornography – or they use aesthetics derived from elsewhere in popular culture as Silk Labo does when it models its *eromen* performers on pop idols. Others use subcultural iconographies, draw on queer culture, or mix together porn, performance and art forms. These pornographies do not take a clear and simple form that tell us something concrete or straightforward about what 'women' like. In some instances a focus on women's bodies emerges as the most important thing; in others women's bodies become invisible as sex between men takes centre stage. Some "female-friendly" porn is gentle and non-explicit, foregrounding sensitive vanilla lovemaking, but elsewhere – in lesbian porn, or in slash and *yaoi*, for example – the sex might be kinky, rough or hard, feature dominant and submissive encounters, and include non-consensual sex.

What is also clear from a brief examination of trends in porn production and consumption for women is the variety of its dimensions for those who engage with it. It may be important for individuals in terms of connecting with their bodies, relieving stress, developing a sense of solo sexuality, preparing for sex with a partner, and creating a fantasy world. It has particular relevance for groups of women who want to share imaginative encounters around porn and particular sexual preferences, and has special meaning for women who are constructing particular sexual identities that are made visible as lesbian or queer. For some women and with some kinds of porn, there is also political importance. This can operate at the level of intervening in the regimes of sex and gender representation; working to challenge, subvert, appropriate or make new kinds of visual and written texts. It may focus on the making visible of a range of body types and sexual identities that are hidden or taboo elsewhere in visual culture. It may challenge the boundaries of what counts as sex. In some cases it may work to provide new models of labour and business. The study of porn made by and for women is still very much in its infancy but the work that has been done so far reveals a complex scenario and one that is deserving of further investigation.

References

Attwood, F. (2007). No money shot? Commerce, pornography and new sex taste cultures. *Sexualities, 10*(4), 441–456.

Attwood, F. (2010a). "Younger, paler, decidedly less straight": The new porn professionals. In F. Attwood (Ed.), *porn.com: Making sense of online pornography* (pp. 88–106). New York, NY: Peter Lang.

Attwood, F. (Ed.). (2010b). Conclusion: Toward the study of online porn cultures and practices. In F. Attwood (Ed.), *porn.com: Making sense of online pornography* (pp. 236–243). Digital Formations, Vol. 48. New York, NY: Peter Lang.

Biasin, E., Maina, G., & Zecca, F. (Eds). (2014). *Porn after porn: Contemporary alternative pornographies.* Milan, Italy: Mimesis.

Blue, V. (2006). *The smart girl's guide to porn.* San Francisco, CA: Cleis Press.

Böhm, M., Franz, P., Dekker, A., & Matthiesen, S. (2014). Desire and dilemma: Gender differences in German students' consumption of pornography. *Porn Studies, 2*(1), 76–92.

Boynton, P. M. (1999). "Is that supposed to be sexy?" Women discuss women in "top shelf" magazines. *Journal of Community & Applied Social Psychology, 9*(6), 449–461.

Bright, S. (2013). The birth of the blue movie critic. In T. Taormino, C. Parreñas Shimizu, C. Penley, & M. Miller-Young (Eds.), *The feminist porn book: The politics of producing pleasure* (pp. 32–40). New York, NY: The Feminist Press.

Busse, K., & Lothian, A. (2009). Bending gender: Feminist and (trans) gender discourses in the changing bodies of slash fan fiction. In I. Hotz Davies, A. Kirchhofer, & S. Leppänen (Eds.), *Internet fictions* (pp. 105–126). Newcastle upon Tyne, United Kingdom: Cambridge Scholars Publishing.

Busse, K., & Lothian, A. (2017). History of slash sexualities: Debating queer sex, gay politics, and media fan cultures. In C. Smith, F. Attwood & B. McNair (Eds.), *The Routledge companion to media, sex and sexuality* (pp. 117–129). London, United Kingdom: Routledge.

Butler, H. (2004). What do you call a lesbian with long fingers? The development of lesbian and dyke pornography. In L. Williams (Ed.), *Porn Studies* (pp.167–197). London, United Kingdom: Duke University Press.

Chao, S.-C. (2016). Grotesque eroticism in the Danmei genre – the case of *Lucifer's Club* in Chinese cyberspace. *Porn Studies, 3, (6)*1, 65–76.

Ciclitira, K. (2004). Pornography, women and feminism: Between pleasure and politics. *Sexualities, 7*(3), 281–301.

Comella, L. (2013). From text to context: Feminist porn and the making of a market. In T. Taormino, C. Parreñas Shimizu, C. Penley, & M. Miller-Young (Eds.), *The feminist porn book: The politics of producing pleasure* (pp. 79–96). New York, NY: The Feminist Press.

DeGenevieve, B. (2007). Ssspread.com: The hot bods of queer porn. In K. Jacobs et al. (Eds.), *C'lick me: A netporn studies reader* (pp. 233–238). Amsterdam, Netherlands: Institute of Network Cultures.

DeGenevieve, B. (2014). The emergence of non-standard bodies and sexualities. *Porn Studies, 1*(1–2), 193–196.

Deller, R. A., & Smith, C. (2013). Reading the BDSM romance: Reader responses to Fifty Shades. *Sexualities, 16*(8), 932–950.

Eck, B. A. (2003). Men are much harder: Gendered viewing of nude images. *Gender & Society, 17*(5), 691–710.

Hambleton, A. (2016). When women watch: The subversive potential of female friendly pornography in Japan, *Porn Studies, 3*(4), 427–442.

Hill-Meyer, T. (2013). Where the trans women aren't: The slow inclusion of trans women in feminist and queer porn. In T. Taormino, C. Parreñas Shimizu, C. Penley, & M. Miller-Young (Eds.), *The feminist porn book: The politics of producing pleasure* (pp. 155–163). New York, NY: The Feminist Press.

Jenkins, H. (1995). Out of the closet and into the universe: Queers and Star Trek. In H. Jenkins & J. Tulloch (Eds.), *Science fiction audiences: Watching Star Trek and Doctor Who* (pp. 237–265). New York, NY: Routledge.

Jenkins, H. (2012). *Textual poachers: Television fans and participatory culture.* New York, NY: Routledge.

Jones, G. I. (2005). Bad girls like to watch: Writing and reading ladies' comics. In L. Miller & J. Bardsley (Eds.), *Bad girls of Japan* (pp. 97–109), New York, NY: Palgrave Macmillan.

Juffer, J. (1998). *At home with pornography: Women, sex, and everyday life.* New York, NY: New York University Press.

Lane, F. S. (2001). *Obscene profits: The entrepreneurs of pornography in the cyber age.* New York, NY: Routledge.

Levi, A., McHarry, M., & Pagliassotti, D. (Eds.). (2010). *Boys' love manga: Essays on the sexual ambiguity and cross-cultural fandom of the genre.* Jefferson, NC: McFarland.

Levin Russo, J. (2007). "The real thing": Reframing queer pornography for virtual spaces. In K. Jacobs et al. (Eds.), *C'lick me: A netporn studies reader* (pp. 239–252). Amsterdam, Netherlands: Institute of Network Cultures.

Madill, A. (2017). Boys' Love, Shonen-Ai, Yaoi and (MxM) Shotacon. In C. Smith, F. Attwood, & B. McNair (Eds.), *The Routledge companion to media, sex and sexuality* (pp. 130–140). London, United Kingdom: Routledge.

Maina, G. (2014). After *The feminist porn book*: Further questions about feminist porn. *Porn Studies, 1*(1–2), 182–185.

McLelland, M. (2000). No climax, no point, no meaning? Japanese women's boy-love sites on the Internet. *Journal of Communication Inquiry, 24*(3), 274–291.

Milne, C. (Ed.). (2005). *Naked ambition: Women who are changing pornography.* New York, NY: Carrol & Graf Publishers.

Mizoguchi, A. (2003). Male-male romance by and for women in Japan: A history and the subgenres of YAOI fictions. *U.S.-Japan Women's Journal. English Supplement, 25,* 49–75.

Mondin, A. (2014). Fair-trade porn+ niche markets+ feminist audience. *Porn Studies, 1*(1–2), 189–192.

Moorman, J. (2009). Gay for pay: Gay for(e)play: The politics of taxonomy and authenticity in LGBTQ online porn. In F. Attwood (Ed.), *porn.com: Making sense of online pornography* (pp. 155–171). Digital Formations, Vol. 48. New York, NY: Peter Lang.

Nagaike, K., & Suganuma, K. (2013). Editorial: transnational boys' love fan studies. *Transformative Works and Cultures, 12.* doi: 10.3983/twc.2013.0504.

Naughty, Ms. (2013). My decadent decade; ten years of making and debating porn for women. In T. Taormino, C. Parreñas Shimizu, C. Penley, & M. Miller-Young (Eds.), *The feminist porn book. The politics of producing pleasure* (pp. 71–78). New York, NY: The Feminist Press.

Neville, L. (2015). Male gays in the female gaze: Women who watch m/m pornography. *Porn Studies, 2*(2–3), 192–207.

Palac, L. (1998). *The edge of the bed: How dirty pictures changed my life.* Boston, MA: Little, Brown & Co.

Parvez, Z. F. (2006). The labor of pleasure: How perceptions of emotional labor impact women's enjoyment of pornography. *Gender & Society, 20*(5), 605–631.

Penley, C. (1992). Feminism, psychoanalysis, and the study of popular culture. In L. Grossberg, C. Nelson, & P. A. Treichler (Eds.), *Cultural Studies* (pp. 479–500). New York, NY: Routledge.

Penley, C., Parreñas Shimizu, C. P., Miller-Young, M., & Taormino, T. (2013). Introduction: The politics of producing pleasure. In T. Taormino, C. Parreñas Shimizu, C. Penley & M. Miller-Young (Eds.), *The feminist porn book: The politics of producing pleasure* (pp. 9–20). New York, NY: The Feminist Press.

Roberts, J. (2015). Girly porno comics: Contemporary US pornographic comics for women. *Journal of Graphic Novels and Comics*, doi:10.1080/21504857.2015.1011398

Ryberg, I. (2013). "Every time we fuck we win": The public sphere of queer, feminist and lesbian porn as a (safe) space for sexual empowerment. In T. Taormino, C. Parreñas Shimizu, C. Penley, & M. Miller-Young (Eds.), *The feminist porn book: The politics of producing pleasure* (pp. 140–154). New York, NY: The Feminist Press.

Sabo, A. G. (2012). *After pornified: How women are transforming pornography and why it really matters.* Winchester, United Kingdom: Zero Books.

Shamoon, D. (2004). Office sluts and rebel flowers: The pleasures of Japanese pornographic comics for women. In L. Williams (Ed.), *Porn Studies* (pp. 80–103). Durham, NC: Duke University Press.

Shaw, S. M. (1999). Men's leisure and women's lives: The impact of pornography on women. *Leisure Studies, 18*(3), 197–212.

Sihombing, F. (2011). On the iconic difference between couple characters in Boys Love manga. *Image & Narrative, 12*(1), 150–166.

Smith, C. (2013). "I guess they got past their fear of porn". In X. Mendik (Ed.), *Peep shows: Cult film and the cine-erotic* (pp. 155–167). New York, NY: Columbia University Press.

Smith, C., Barker, M., & Attwood F. (2015). Why do people watch porn? Results from PornResearch.org. In L. Comella & S. Tirrant (Eds.), *New views on pornography: Sexuality, politics, and the law* (pp. 277–296). New York, NY: Praeger.

Sprinkle, A. (1998). *Annie Sprinkle: Post-porn modernist: My 25 years as a multi-media whore*. San Francisco, CA: Cleis Press.

Stryker, K. (2015). An open letter to the Feminist Porn Awards. Retrieved from http://kittystryker.com/2015/03/an-open-letter-to-the-feminist-porn-awards/

Stüttgen, T. (Ed.). (2009). *Post/porn/politics. Queer-feminist perspectives on the politics of porn performance and sex-work as culture production*. Berlin, Germany: b_books.

Tisdale, S. (1995). *Talk dirty to me: An intimate philosophy of sex*. New York, NY: Anchor Books.

Voss, G. (2014). Tristan Taormino interviewed by Georgina Voss. *Porn Studies, 1*(1–2), 203–205.

Ward, J. (2013). Queer feminist pigs: A spectator's manifesta. In T. Taormino, C. Parreñas Shimizu, C. Penley, & M. Miller-Young (Eds.), *The feminist porn book: The politics of producing pleasure* (pp. 130–139). New York, NY: The Feminist Press.

Williams, L. (1990). *Hard core: Power, pleasure and the "frenzy of the visible"*. London, United Kingdom: Pandora.

Wilson-Kovacs, D. (2004). *Women, pleasure and everyday life: An ethnographic investigation into the cultures of sexual intimacy* (Unpublished doctoral thesis). University of Exeter, United Kingdom.

Wood, A. (2006). "Straight" women, queer texts: Boy-Love manga and the rise of a global counterpublic. *Women's Studies Quarterly, 34* (1–2), 394–414.

Wood, A. (2013). Boys' Love anime and queer desires in convergence culture: Transnational fandom, censorship and resistance. *Journal of Graphic Novels and Comics, 4*(1), 44–63.

CHAPTER THREE

POSTFEMINIST SEXPERTISE ON THE 'PORN AND MEN ISSUE': A TRANSNATIONAL PERSPECTIVE

Laura Favaro

Focussing on women's online magazines produced between 2012 and 2014 in the UK and in Spain, this chapter examines peer responses to women feeling distressed about their male partners' consumption of pornographies, in addition to editorial content around the subject. Moving beyond 'for and against' positions, and driven by a social justice agenda, the chapter utilises this commentary about hetero-male-oriented pornographies as a point of analytical entry into the kinds of gendered and sexual pleasures, bodies, subjectivities and intimate relational possibilities contemporary (new) media and public sex and relationship advice bring into being and render (un)intelligible. In doing so, it seeks to contribute to feminist interrogations of the politics of mediated intimacy and pornification under neoliberalism and postfeminism, incorporating a much-needed transnational perspective.

Background: mediated intimacy, pornification and postfeminism
To an unprecedented degree intimacy penetrates the media and intimate lives are mediated. Especially in the global North, intimate relationality is increasingly constructed, negotiated and lived in and through media and communication technologies. More and more digital platforms are used to build, maintain and discuss intimate relationships, as well as engage in sexual practices. Many others create and disseminate personal intimate material, notably sexually explicit content, as

part of a convergence culture of fluid boundaries between the public and the private, content and connectivity, consumption and production. Representations of intimacies – particularly concerning sex – dominate the media, arguably now the central site for defining regimes of sexual desire and conduct. Alongside the multiplication of well-established genres such as sex and relationship advice books and magazine problem pages, newer forms of 'sexpertise' (expertise in sex) have rapidly proliferated – spanning from 'celebsexpert' media (Harvey & Gill, 2011), the seduction or pickup community-industry (O'Neill, 2015), to peer-to-peer online communications, as explored in this chapter. Notwithstanding differences, they all share a number of features characterising the terrain of mediated sex/uality in the contemporary postfeminist neoliberal climate. This includes ties to corporate culture, commodification and recreationalisation, in addition to an obsessive concern with 'great (hetero)sex' – as vividly expressed by exhortations in women's magazines like: "Don't just be good in bed, be GREAT!"(sofeminine.co.uk). Depicted as the "'truth' of subjectivity and the cement of relationships" (Harvey & Gill, 2011, p. 491), and emerging as normative imperative, 'great sex' broadly refers to consistently high amounts of sex, skilful performance, and the constant introduction of novelty. In this sense, and despite the current abundance of information, commercial pornography has surfaced as *the* source of knowledge and new techniques across sex advice media (Farvid & Braun, 2014).

A related and much debated shift pertaining to the media more generally concerns the blurred lines between pornographic and mainstream representations of bodies, sex and sexuality. This has been associated with a broader contemporary Western phenomenon often referred to as 'pornification' (also 'pornographication' and 'sexualisation', see

Gill, 2012). Such a term indicates the perception of societies as saturated by sexual imagery and discourse (as well as products and services), and more specifically of culture as transformed by an increasingly influential and porous commercial sex industry – particularly pornography (García-Favaro & Gill, 2016). Pornographic and strip culture aesthetics, scripts and values have entered the everyday, reconfiguring sexual sensibilities, identities and practices. Porno or stripper chic has become a dominant representational practice across the media, and fashion style across the high street. Many porn stars and sex workers have emerged as celebrities, bestselling authors, sex advisors, and more generally often icons of empowered female sexuality. Further, practices once associated with commercial sex are repackaged as leisure and corporate entertainment – largely for men – as well as recreational and fitness pursuits – predominantly for women: for example, 'strippercise', 'stiletto strength', burlesque, lap- and pole-dancing classes. The participation of women in these activities together with their consumption of pornographic material is situated within a neoliberal politics of individualism, consumerism and choice and, in particular, celebrated through postfeminist discourses of personal sexual liberation, entitlement and empowerment (McRobbie, 2008).

According to Rosalind Gill (2007, p. 255), at the centre of the postfeminist cultural sensibility is a shift from objectification to the "sexual subjectification" of (some) women. Here sexual objectification is (re-)presented as the freely chosen wish of active, autonomous, confident, desiring female subjects; thus constituting a new, more pernicious and distinctively neoliberal disciplinary regime where power "constructs our very subjectivity" (Gill, 2007, p. 258). In the 1990s, Hilary Radner (1993, p. 59) observed the cultural pervasiveness – ignited by Helen Gurley Brown's *Cosmopolitan* magazine – of a new, 'modernised' mode of femininity that had replaced virginity, goodness, innocence or virtue as women's value/object of exchange in the heterosexual contract with a "technology of sexiness" organised around the body, sexual expertise and consumer display. More recently authors have underscored the centrality of psychological transformation to this technology of the self, which now demands a female subject who is compulsorily sexy and sexual, sexually agentic and confident, as well as knowledgeable and skilled in an ever-expanding variety of practices (Evans & Riley, 2014; Harvey & Gill, 2011; Gill, 2007, 2009). Building on the Foucauldian-inspired concepts of "technologies of sexiness" (Radner, 1993, p. 59) and "sexual subjectification" (Gill, 2007, p. 255), Laura Harvey and Rosalind Gill (2011, p. 52) have developed the notion of "sexual entrepreneurship" to capture this new postfeminist neoliberal feminine subject. The "sexual entrepreneur", Harvey & Gill (2011, pp. 56, 64) observe, "is interpellated through discourses in which sex is work that requires constant labour and reskilling (as well as a budget capable of stretching to a wardrobe full of sexy outfits and drawers stuffed with sex toys)" and "made intelligible through discourses of sex produced by the mainstream self-help genre".

But what about the newer user-led spaces of mediated intimacy? How does the sexpertise elaborated by members of the public relate to that disseminated in the edited content of experienced advisors like 'agony aunts'? Also, what happens if women fail or refuse to undergo the adjustments demanded by postfeminist sexualised culture? What are the consequences of failing to provide the sense of female consent and enthusiastic participation that is so fundamental to it? This chapter begins to deal with these broad questions by zooming in on a moment of 'postfeminist disorder', namely women struggling with the presence of pornography in their everyday intimate lives.

Pornographies

The study: technologies of gender and mediated intimacy

Despite the ongoing proliferation of new media forms, the women's magazine remains an inescapable feature of the dominant cultural landscape of femininity in contemporary Western societies and a prevailing locus of ideas about gender, sex, sexuality and intimate relationality. However, printed publications are fast being displaced by online versions. These offer free of charge editorial content and significantly greater opportunities for interaction, including forums or discussion boards. This chapter is part of a larger research project examining producer interviews, editorial content and forum discussions in four such publications targeting millennial women: the UK-based cosmopolitan.co.uk and femalefirst.co.uk, and the Spain-based elle.es and enfemenino.com. These popular sites cross national borders, respectively having users from the USA and India, and several Latin American countries, among others. I therefore consider them transnational technologies of gender and mediated intimacy (De Lauretis, 1987; Foucault, 1988).

In this chapter, I explore a recurrent thread in the forums: (self-identified) young women expressing confusion, concern, disappointment, hurt and/or self-doubt, and asking for advice, upon discovering that their male partners consume various pornographies. This primarily encompasses mainstream soft- and hard-core pornography targeting heterosexual men, but also online live chats and shows. The following are illustrative of such thread-initiating messages.

> Subject: Your boyfriend watching porn
> Hello, is it normal for your partner (in this case a guy) to watch porn and to comment with his friends[1] photos that

---

[1] The website material cited in this chapter is reproduced as posted online (apart from omitted material shown by an ellipsis: '…').

Postfeminist Sexpertise on the 'Porn and Men Issue'

> they send each other of women showing their boobs etc. ... he says it's for fun, but I tell him that it bothers me (not because I'm jealous) but because I don't like him commenting "what a pair of tits, she is so hot"... and he says there is nothing wrong with it (enfemenino.com, 2013)

> Subject: Boyfriends and Porn!
> Ok, so this thread has kinda come from a lot of comments on other threads concerning boyfriends or husbands watching porn.
> I commented on one saying I didn't think my OH [other half] watches porn. I was wrong. ...
> Now – first point first, I have NO problem with my OH masturbating and that is not the point of this thread; I do it too.
> Second of all – I KNOW from previous threads that it's entirely normal for him to watch porn and that it is genuinely something we girls have to accept. And that it does not mean they like the girl in the porn more than us.
> However – although I know I shouldn't, I do feel a tiny bit bothered by it (cosmopolitan.co.uk, 2014)

As this chapter will show, both posts are responding to dominant discourses on the subject of pornography circulating these sites ("not because I'm jealous", "I know ... it's entirely normal for him to watch porn"). Echoing my own position, a cosmopolitan.co.uk forum user wrote in 2014: "I find this topic interesting as it seems to be something that comes up time and time again". It was so recurrent that some women even apologised for starting yet another thread on the topic: "OH & Porn – AGAIN! Sorry! Right, I know this topic has been talked about to death!, but ..." (cosmopolitan.co.uk). Moreover, whilst the (relative) anonymity of the Internet facilitates the release of inhibitions and this often means that online discussion forums are highly affectively charged spaces, this specific topic provoked a particularly intense response. This was even noted by forum users, who for instance spoke about "the porn watching topics" as "explosive threads" (cosmopolitan.co.uk). All this suggested the need for a close feminist inquiry.

To this end, I gathered a substantial but manageable sample comprising 102 threads about 'the porn & men issue' (cosmopolitan.co.uk), which resulted in 2,096 peer-to-peer messages posted between the years 2012 and 2014. A second dataset consisted of 32 editorial features, including 'agony aunt' texts, published in the same period and discussing the same scenario, or pornographies more generally. The collected material was uploaded to NVivo qualitative data analysis software. Aiming to ascertain the diversity of discussion, I used an inductive coding method. This involved several close readings of the whole corpus and various reorganisations of data-driven codes before I identified a stable set of pattered themes.

There are certain contrasts between the editorially authored and user-generated content, and the websites hosted in the UK and in Spain. Especially in the Spanish forums, the pathologising discourse of (male) (cyber)porn/sex addiction is occasionally mobilised. Contrastingly, also shaping the contours of the debate across the Spain-based sites is a critique of women as upholding conservative and archaic views, at times associated with the influence of religion. Pornography is championed as exemplifying sexual liberation, modernity, and freedom from old taboos and religious indoctrination. In the UK data, this seems to stand as a commonsensical understanding unwarranting explicit verbalisation. Here there is instead great preoccupation with the notion of men's privacy having been invaded. Women are figured as psychologically disturbed and shamefully untrustworthy individuals for looking through their partner's belongings (principally computers and phones), and as somehow deserving their distress for "asking for trouble" (cosmopolitan.co.uk).

Drawing on a feminist discursive approach informed by poststructuralism (e.g. Gill, 2009), in what follows I unpack three interrelated ideological formations permeating all datasets: first, the articulation of 'postfeminist biologism', promoting a sexual regime based on male immutability and female adaptation; then, in turn, the motifs I have labelled 'toxic insecurity' and 'porn(ified) upgrade'. These fundamentally revolve around positioning women as the problem and self-transformation as the solution. They thus clearly exemplify the tendency across my data to turn the critical gaze away from men's pornography consumption and towards the women starting the thread. The identified discursive landscape is theorised in relation to the (trans)cultural penetration of postfeminist and neoliberal rationalities, technologies of governmentality and modalities of sexism.

Analysis: on the "porn and men issue"
Postfeminist biologism
Throughout the datasets, pornography is represented as intrinsic to male sexuality through pseudo-technoscientific discourses and figurations of body-subjects. These are intertwined with postfeminist discursive formations and genres of argumentation, including: the heteronormative 'Mars and Venus' framework, which purportedly advocates a 'no-blame' approach to tensions and conflicts between women and men, positioned as – innately and thus rightly and valuably – 'different but equal'; a related 'cruel but true' credos, which acknowledges some forms of gender-based inequities, but renders these asocial and so non-ideological; an assumed pastness of sexism, and an attendant "overing" of feminist critique (Ahmed, 2012, p. 179). I see the concrete articulation of such ideological elements at the current conjuncture as giving

rise to a highly ideological and pernicious sex/gender power/ knowledge regime: 'postfeminist biologism'.

The data is littered with high modality statements establishing an intimate link between pornography and men. Examples from the cosmopolitan.co.uk forum include: "ALL men have stashes of porn, it's a fact of life" and "Men look at porn period". Often forum users expressed a sense of frustration and/or exhaustion regarding this discussion. For instance: "It is Normal, how much longer is it going to take until women understand that all men watch porn on a daily basis" (enfemenino.com forum). These claims to 'porn debate fatigue' work to silence women and police what are legitimate topics for the forums and, arguably, public conversation about sex and sexuality more generally. Furthermore, in a distinctly postfeminist manner, they operate to render obsolete and disenfranchise any critique of pornography, and with that associated feminist vocabularies and imaginaries.

Rather than collective politicised consideration, for those experiencing 'porn debate fatigue' all that is required to solve the "porn problem" (cosmopolitan.co.uk forum) is women assuming the 'truth' of pornography consumption as inherent to male sexuality, ultimately so that women can: "get over it!" (elle.es and female.first.co.uk forums). This reflects the postfeminist 'double move' permeating the data, namely the repudiation of sexual politics and simultaneous reassertion of sexual difference, grounded in a heteronormative framing of gender complementarity (Gill, 2007). Certainly, many contributors drew on postfeminist (media) culture's favourite metaphor of difference: "they are men and are driven by entirely different forces than us girls. ... its a mars venus thing" (cosmopolitan.co.uk forum).

Repeatedly, the forum users of women's magazines pathologised and attacked women for ignoring or overlooking gender differences and thus the allegedly natural connection between pornography and male sexuality. Epitomising the widely unempathetic and at times vicious peer-to-peer responses that this particular topic attracted, a self-identified woman wrote: "Girl, you're not well, men's nature is different to ours ... please, what planet are you from?"; and a self-identified man said: "You are an idiot or inexpert. ALL MEN [WE] WATCH PORN" (both enfemenino.com). Due to the perceived gravity of ignoring or feeling affected by what was perceived as a simple but fundamental 'fact of life', women were often (re)directed to the expert tutelage of psychology. For example, one femalefirst.co.uk forum user wrote: "get over it. men watch porn. if you're going to be hurt by a simple fact of life, you probably have some bigger issues going on that need some looking into. i suggest counselling." The women posting their concerns received a similar response in the Spain-based sites: "So the problem is you, look for psychological help to be guided regarding the reality of life" (enfemenino.com). These posts reflect the omnipresence of psychological (highly selected) knowledges, techniques and practitioners across popular sex and relationship advice media, including women's magazines. They likewise speak to the significance of psychology under neoliberalism, and the centrality of practices of subjectification through technologies of self-regulation in the constitution of femininity.

Most forum contributors additionally took it upon themselves to instruct women about 'the reality of life', that is, purportedly natural sexual differences as explanation to why "men need porn" (cosmopolitan.co.uk). A pervading theme involves the well-rehearsed socio-biological idea that: "Men are turned on by the visual, Women by the emotional" (femalefirst.co.uk); dichotomous psychosexualities which were straightforwardly correlated to media consumption: "Watching porn is for men like watching rom coms is for women" (cosmopolitan.co.uk). Another instance is this 'agony aunt' explanation:

> Men are very visual creatures and so porn is a great way for them to get themselves off – whereas women need more of an emotional connection. This is not his fault, simply a part of his biology. … It may be difficult for him to understand how you feel, given than we are programmed differently to each other. (femalefirst.co.uk)

Therefore, discursive closure on the subject is orchestrated through claims to biologically determined – and thus immutable and unaccountable – masculinity. Note also how women are expected to undergo the non-reciprocal emotional work of understanding men. Indeed, the heterosexual contract promoted in the data rests upon a profoundly unequal distribution of labour, lack of mutuality and consensus building. This is again suggested by repeated messages both in the UK- and Spain-hosted forums to women like: "EVERY man will watch it, … and EVERY (straight) man will find other women attractive. It's something you just have to grin and bare!"(cosmopolitan.co.uk forum) and "learn to resign yourself" (enfemenino.com forum).

As I discuss elsewhere (García-Favaro, 2015), postfeminist biologism is deeply informed by the logics and narratives of evolutionary psychology. Briefly, this involves the association of female sexuality with a greater desire for emotionally close, committed relationships; and emphasis upon the "deeply visual nature of male sexuality" (in order to identify "mate value") (Salmon, 2012, p. 154). As a result of such male ancestral adaptation to maximise reproductive success, male-oriented "modern pornography is exactly what should be expected" (Salmon, 2004, p. 226). Evolutionary psychologists additionally maintain that hard-core pornography caters to "what's at the root of male psychology", namely "to have mating access to endless women" (Saad, 2013, p. 68) and "low cost, impersonal sex" (Salmon, 2012, p. 154). Again, these ideas are closely reproduced throughout my data. For example, in the following forum posts men's desire/need for pornography is naturalised through a connection to polygamy as male biological imperative to ensure genetic legacy: "Males in nature are programmed to spread their seed, their genes. ... men are polygamous" (cosmopolitan.co.uk forum) and "That's the way life is. Men are polygamous by nature and need to contain all that sexual charge somehow" (enfemenino.com forum). It is troubling that a key aspect of the "cultural scaffolding of rape" (Gavey, 2005), namely the construction of male sexuality as voracious and emotionally detached, is still pervasive and reproduced so boldly across the datasets, as well as in some scholarly work (e.g. Salmon, 2004, 2012; Saad, 2013).

In the data, men are constructed as innately potential cheaters and pornography is advanced as a technology of male infidelity prevention. Women are thus explicitly encouraged to see their partners' consumption in a positive light: "be glad he's satisfying himself that way rather than cheating" (cosmopolitan.co.uk forum). Suggesting the powerful influence of this media, another forum user of cosmopolitan.co.uk wrote: "i cant stand the idea of porn! never could. ... but i read an issue of cosmo which said lads who have a healthy porn habit are less likely to cheat!!" Somewhat differently but similarly calling for a 'rational' cost-benefit approach, others exhort women to welcome such activity "If you want a man that is any good in the sack" (femalefirst.co.uk forum). This relates to the current status of pornography as the best source of sexual knowledge, alongside the continued association of masculine sexual subjectivity with physical performance, technique, efficiency, prowess, control/leadership and stamina. The following cosmopolitan.co.uk editorial combines both narratives:

> Far from getting bothered by it, you should try to realise that your fella watching porn is actually a good thing (bear with me here). One: it could stop him cheating. By alleviating his sexual curiosity and satisfying his erotic appetite, porn will make him less likely to play away. Two: by watching porn, your man will be able to learn all kinds of new positions and techniques that he'd never even know existed otherwise. Think of it as a how-to guide, but with moving images. And three: male porn-stars have incredible stamina. He'll see this and want to emulate them, so will work on becoming a more tireless lover.

The widespread naturalisation of male promiscuity seen in the data can produce feelings of insecurity and construct men's (potential) cheating as a normative concern for all heterosexual women. In addition, it functions to position women in competition against each other for men's attention and (lasting) affection and to legitimise the demand for women to relentlessly work on their sexual appeal and practice (see below). Overall, this analysis section has shown that while men's consumption of pornography is established as that which is strictly not open for debate, women are expected to promptly abandon their negative feelings about pornography – plus their partner's lying – through a recognition that men are "biologically programmed" to consume such material (or cheat) and to reconstruct themselves as wiser, better-adapted, porn-embracing postfeminist subjects. This is discussed further in the remainder of the chapter.

Toxic insecurities

As seen above, respondents to the "porn trouble" (cosmopolitan.co.uk) threads repeatedly position women as 'the problem'. This often involves exhortations to surveil, work on and transform their 'inner' selves. Women's hesitant or negative feelings towards their partners' pornography use are depicted as rooted in individual psycho-affective faults such as ignorance about or inability to deal with 'reality' (i.e. 'natural' sexual difference). Another perceived female deficiency is irrationality: "it's your problem. you need to get over it. Deal with why it bothers you. ... your feelings are irrational" (femalefirst.co.uk forum). Forum users also consider that the women posting their concerns demonstrate immaturity: "you need to look for the solution: IN YOURSELF. And in your maturity" (enfemenino.com forum). Therefore, what is a sociopolitical issue is translated into narratives of women's individual psychological maladaptation, pathology or failing.

Self-reflexivity, management and adaptation are advanced as the only intelligible responses for women, thereby conjuring gendered neoliberal logics and modes of regulation. Neoliberalism is structured by an ethos of autonomous individualism and self-determination that replaces – renders unthinkable even – any notion of social/external pressures, constraints or influences. Individuals are interpellated as self-reliant and self-regulating, freely choosing, perpetually transformative, adaptive and entrepreneurial actors who are accountable for their life biographies, and whose value is largely measured by their capacity to self-care and self-improve (Gill, 2007; Ringrose & Walkerdine, 2008). Again reproducing neoliberal logics, people posting depict women as responsible for their feelings of vulnerability: "You yourself, position yourself as a victim" (enfemenino.com). A second, remarkably unempathetic and disciplining example is:

> I'M SORRY, BUT THAT 'OOOHH IT UNDERMINES MY SELF-ESTEEM'... YOU CHOOSE HOW TO TAKE THE SITUATION, WHAT AFFECTS YOU AND WHAT DOESN'T ... ONE HAS TO BE RESPONSIBLE FOR WHAT ONE

FEELS/DOES WITH RESPECT TO A SITUATION, NOT SEE ONESELF AS A VICTIM OF SITUATIONS ...
(enfemenino.com forum)

Informing these claims is the neoliberal (re)configuration and elevation of 'freedom', 'choice' and 'agency' as indisputably and straightforwardly defining contemporary existence, and the related association of notions of vulnerability or victimhood with "self-pity, insufficient personal drive and a lack of personal responsibility for one's own life" (Baker, 2010, p. 190). In the data, experiencing a sense of fragile self-esteem, helplessness or victimisation is coded in strictly individualised terms as a personal attitude or behaviour, rather than a relational – let alone structural – situation. It is reprehended as something the individual woman actively chooses, with the concurrent implication that she can also simply choose to feel better or even good about herself or her situation. As such these peer-to-peer communications reproduce the ideas promulgated by the commercial 'love your body' (LYB) discourses that have been increasingly targeting women over the last decade with seemingly affirmative messages about bodies (Gill & Elias, 2014). Women's magazines are at the centre of this market for female self-esteem (Banet-Weiser, 2013), whose preoccupations are a guiding feature of the sexpertise under my analytic gaze.

Regardless of the nature of their posts women are persistently told that the reason why they do not appreciate their partner's consumption of pornography is because they are insecure or, moreover, as one commenter from enfemenino.com put it: "something is wrong with your self-esteem". Illustrative peer-to-peer posts from both contexts are: "The emotions you perceive are only the result of your insecurities, otherwise you would not care about that" (enfemenino.com); and: "If this bothers you, you need to improve your own self esteem, thats the issue here ... So improve your self confidence and porn

Postfeminist Sexpertise on the 'Porn and Men Issue'

wont seem like an issue anymore" (cosmopolitan.co.uk). In addition to this deceptively simple panacea, respondents urge women to work on their self-esteem through an ideological discourse of 'toxic insecurity'. Here women are not only blamed for feeling unconfident, but also for putting the relationships at risk, and unjustly affecting their male partners. Rather than to accomplish greater personal well-being and happiness, women's labour of self-confidence is presented as crucial relationship preservation work. Two examples from forums are: "If you don't resolve your insecurity problems your relationship is going to end BADLY" (enfemenino.com) and "Insecurities are recipes for disaster and it is NEVER OK to inflict them on others" (cosmopolitan.co.uk). For some forum users, women's insecurities are toxic to the extent of incompatibility with a heterosexual relationship: "If such a little thing has 'knocked your confidence' then you shouldn't be in a relationship, you need to work on your insecurities instead of offloading them on your poor boyfriend" (cosmopolitan.co.uk).

In their thread-initiating posts, some women do speak of feeling inadequate and/or unconfident about their own bodies ("It makes me feel ugly, inadequate and just not good enough") in light of the material their partners enjoy (usually "websites with naked ladies with huge boobs" and "perfect bodies") (both cosmopolitan.co.uk). Respondents often translate this into notions of jealousy, which is again rendered the exclusive responsibility of the individual woman and pathologised as evidence of toxic low self-esteem. Likewise, to fail to be immune and emotionally detached from media representations is put forward as symptomatic of a personal psychological disturbance requiring individualised self-work: "i would say that the problem lies with the person who is jealous of a picture, rather than the person looking at a picture" (femalefirst.co.uk forum). Another illustration is: "Girls who feel insecure and freak out on their boyfriends because they compare themselves to airbrushed women in magazines need their head checked. I mean seriously, get a grip – those women are entertainment only" (cosmopolitan.co.uk forum). This recurrent response suggests a surfaced normativity of certain articulations of 'media literacy', and how this can operate in the service of the neoliberal programme, rendering each individual consumer responsible for their own engagements with texts, and silencing all those important, complex questions about subjectivity and representation (Gill, 2012).

Another reviled form of emotional vulnerability to external factors concerns women's self-esteem depending on their partner's acts, validation or appreciation. Once more, in line with neoliberal logics, women are expected to be hyper-autonomous rational subjects of 'choice'. And, again, their insecurities are often derided and portrayed as a threat to the relationship. For example: "Really, that the self-esteem of a person should depend on someone else or what someone else does ... instead of enjoying the relationship, you come with silly complexes. It's as if you don't want to enjoy it and want your relationship to fail" (enfemenino.com forum). Particularly in the magazines' editorial advice, this idea is also conveyed by drawing on the rhetoric and language of LYB. For example, in response to the reader letter "He has pictures of other women on his phone!", which includes the comment "All I ever find on his laptop is porn and photos of women's bodies, mostly porn stars", femalefirst.co.uk advises: "work to build your self-esteem so you don't need your partner's validation to know how sexy you look".

The data reflects how in the current postfeminist climate the regulatory work that women are required to undergo includes the disciplining of subjectivity through a 'madeover' ethical relationship to the self (Gill, 2009), with self-confidence becoming an increasingly crucial part of this intensified incursion of the operation of power into the psychic (Gill & Elias, 2014). The emergent gendered technology of neoliberal governmentality I have elsewhere called 'confidence chic' (Favaro, 2016) interpellates a hyper-autonomous, deeply individuated woman who can thereby more effectively meet the demands emanating from patriarchal capitalism, not least by re-conducting the desire for change towards the self. Against this backdrop, the diagnosis of 'lacking self-confidence' can be seen as a responsive effect of power to deviance or resistance.

'Confidence chic' (re-)presents women's insecurities as individual – or at times intrinsically female – maladies, instead of a socio-political issue deserving collective anger at both old and new realms of injury and injustice, including a media culture obsessed with women's bodies – bodies that are simultaneously a source of power and always already unruly (Gill, 2007). Indeed, the practice of female governmentality through confidence also accomplishes the important ideological work of obfuscating the continued hostile surveillance and judgement of women's bodies, and, increasingly, sexual practice. It is to this last theme that I now turn.

Porn(ified) upgrade
In addition to the psychic makeover women are expected to undergo, and coexisting alongside calls to confident femininity, the sexperts in the online spaces under scrutiny here construct a female subject whose sexual appeal and practice is failing or lacking and needs (ongoing) scrutiny, discipline and work. This operates through the portrayal of men's consumption of pornography as a response to inadequate lust stimulus: "do you maintain your sex appeal for your husband?" (enfemenino.com forum). Also blamed is women's supposedly unsatisfactory sexual upkeep: "it is very probable that he is sexually unsatisfied" (enfemenino.com forum). This obligatory labour

involves providing men good enough sex both in terms of *quantity* and *quality*, for example: "in a healthy relationship you should be having enough sex that he doesnt need to watch t every day" (cosmopolitan.co.uk forum), and "maybe you are falling short in bed, find out what he likes" (enfemenino.com forum).

On the basis of the premise that men watch pornography because they are sexually unsatisfied, women are exhorted to engage with a narrow repertoire of commodified sexual practices to regain men's interest and ensure their satisfaction. This feminine labour entails "visual stimulation" by wearing make-up, and "keeping in shape, wearing nice clothes/high heals around him" (femalefirst.co.uk forum), besides practices now considered compulsory for women in relationships, such as "surprising him with a bj" (blow job) and "doing a sexy striptease", as well as constantly working to "expand your sexual repertoire" (all cosmopolitan.co.uk forum). In this sense, users of the cosmopolitan.co.uk forum recommend creating "topless selfies" and to "try something new in the bedroom like some more kinkiness" as "showing a more adventurous side to yourself can really turn a man on". The advice in these sites thereby props up the feminine 'sexual entrepreneur' (Harvey & Gill, 2011), including her newer – post-*Fifty Shades Of Grey* (James, 2011) – 'kinky chic' or 'bondage babe' element. As a neoliberal subject, this inhabitant of a strictly policed and delimited sexual matrix is incited to relentlessly self-improve and renovate through entrepreneurialism and "consuming the self into being" (Ringrose & Walkerdine, 2008, p. 227). A link between sexuality and commodity culture suffuses both the editorial and user-generated content, as in: "You could suggest dressing up for him or introducing some sex toys into your sexual play to make things more exciting" (editorial, femalefirst.co.uk), "you could try and spice your sex life up a

Postfeminist Sexpertise on the 'Porn and Men Issue'

bit, next time your in town casually take him into Ann Summers [retailer of sex toys and underwear]", and "Get some sexy lingerie like a baby doll and stockings" (both cosmopolitan.co.ukforum). The first quotation clearly testifies to the commercial imperative of the sites: femalefirst.co.uk has a lingerie shopping section, and is littered with advertorials and links to retail websites for sex toys and costumes. Concerning the widespread reproduction of such consumerist discourses in the forums, this adds as yet another form of free immaterial labour performed by digital media users benefiting corporations (Campbell, 2011). Ultimately, it points to the commercial conquest of the sphere of sexuality.

In these transnational spaces, being sexually compliant to men's sexual desires, regardless of personal views or wants, is normalised as what women in love do. Furthermore, a number of forum contributors advance this as a requirement to prevent men from leaving. In addition to such a threat, the post below also suggests the casual normalisation of women's incorporation of commercial sex aesthetics and activities to satisfy men while in (and for the good of) committed heterosexual relationships:

> You will lose him being like this. I am not telling you to like what he likes ... if he likes porn so much, lose your inhibitions, stimulate his visual sexuality by buying a really sexy lingerie set and doing for him a phenomenal striptease as if you were a true porn actress (enfemenino.com forum)

No other feminine subject weaves together more perniciously aesthetic, sexual and psychic labour than the 'sexual entrepreneur' (Harvey & Gill, 2011). In the data, her 'technology of sexiness' (Radner, 1993) also entails being 'confident' and 'cool' with (men's) pornography. Two illustrations from the cosmopolitan.co.uk forum are: "a woman who is confident with regards to porn is sexy" and "women who are cool about these kind of things are considered very sexy by a lot of men, whereas 'needy' behaviour like freaking over things like this just pushes them further away".

It is remarkable how unequally distributed care and empathy are. While any sign of female emotional fragility or dependency is resolutely not tolerated, cast as pathological, indisputably repulsive and toxic for relationships, women are expected to be permanently attentive and responsive to – even anticipatory of – men's needs, desires and insecurities. Moreover, women's wishes or anxieties are rendered invisible through an emphasis on those potentially experienced by men (as projected by respondents). The femalefirst.co.uk editorial response to the reader letter "He's having live chat sex with other women!" includes: "Perhaps he is craving for something new from you in the bedroom but too shy to ask?" In a similar manner, the peer-to-peer messages both in Spanish and in English offer the following advice: "ask him if he would want to treat you like a porn star, maybe he's just imagining That which he is too afraid to ask" (cosmopolitan.co.uk forum), and "Maybe he wants to realise a fantasy and is shy to tell you, watch porn with him" (enfemenino.com forum).

Indeed, there is an overwhelming consensus both in the editorial and user-generated content in the Spain- and UK-based websites that the solution to women's dilemma is to watch pornography with their partner. This is variously depicted as normatively demanded instrumental behaviour to satisfy men and for the benefit of the relationship, and, to a lesser extent, as an empowering and pleasurable activity. In this sense, some self-defined women point to their own use and enjoyment of pornography: "I love watching porn!" (cosmopolitan.co.uk forum). Others draw on a hedonistic discourse of shared playfulness and pleasure, for example: "see how much fun you can have with each other" and "its such a turn on we always end up having great sex" (both cosmopolitan.co.uk forum). These messages thus make a strong gesture to the 'Fun, Fearless Female' of the global *Cosmopolitan* brand, to the playful, feisty, pleasure-seeking and sexually desiring version of femininity of much postfeminist media and advertising.

More recurrently, however, "watching porn with your OH" (cosmopolitan.co.uk forum) is depicted in instrumental terms as sex-life enhancing. One instance of this pervasive piece of advice is the following from the cosmopolitan.co.uk forum: "Why don't you watch porn with him. ... Watching it together and commenting on it (dirty talk) can enhance your sex life". The editorial content of this women's magazine equally suggests: "Instead of losing sleep over it, why not join him? Watching porn together can be a great way to expand your sexual repertoire". Women are also encouraged to – enthusiastically and actively – engage in this activity simply because, as an article in elle.es explains: "to watch a porn film with a girl is the fantasy of many men". Namely, as an act of love: "He will love you for it" (cosmopolitan.co.uk forum), and "If you care about your boyfriend, you can show interest in a pleasant way in his virtual pastimes" (enfemenino.com forum).

In addition to embracing pornography consumption as a pleasure producing device or, more recurrently, in instrumental ways to spice up sex and please (to keep) men, women are advised to fashion themselves according to the pornographic aesthetics from, and to engage in the sexual acts depicted in, the material their partners enjoy. For example, the 'agony aunt' in female.first.co.uk suggests: "maybe have a sneaky look at the girls in the porn films to see what they are wearing and try and match it", and "Why not try to get more involved with it – watch it together or play out one the fantasies in the recording?" The forum users of this publication equally advise: "Does he look at any particular genre? If so, pay attention to those, and try to work them into your bedroom activities". This chapter hence provides further evidence that pornography consumption, along with sex industry aesthetics and practices, is being normalised as part of a modern (particularly young) woman's sexual repertoire (Gill, 2009), showing that this is not limited to Anglo-American media, but is very much part of the sexpertise circulating online in women's journalism as well as peer networks across and beyond national contexts.

Conclusion: postfeminist sexpertise

Focussing upon commentary about the "porn and men issue" in online women's magazines, this chapter has unpacked three interrelated ideological formations – 'postfeminist biologism', 'toxic insecurity' and 'porn(ified) upgrade' – crossing conventional boundaries of authorship and genre, language and nation-state. The identified (re-)mediations of gender and intimacy advance a depoliticised, individualised interpretation of women's situation and discontents, built according to, and mystified by, neoliberalism and postfeminism. In this context, much like sex and gender relations, pornography is becoming increasingly unknowable as a political or feminist issue. Such a manoeuvre works to disarticulate the potential for solidarity and politicised collectivity among women, which are further discouraged by the attack on social empathy nourished by the neoliberal ethos, and are rather rechannelled into technologies of self-governance through confidence and entrepreneurism.

The identified sexpertise operates to discipline female bodies, affect and thought into deeply injurious and unjust psycho-social arrangements. While men are deemed as entitled to more understanding, the female user is expected to adopt a position of compliance, to resign herself to the biological inevitability of male sexuality. Further, she is expected to subjugate her feelings, views and needs – which are stringently policed, pathologised, ridiculed and cast as toxic – and instead adapt and respond to her partner's. Positioned as failed subject-objects of desire-consumption, working on constructing an upgraded – pornified – selfhood is advanced as women's only intelligible response to male consumption of pornography. These critical readings do not negate the potential pleasures enjoyed by those who give and take up the advice, but rather respond to my aspiration for our mediated intimacies to place compassion, consensus and consent at the centre of relationships, along with a sexual liberation grounded on erotic justice for all.

References

Ahmed, S. (2012). *On being included: Racism and diversity in institutional life*. Durham, NC: Duke University Press.

Baker, J. (2010). Claiming volition and evading victimhood: Post-feminist obligations for young women. *Feminism & Psychology, 20*(2), 186–204.

Banet-Weiser, S. (2013). Am I pretty or ugly? Girls and the market for self-esteem. *Girlhood Studies, 7*(1), 83–101.

Campbell, J. (2011). It takes an ivillage: Gender, labour, and community in the age of television-Internet convergence. *International Journal of Communication, 5*(11), 492–510.

De Lauretis, T. (1987). *Technologies of gender: Essays on theory, film and fiction*. Bloomington & Indianapolis: Indiana University Press.

Evans, A., & Riley, S. (2014). *Technologies of sexiness: Sex, identity and consumer culture*. New York, NY: Oxford University Press.

Farvid, P., & Braun, V. (2014). The "sassy woman" and the "performing man": Heterosexual casual sex advice and the (re)constitution of gendered subjectivities. *Feminist Media Studies, 14*(1), 118–134.

Favaro, L. (2016). "Just be confident girls!": Confidence chic as neoliberal governmentality. In A. S. Elias, R. Gill, & C. Scharff (Eds.), *Aesthetic labour: Rethinking beauty politics in neoliberalism*. London, United Kingdom: Palgrave Macmillan.

Foucault, M. (1988). Technologies of the self. In L. Martin, H. Gutman, & P. Hutton, (Eds.), *Technologies of the self: A seminar with Michel Foucault* (pp. 16–49). London, United Kingdom: Tavistock.

García-Favaro, L. (2015). "Porn trouble": On the sexual regime and travels of postfeminist biologism. *Australian Feminist Studies, 30*(86), 366–376.

García-Favaro, L. (2016). From produsers to shareaholics: Changing models of reader interaction in women's online magazines. *tripleC: Communication, Capitalism & Critique, 14*(2), 346–379.

García-Favaro, L., & Gill, R. (2016). "Emasculation nation has arrived": Sexism rearticulated in online responses to Lose the Lads' Mags campaign, *Feminist Media Studies, 16*(3), 379–397.

Gavey, N. (2005). *Just sex?: The cultural scaffolding of rape*. London, United Kingdom: Routledge.

Gill, R. (2007). *Gender and the media*. Cambridge, United Kingdom: Polity Press.

Gill, R. (2009). Mediated intimacy and postfeminism: A discourse analytic examination of sex and relationships advice in a woman's magazine. *Discourse and Communication, 3*(4), 345–369.

Gill, R. (2012). Media, empowerment and the 'sexualization of culture' debates. *Sex Roles, 66*(11–12), 736–745.

Gill, R., & Elias, A. S. (2014). 'Awaken your incredible': Love your body discourses and postfeminist contradictions. *International Journal of Media & Cultural Politics, 10*(2), 179–188.

Gray, J. (1992). *Men are From Mars, Women are from Venus*. London, United Kingdom: Thorsons.

Harvey, L., & Gill, R. (2011). The sex inspectors: Self-help, makeover and mediated sex. In K. Ross (Ed.), *Handbook on gender, sexualities and media* (pp. 487–501). Oxford, United Kingdom: Blackwell.

James, E. L. (2011). *Fifty Shades of Grey*. New York, NY: Vintage Books.

McRobbie, A. (2008). Pornographic permutations. *The Communication Review, 11*(3), 225–236.

O'Neill, R. (2015). The work of seduction: Theorising sexual subjectivity and mediated intimacy in the London 'seduction community'. *Sociological Research Online, 20*(4), 5.

Radner, H. (1993). Pretty is as pretty does: Free enterprise and the marriage plot. In H. Collins, H. Radner, & A. Preacher (Eds.), *Film theory goes to the movies* (pp. 56–76). New York, NY: Routledge.

Ringrose, J., & Walkerdine, V. (2008). Regulating the abject. *Feminist Media Studies, 8*(3), 227–246.

Saad, G. (2013). The consuming instinct: What Darwinian consumption reveals about human nature. *Politics and the Life Sciences, 32*(1), 58–72.

Salmon, C. (2004). The pornography debate: What sex differences in erotica can tell us about human sexuality. In C. Crawford & C. Salmon (Eds.), *Evolutionary psychology, public policy and personal decisions* (pp. 217–230). Mahwah, NJ: Erlbaum.

Salmon, C. (2012). The pop culture of sex: An evolutionary window on the worlds of pornography and romance. *Review of General Psychology, 16*(2), 152–160.

CHAPTER FOUR

REVOLTING WOMEN: PERFORMING THE 'NEW EXPLICIT'

Emma L. E. Rees

It may seem strange, but bear with me, to begin a chapter in a book about pornography, and to articulate for the first time a concept – the 'New Explicit' – by considering an image not of oiled and lissom bodies intertwined in the throes of priapic agitation, but of the assembled participants of the G8 forum (the leaders of the world's largest industrial democratic nations). It is an easy enough photograph to find on the Internet (I'm referring to the G8 picture, here, although numerous versions of the other one are, these days, just as easily accessed), and what is immediately striking about it, year in and year out, is how utterly homogeneous it is. The G8 leaders are hegemony and the patriarchy in formation. The picture will, inevitably, show a row of men in an unimaginative uniform of suits and ties, offset by just one woman (still in a trouser suit, but dressed a little more colourfully than her male counterparts). This is a disturbing image: here is where real power resides, in the hands of gurning, well-fed men in suits.

At the heart of this chapter is rage. But it is not rage directed, as it ought to be, at the structural gender inequalities personified in the bogus rictus of world leaders, and perpetuated in their policies. Nor is the rage focussed on the monolithic powers of the military-industrial complex, nor even at the futile deaths of small children in Damascus. It is a rage directed instead at a softly spoken Australian woman called Casey Jenkins. What moves newspaper readers to rage? Not Trident, nor austerity; not famine, nor poverty (although these issues do, of course, generate their own *Sturm und Drang* in some publications), but vaginas. In this instance, one vagina in particular: the artist Casey Jenkins's vagina. It has been noted (Valentine & Wilchins, as cited in Karkazis, 2008, p. 147) that, pound for pound, genitals account for only about one per cent of the body's total surface area. But what a contested little percentage that is. Wars have been started and lives lost because of the urgings of that 1%; and, depending on who does what with their 1%, and with whom, the online comments sections of newspapers become a breeding ground for cultural anxieties and moral indignation.

The word 'explicit' derives from the Latin 'explicare' – to unfold. It is a word often used to shock and sensationalise, having moved away from its etymology to become synonymous with 'hard-core' or 'full on'. An 'explicit' image is, then, one which lacks nuance or complexity: its meaning is overt. It is denotative more than it is connotative or representational. But a return to the word's roots can be rewarding, and, yes, revealing. In coining the term the 'New Explicit' my aim is to reclaim nuance, connotation and depth, through a sometimes literal 'unfolding'. But it rapidly becomes apparent that when a female artist or performer takes control of the New Explicit, of that unfolding or revelation of her sexual identity, rage, not sexual arousal (the principal objective of pornography) is the overriding response.

The unfolding of the sexual self is threatening in a way that pornography is not. For a start, the New Explicit cannot be monetised in the same ways as pornography. Second, it has depth and also, third, self-containment – it does not depend for its meaning on the presence of an observer. Finally, its empowerment of women performers threatens the hegemony: until the day comes that the G8 roll-call photograph shows a line of women, women who demonstrate independence and creativity will remain routinely denigrated. There is a genealogy for the New Explicit, as this chapter shows, and it is a notion that resonates with what Linda Williams has called "hard-core art film", which is "hard-core in its explicitness, yet not pornography in a primary desire to arouse" (Williams, 2014, p. 29). To unfold oneself is to engage in a series of self-determined, explicit acts in which the power dynamic is far removed from another unfolding, this time of that now outdated porn phenomenon: the centrefold.

In constructing a genealogy for the concept of the New Explicit, I have looked at the work of five women artists spanning the last half century. While these women do not directly reference one another, to my mind they are all placed squarely on the same powerful cultural continuum. These are revolting women, where 'to revolt' entails a turning away from, and rejection of, the dominant images, discourses, and power dynamics that inhere in 'hegemonic' pornography. Porn is no longer quite the "outlaw discourse" (Attwood, 2002, p. 93) that it once was.

As far back as 1998, Lynn S. Chancer argued that "hegemonic pornography" is an inevitable by-product of patriarchy, since "as long as a given society remains largely controlled by men in terms of who hold a preponderance of economic, political, and technical power, certain sexual representations are likely to become ideologically predominant over others" (p. 77). What Chancer could not have foreseen twenty years ago was how much the Internet, and the rise of user-generated content, would change things. Without realising it, Chancer was effectively anticipating the emergence on almost anyone's computer, tablet or smartphone, of sub-genres and styles such as alt or gonzo porn. What were once niche tastes in porn, presumably gratified only in the basements of sleazy 'private' shops, are now easily accessible, even though it

Revolting Women: Performing the 'New Explicit'

is still the case that most pornography "manifests a rather remarkable and somewhat ironic homogeneity amid its apparently rich and ultracommodified diversity" (Chancer, 1998, p. 77).

The ready availability of a staggering array of different types of porn today has not led to a concomitant rise in more tolerant responses to women who engage in explicit activities with their own bodies. Because these activities are not designed with the needs of an onlooker as the chief focus, the bodies that are implicated become designated not only as revolting against the hegemony, but also as being 'revolting' in the sense of 'disgusting'. Autonomous female sexual bodies inspire far more revulsion than they do admiration. Their explicitness demonstrates how much more exists beyond being an object for the sexual arousal of a third party. 'You' simply do not figure in their performances. 'Your' role is thus problematised: in pornography, 'you' are indispensable in giving purpose and meaning to the images on which you gaze. In consuming porn 'you' acquiesce to a fundamentally dialogic relationship, where "Consciousness of self is possible only on the basis of differentiation: 'I' cannot be signified or conceived without the conception 'non-I', 'you', and dialogue, the fundamental condition of language, implies a reversible polarity between 'I' and 'you'" (Belsey, 2002, p. 49). The New Explicit, by contrast, exposes the precarious ontology of the viewer.

Shigeko Kubota (b. Japan, 1937), Carolee Schneemann (b. America, 1939), Annie Sprinkle (b. America, 1954), Megumi Igarashi (b. Japan, 1972) and Casey Jenkins (b. Australia, 1979), are the women who, in their art and performances, exemplify the ethos of the New Explicit. If porn is designed to arouse and to eschew any kind of interpretive difficulty that might produce a barrier between the viewer, or consumer, and his or her orgasm, then what these women do is the polar opposite of that.

Pornographies

Their bodily texts urge intellectual, not sexual, activity on the viewer's behalf (assuming a viewer is even present – it is not a prerequisite for the New Explicit), and encourage high-level conceptual engagement that transcends the dynamics of porn. (That said, given the dazzling variety of porn's sub-genres, there probably are people who are sexually aroused by aspects of the New Explicit, but such arousal is not its primary aim.)

My aim here is not to focus on tired, well-rehearsed debates around porn, for it is the case that, "what was once definable as essentially a social problem has now become a social phenomenon" (Ribner, 2014, p. 376). Instead, I shall consider the antecedents and trailblazers; the women who demonstrate physical and psychical self-containment in their explicit art. And it is precisely this autonomy that riles commentators – my analysis of the user-generated comments on a newspaper article about the artist Casey Jenkins illustrates this. Those who left comments are not the 'ideal' viewers of junk, and many of them report revulsion at Jenkins's closed-off, yet open, body. She, as I'll show, is one of the most recent in a tradition of women who use their bodies against the hegemony and against pornography; they have shaken themselves free of a need to perform with their bodies in a way that pleases others – the 'you' of Belsey's formulation. Their autonomy is revolting to readers, ironically, given that many of those same readers have their own vaginas and menses. And many other readers consume pornography that features, at the very least, vaginas, if not menses too (Jenkins's "Vaginal Knitting", as I shall argue, intentionally brought to light those bodily secretions, including menstrual blood, that are more commonly kept hidden). In other words, 'explicit' is acceptable when it is serving the purpose of sexually arousing a third party; when it doesn't depend on a third party for its meaning, it is offensive. Women pleasing themselves *for themselves* are socially constructed as offensive, not least in their rejection of the supply and demand exchanges of the market economy. New Explicit acts demonstrate breathtaking autonomy in their self-referential significations.

New explicit performers
In the 1960s, the conservative American art establishment was shaken by the activities of what became known as the Fluxus movement of iconoclastic, experimental artists. At a Fluxus gathering in New York in 1965 a young Japanese artist called Shigeko Kubota created her "Vagina Painting". Kubota squatted over a large sheet of paper, which had been placed flat on the floor. Using a paintbrush, which appeared to extend from her vagina, she began to draw calligraphic brushstrokes in menstrual blood-red paint. There was, in Kubota's performance, the powerful self-containment that I argue typifies the New Explicit. On some level, she was appropriating the phallic brush in a riposte to the painted ejaculatory splatters of Jackson Pollock, the abstract expressionist who had died in 1956. Further, she was being simultaneously avant garde and traditional, in co-opting traditional Japanese calligraphy or brushwork, and also by reimagining the geisha tradition of grabbing on to Ben Wa balls using vaginal muscles. Despite these implied gestures to cultural rituals, it is the closed loop of Kubota's explicitness that is most important here. That is, 'the artwork' is both finished product (the brushstrokes on the paper) and process: neither fully makes sense without the other. In creating her "Vagina Painting", Kubota's body was at once origin and destination, and the vagina, that into which things – any number of different things – are routinely inserted in a pornographic context, instead unfolds, and creates meaning. In the New Explicit, the vagina *does*, more than it is done *to*.

Pornographies

Carolee Schneemann first performed her "Interior Scroll" ten years after Kubota's "Vagina Painting", again in New York. Naked, Schneemann stood on a table, and "began to remove a long (36" × 2.25") concertinaed paper scroll from her vagina, reading from it, inch by inch" (Rees, 2015, p. 227). In an act of literal unfolding, and revelation, Schneemann slowly brought the scroll into the arena of the observed, and of the interpreted. On the scroll were Schneemann's own writings and drawings, aimed at puncturing the rhetoric around gender equality: "he ['a happy man / a structuralist filmmaker'] told me he had lived with / a 'sculptress' I asked does / that make me a 'film-makeress'? / 'Oh no,' he said. 'We think of you / as a dancer'" (Schneemann, 2002, p. 160). As with Kubota – and unlike many porn scenarios – in Schneemann's art the vagina explicitly and actively produces and creates. It is not a passive receptacle for semen, sex toys, or the projected fantasies of a viewer. Schneemann is both subject and object within a framework of complex signs, controlled by her and existing without accountability to the needs or desires of anyone else.

The former porn actor and activist Annie Sprinkle is, as I have argued elsewhere (Rees, 2015), a key practitioner in the emergence of what I term the New Explicit. Her most celebrated and controversial performance art sequence, "Public Cervix Announcement", was viewed live in the late 1980s and early 1990s by around 25,000 people altogether. In "Public Cervix Announcement", Sprinkle set out to dictate the sexual uses of her own body on her own terms: "I felt I was fixing taboos that were not in our best interest, like using a speculum without a medical degree and looking at our beautiful genitals in bright light and in public" (Sprinkle, cited in Rees, 2015, p. 230).

In "Public Cervix Announcement" Sprinkle is simultaneously commentator and actor; subject and object; unmistakeably in control. And that 'control' is not simply fiscal; it is about epistemic and aesthetic autonomy, too. After an onstage douche during which Sprinkle chatted comfortably with the audience, she would insert a metal speculum so that around forty audience members could, one-by-one, hold a little torch and peer at Sprinkle's cervix. This is a literally explicit act: the folds of the labia have been parted, the speculum inserted, and the cervix made visible.

Similarly, in her piece "Deep Inside Annie Sprinkle", the artist disrupted theatrical conventions by breaking the fourth wall in order to interact with on-screen images and viewers. This interaction unsettled the 'safe' distance that usually exists between porn actor and the porn consumer: Sprinkle recounts how she would go "into a movie theater where one of my porn movies is playing and have sex with several of the porn fans who are watching me on screen" (Sprinkle, quoted in Cody, & Sprinkle, 2001, p. 7). In these iterations of the New Explicit, Sprinkle unsettles the traditional dynamic of the pornographic gaze; she can look at the viewer who is looking at her, creating an immediacy and relationship which is absent from hegemonic porn.

In 2013 the video of Australian Casey Jenkins's "Vaginal Knitting" craft/performance piece went viral. In the three-minute film, called "Casting off my Womb", Jenkins recorded the knitting she did every day for twenty-eight days, using skeins of wool that she had carefully inserted into, and then drawn out from, her vagina. Menstrual blood (that is, 'cast off' endometrial cells) stained some of what slowly became a long scarf; other sections of it appeared pristine and white. Like Kubota, Schneemann, and Sprinkle, Jenkins was making her sexual organs explicit *on her own terms*. And it is precisely this autonomy, I'd argue, and as I'll shortly demonstrate, that made commentators so venomous in their assessments of "Casting

Off". This is the New Explicit: Jenkins refuses to feel shame in setting the parameters for the representation of her own body.

The final artist I want to situate in this emerging tradition of the New Explicit is Megumi Igarashi. Igarashi was arrested by the Japanese authorities in 2014, released, and then charged again. She stood trial in 2015, accused of obscenity for circulating online images of her vulva. Some of the images had been 3D-printed and made into a full-sized, fully functional canoe. In an interview with David McNeill, "Artist says her vagina creations confront a Japanese taboo" (McNeill, 2015), Igarashi identified a degree of hypocrisy in Japanese culture over sexualised images and who controls and has access to them. "Japan is inconsistent", Igarashi is reported as saying: "If you ride the train you're confronted with adverts with sexual images and you cannot avoid looking at them. All these notions are based on the men's viewpoint and there is a lack of empowerment of women" (McNeill, 2015). She was charged under the obscenity laws of a country that only made being in possession of images of child sexual abuse illegal in July 2015. Igarashi's explicit autonomy was, ultimately, what meant that she fell foul of the laws of a country where it is still not an offence to possess anime illustrations of images of child sexual abuse.

New explicit commentators
One need look no further for an indication of prevalent social attitudes and moral panic than the "comments" sections found under articles or op-eds in most online newspapers and forums. Reading the comments is, usually, ill-advised, not least because of what Cohen-Almagor (2015) has identified as their non-reflective, rushed nature. "The processes of production, editing, and diffusion are now squeezed into brief moments", he writes: "The ease of pressing a button tempts many to post half-baked

thoughts, instinctive reactions, and impulsive rather than thoughtful comments" (Cohen-Almagor, 2015, p. 93). At best, 'comments' sections are hardly a paean to user-generated content; at worst they constitute a tawdry, often unregulated repository for humanity's least ennobling suppositions.

On 6 December 2013, the *Daily Mail* ran a story about Casey Jenkins headlined "She didn't learn THAT at WI: 'Vaginal knitter' spends 28 days making scarf from wool stored inside her" (Winter, 2013). Jenkins was the main feature of the piece (the newspaper provided a link to the YouTube video of her "Casting off my Womb"), but mention was also made of the art of the Chilean Carina Ubeda's work (Ubeda displayed five years' worth of menstrual blood collected on fragments of cloth, suspended from the ceiling in small embroidery hoops next to blackened apples). The presence of menstrual blood in the work of both Jenkins and Ubeda kindles primal fears in observers. Although the painter and photographer Vanessa Tiegs has attempted to create and participate in a movement that she terms "Menstrala Art", the extreme taboo remains: menstrual blood is blood lost (usually) without signalling danger – it is a marker of a uterus that has not 'done its job' of procreation. To make menstrual blood visible is to unfold or reveal what many would prefer remained the "mysteries" of female sexuality.

Comments on the *Daily Mail* article were, for some reason, unmoderated. A total of 282 were posted (some users posted more than one comment) from the date of the article's publication through to about July 2014. I grouped the comments into six categories. In the first category I placed comments that focussed on the readers' responses and feelings of revulsion (a fairly typical response here would be: "I'm sorry. That's disgusting."). Some readers intimated that Jenkins had to be mentally ill ("Certifiable!!"). I placed these comments into a second group. In the third group were comments that, often in a non-aggressive way, expressed bewilderment ("What did I just read?"); and comments that attempted humour went into the fourth ("Beyond ridiculous. It'll be someone's crocheting from their bottom next"). There was a small category for those comments which simply didn't fit into one of the others and, finally, there was a tiny category of positive comments.

Of the commentators, 69% (I have rounded percentages up or down to the nearest whole number) reported themselves as being UK-based (an unsurprising majority, given that the *Mail* is a British newspaper); 12% stated that they were from the USA. The remainder came from countries throughout the world, and one claimed to be from the Moon (a reach of which most daily newspapers can only dream). I am aware, of course, of the potential pitfalls of extrapolating from the 'found data' of comments left in response to Internet pieces: they may present a skewed impression of dominant cultural opinions. For example, the impetus to comment may arise more easily out of anger than from joy and approval. But, as Christine Hine argues, "Collections of fragments that are similar in some way may be brought together in order to explore patterns, and to highlight similarities and differences which may tell us something about underlying structures and values", and "An ethnographic treatment of found data can permit a focus on what common forms of expression and structures of meaning are found in a population" (Hine, 2015, p. 162).

One-third of all of the comments expressed revulsion at Jenkins's art (it was her work that seemed to garner almost all of the attention, despite the mention of Ubeda in the same article). These comments ranged from the very brief – "Pukesville", "Vile", "Eeeeew!!!" – to the more expansively vitriolic: "This is just disgusting! Feminist art? What a load of old rubbish! It's just some strange fetish that she wants to share with the world! Horrible dirty woman". Another commentator

Revolting Women: Performing the 'New Explicit'

wrote: "grosssssssssssssssssss! why was there a need to even publish this garbage? and who is going to want her knitted piece? with all her cooter juice on it not to mention blood sick and just plain gross! plz stop giving there[2] ppl any attention".

The pleasurable arousal, which is the chief objective of porn, is completely absent from these comments. Jenkins's self-containment leads to ejaculations that are quite different from those to which porn gives rise. Her work is repeatedly denigrated as arousing unpleasant bodily responses in observers. Jenkins revolts against dominant cultural imperatives about her genitals, and the result is that the somatic feelings provoked by her explicitness are powerful – and negative. "I've just been sick in my mouth", reads one comment; "just thrown up in my mouth" reads another; and "I feel sick :o(" goes a third.

Around 21% of the comments suggest that Jenkins must be mentally ill to be doing what she is doing: "as a healthcare professional i thought i had heard it all … she needs sectioning!" "Sometimes", opined another commentator, "the word 'Art' is used to disguise serious mental illness". And this, in another comment: "If you captioned it 'mental patient post lobotomy' i would have believed you more. She looks short of a few things upstairs in that first pic. Jeepers".

Is the intimation, then, that a woman doing things with her own body for her own ends without reference to culturally designated notions of appropriateness (and this isn't just about a chaste 'respectability' – hegemonic porn also operates to perpetuate a narrative of acceptable female behaviour), must be somehow 'mad'? The suspicions which circulate around the autonomous woman who subverts the 'feminine role' were

---

[2] The website material cited in this chapter is reproduced as posted online (apart from omitted material shown by ellipses: '…').

encapsulated by Jane Ussher (1991): "To be a woman is often to be mad. If we stay inside our prescribed roles and routes ..., or if we speak out, or move outside our designated paths we become mad" (p. 6). This is a no-win situation, and it is one into which her detractors are quick to condemn Jenkins: "what a bloody fruitcake, she needs help"; "Disgusting, she must be bonkers"; "Bonkers!"; and "Fruitloop". Finally, one comment asks: "Err can the last person on planet insanity please put the cat out[?]".

For women in the West, the expression of sexual autonomy in the capitalist paradigm is fraught. As Chancer (1998) wrote: "To challenge sexism and feel sexually free still calls for assiduous negotiations, and often unsatisfactory compromises; many women seem unable to realize a comfortable combination" (p. 62). This is not least because of the "chasm that separates the acts of confronting sexism and liberating sexuality" (Chancer, 1998, p. 62). "Sexual freedom" has not always been liberating for women, since it "has never really been about *sexual justice between men and women*. It has been about maintaining men's superior status, men's power over women; and it has been about sexualising women's inferior status" (Stoltenberg, 2000, n.p.).

To engage with the New Explicit is to leave entrenched societal norms behind, and, evidently, is to baffle commentators. The cultural violation enacted by the proponent of the New Explicit is manifold: not only are traditional 'feminine' qualities of compliance and decorum being overturned, but so too are the unwritten rules and expectations of hegemonic porn. Jenkins, like Kubota, Schneemann and Sprinkle before her, and as Igarashi does, too, is putting a new iteration of the sexual female body firmly on to centre stage.

Irony and reflection get lost in the thicket of negative comments, to the point where, apparently oblivious to the interconnectedness of hate and fear, one commentator was moved to remark that: "Nobody this side of the Spin Ghar mountains [the natural frontier between Pakistan and Afghanistan] has a 'fear' of female genitalia. What a load of feminist nonsense!" But it is "fear" that does ooze out of the majority of the comments: "Whatever next?! Dread to think", and "Omg this is disgusting, why do we need to know[?]".

One comment made an attempt to situate Jenkins in a wider artistic or ideological tradition, but in negative and dismissive terms: "Not really sure knitting as part of the performance piece highlights a protest against gender roles but rather stereotypes in a less than negative way her own preconception of gender roles … these methods of feminism (Wool-knitting) through Art were used originally in the 1970's and it is a shame that this piece of work does not comment on the advances made by the second wave feminists but instead undermines her/our predecessors". My own favourite comment (because of its non sequitur character) came from a reader in Australia who felt moved simply to remark: "Lots of typos in this article".

Some commentators tried to calm their feelings of unease by attempting humour. "OK I'm going to make my singing foreskin public now. Just you wait" went one remark, while another writer asked: "What's next for her then … decorating the xmas tree with her used tamp*ns? and letme guess … she'll perch herself on the top as the angel!" This same commentator, "Jane" from Edinburgh, got on a bit of a roll, despite evidently being perturbed by the word 'tampon'. She also wrote: "My husband just offered to insert a ball of wool into his backside and knit me a pair of mittens for the cold spell".

Others felt compelled to defend Art in their comments. "I think this woman's just cross[ed] the line", wrote one American commentator, continuing: "Art?? Really!!!! For me that's a violation to every woman intimaty, including her self. Like others says, whats next?? We need to relearn self respect". "Will" from Lichfield in the UK also expressed aesthetic disappointment, as well as a concern for commuters: "I hope she stops when she gets on the bus, sorry but this just made me laugh if a normal person did this they would prob section them but its ok as its in the name of art, personally I think she needs some help". And some were offended by the newspaper running the story at all, apparently forgetting that they were not actually compelled to read, or comment on, it: "Art? Er – mentally unstable ... She'll probably end up with an infection. This is the very worst kind of feminist crap – don't give her the publicity ... revolting creature". And "Bo Roberts" from Los Angeles was motivated to comment: "WARNING: One more undeserving story like this, and I'm unsubscribing to your Publications" (I especially liked the comment immediately following Bo's: "I am sure we'll manage without you dear").

Comments that might broadly be termed "positive" about Jenkins and her work (the two are, more often than not, conflated by readers) make up under 1% of the total number of contributions. There were just two: "Thank you! You are so lovely! Thank you so much for doing this!!" came one comment from Portugal, and another commentator offered the slightly more qualified remark: "I think she[']s very brave if a little out there, shows how robust the female antomy is and is something to be proud of and celebrated it[']s not as if anyone is wearing the scarf is it[?]".

The 2015 Gallup "Morals and Beliefs" survey found that 43% of adult American men and 25% of adult American women said they found pornography "morally respectable". However, to use the term 'pornography' in a context like this is about as helpful as using the term 'food' when what you really want to know is if someone likes broccoli or not. If you ask them if they like 'food' they will probably answer 'yes'. But if you're more specific, the reply will change. 'Is food OK?' is not the same question as 'Do you find cruciferous vegetables to be gastronomically desirable?' Similarly, 'Is porn "morally respectable"?' is not the same question as 'Is an image of fisting "morally respectable"?', and the answers would indicate this.

What the Gallup statistics do tell us, however, is that, assuming British and American adults share dominant cultural tastes and attitudes, then many of those 282 comments on the *Daily Mail* website were left by people who consume, and presumably enjoy, what might be termed 'pornography'. The revolting woman, though, opts out of the producer/consumer dynamic of porn, and instead exhibits autonomy and a refusal to be anyone else's object. She quite literally cannot, if the comments that focus on emesis are anything to go by, be stomached ("Revolting repulsive disgusting vomit inducing. I can go on for days. I am a woman but this is not celebrating women, this is celebrating crazy filthy yuck").

There is something explicit yet unerotic about Jenkins's activity. She resists using her body according to the unwritten rules and precepts that inform how women's bodies are used in porn. Like Schneemann, Kubota and Sprinkle, Jenkins is calling the (money) shots and resisting what's paradoxically portrayed as 'acceptable' modes of displaying the female body – either in an attitude of modesty and impermeable, near-hermeneutic submissiveness, or in a way that pays obeisance to the hegemony. Indeed, the New Explicit is a crucial riposte to hegemonic pornography. It is a renegotiation of outmoded power structures and pornographic cultures of dependence or even interaction; it is women saying loud and clear what they want to do with, and to, their own sexual organs.

New explicit futures

If the insertion of the self into a dialogue with pornographic images leads to masturbation, then it is clear that engagement with the *Daily Mail* leads to mass perturbation. The vitriol, as the comments demonstrate, is the almost inevitable consequence of a woman using her body sexually, but not in order to arouse. And the irony is that it is in the nature of being human that we ordinarily desire explication more than we revile it. That may, of course, account for how porn is shaking itself free of its cultural 'outlaw' status. As recently as 2014, David S. Ribner defended a piece of his writing thus: "This is not an editorial promoting pornography; it is an editorial advocating an acknowledgement of reality" (Ribner, 2014, p. 375).

If we do not make porn academic, or if we fail to engage with its ubiquity and traction, then we are creating a cultural blind spot that makes us unqualified to be cultural commentators. We are in danger of wilfully ignoring a major facet of modern life, and we are thereby refusing to engage with the complexities of the contested political and ideological space of women's bodies. In writing this chapter for *Pornographies: Critical Positions*, I have argued for an unfolding of the meanings that pervade some kinds of explicit images. Whether the New Explicit finds expression in painting (Kubota), writing (Schneemann), education (Sprinkle), knitting (Jenkins), or even in making a small boat (Igarashi), it is about women exercising a kind of power and autonomy which porn often negates.

We need, as Heather Berg puts it, to "un-exceptionalize" (Berg, 2014, p. 75) porn, in order to locate it firmly in relation to dominant cultural beliefs about gender, conformity and power. Recognising the New Explicit is one way to do this and, arguably, the discussions that are happening around feminist porn have applicability here, too. Feminist porn has been characterised, much as the New Explicit is being characterised in this chapter, as "a sentient, interactive and responsive counter-public culture, as genre, as industry, increasingly as social movement itself driven by ethical questions of intention, effect, process and conditions of production vis-à-vis who makes its product, under what labour and production conditions, how it is distributed and who consumes it, and, most importantly, who defines it when, where, why and how" (Noble, 2014, p. 107).

Jenkins is continuing a tradition of self-referential explicitness pioneered by Schneemann, Sprinkle and others. These women reignite the 'Yes, but is it art?' debate in an ultimately productive way. To engage with New Explicit genealogies is to traverse divisions between 'new' media and 'old', and to cut across theoretical 'waves'. For all of our sophisticated academic posturing, though, explicit porn is still about masturbation and, importantly, about maintaining hegemonic power structures. By contrast, explicit performance pieces are about subversion. Dissemination is another key difference – what was previously a piece performed in the presence of a couple of hundred people now has global reach equal to that of porn because of, for example, YouTube. Factors such as this make the New Explicit even more deserving of critical engagement and debate.

References

Attwood, F. (2002). Reading porn: The paradigm shift in pornography research. *Sexualities,* 5(1), 91–105.

Belsey, C. (2002). *Critical practice.* London, United Kingdom: Routledge.

Berg, H. (2014). Labouring porn studies. *Porn Studies,* 1(1–2), 75–79.

Chancer, L. S. (1998). *Reconcilable differences: Confronting beauty, pornography, and the future of feminism.* Berkeley, CA: University of California Press.

Cody, G., & Sprinkle, A. (2001). *Hardcore from the heart: The pleasures, profits and politics of sex in performance.* London, United Kingdom: Continuum.

Cohen-Almagor, R. (2015). *Confronting the Internet's dark side: Moral and social responsibility on the free highway.* New York, NY: Cambridge University Press.

Gallup. (2015). Morals and beliefs. Retrieved from http://www.gallup.com/poll/183719/men-women-differ-morals-sex-relationships.aspx

Hine, C. (2015). *Ethnography for the internet: Embedded, embodied and everyday.* London, United Kingdom: Bloomsbury.

Karkazis, K. (2008). *Fixing sex: Intersex, medical authority, and lived experience.* Durham, NC: Duke University Press.

McNeill, D. (2015, 4 July). Artist says her vagina creations confront a Japanese taboo. *South China Morning Post.* Retrieved from http://www.scmp.com/lifestyle/arts-entertainment/article/1831922/artist-says-her-vagina-creations-confront-japanese

Noble, B. (2014). Porn's pedagogies: teaching porn studies in the academic–corporate complex. *Porn Studies, 1*(1–2), 96–113.

Rees, E. L. E. (2015). *The vagina: A literary and cultural history.* New York, NY: Bloomsbury.

Ribner, D. S. (2014). The pornography question. *Sexual and Relationship Therapy, 29*(4), 375–376.

Schneemann, C. (2002). Interior scroll. In C. Schneemann (Ed.), *Imaging her erotics: Essays, interviews, projects* (pp. 151–161). Cambridge, MA: The MIT Press.

Stoltenberg, J. (2000). *Refusing to be a man: Essays on sex and justice.* London, United Kingdom: UCL Press. Retrieved from http://www.feministes-radicales.org/wp-content/uploads/2010/11/Stoltenberg-Refusing-to-be-a-Man.pdf

Ussher, J. (1991). *Women's madness.* Hemel Hempstead, United Kingdom: Harvester.

Williams, L. (2014). Pornography, porno, porn: Thoughts on a weedy field. *Porn Studies, 1*(1–2), 24–40.

Winter, K. (2013). She didn't learn THAT at WI: 'Vaginal knitter' spends 28 days making scarf from wool stored inside her. *Daily Mail*, 5 December 2013. Retrieved from http://www.dailymail.co.uk/femail/article-2518107/Vaginal-knitter-artist-Casey-Jenkins-makes-scarf-wool-stored-inside-vagina.html#ixzz3fUmYRpCL

CHAPTER FIVE

'SLUTTY & SLUTTIER, STARRING ...': THE RISE OF THE POSTFEMINIST PORN STAR IN CONTEMPORARY CELEBRITY CULTURE

Camilla A. Sears

In 2014, *Slutty and Sluttier* won 'Best Continuing Series' at the 2014 AVN Awards. These awards, also known as the 'Oscars for Porn', provide a platform to celebrate actors for their roles in the latest adult pornographic offerings. Fans flock to the Hard Rock Hotel in Las Vegas for a chance to see their favourite porn stars and starlets. This 'celebration' appears to endorse porn culture and promote the legitimation of a once 'problematic' cultural phenomenon. Thus, no longer is adult pornography rendered invisible, but instead it has been rebranded, and now "sits quite comfortably within the mainstream of popular culture" (McRobbie, 2004, para. 4). Such a societal transformation has not gone unnoticed and scholars have paid attention to understanding this sexualisation of culture and in what ways it sustains or alters gendered practices and expectations. In particular, "the respectabilisation of pornography" (McRobbie, 2004, para. 5) has been considered in a postfeminist context to grasp what it tells us about "contemporary articulations of female sexuality" (Attwood, 2009, p. 17).

This chapter will expand on these debates by addressing further how celebrity and sexuality intersect. It will explore the rising fame and star quality of female actors within the adult pornographic genre. By building on earlier research findings, I will develop my concept of 'the postfeminist porn star' and discuss its role within "current representations of celebrity" (Evans & Riley, 2013, p. 2). Rather than adopting the role of victim, female porn stars within the mainstream have been constructed as the ultimate embodiment of the postfeminist subject; empowered and agentic. By focussing on paratextual elements of the adult pornographic film, such as interviews conducted with female performers, this chapter will delve into understanding these new notions of female success and consider the consequences of them for young women.

Overall, what is evident is that through various discourse strands, the postfeminist porn star exists as the hegemonic discourse within the current socio-cultural landscape. In a position of privilege, the voices of women who talk about their love of pornography showcase it as a viable career choice rather than a desperate measure taken in desperate times; the latter now relegated to the position of a subjugated knowledge. Although not easy to critique articulations of female empowerment and agency, it is important to recognise that whilst seeming progressive, there is a lack of diversity in the interviews, serving to make invisible the power of subjectivities in women's lives.

The postfeminist porn star

Since the 1980s and the rise of Ronald Reagan and Margaret Thatcher, there has been a distinct transformation within the socio-political landscape. Instead of committing to a welfare state, government has moved to modes of "governing at a distance" (Miller & Rose, 2008, p. 34) and adopting a neoliberal ideology (a dramatic shift away from welfare and social reform concerns). In such a way, neoliberalism has become "a wide-ranging political *and* cultural project" (Duggan, 2003, p. xi; emphasis added) where citizens are encouraged to see themselves as individualised and active subjects responsible for enhancing their own well-being and self-care.

To explore the impact of this governmental rationality, I conducted a discursive analysis of Canadian case law from

1959–2009 (Sears, 2014). My focus centred on the legal regulation of adult pornography and in what ways a neoliberal ideology might be present in the judicial rulings. What emerged was both an implicit and explicit trend within the legal realm to adopt neoliberal language and concepts, such as individual responsibility and freedom. This shift towards a free-market mentality constructed a new regulatory framework in Canada in which individuals were increasingly encouraged to self-regulate and police their own pornographic behaviour and consumption. Further, this shift also translated into a reshaping of both girlhood and womanhood, "to fit with [these] new or emerging (neo-liberalised) social and economic arrangements" (McRobbie, 2007, p. 721). Through various judgements, there is commentary that points to the ideas of Rosalind Gill. Gill (2007a) talks about the movement away from sexual objectification towards sexual subjectification and sexual agency, which demonstrates the surfacing of individual choice and autonomy. For example, women now choose to be sexy, rather than it being a result of objectification by men. In this way, women are 'can-do' girls who are "active, desiring sexual subjects" (Gill, 2007a, p. 151).

From the case law, I argued that these ideas are implicitly established through the observations of the judges – to a point where the postfeminist porn star emerges (Sears, 2014). Such a concept represents the judicial trend of viewing women as having achieved equality and no longer needing legal protection from the pornography industry; an industry that they enjoy and are now choosing to be involved in. For example, this idea is evident in judicial comments made on the growth and success of the industry. The consequences of such success are highlighted by Provincial Court judge Payne, who remarks on the rising fame and star quality of those involved in these films, along with the increasing 'attractiveness' of its participants. He states that:

> there appears certainly to be an *upgrading* of the participants in such movies, in that both male and female persons who are involved are at least physically attractive. The women, in particular, are quite physically attractive and it may be some advancement in the industry, that these people now permit their names to be attached to these movies and they are described as starring, and the names of the director and the producer of this type of movie are shown with what appears to be a great deal of pride. As I recall, the old eight millimetre movies on this subject, they were all filmed in bad light, by a lot of scrawny individuals who didn't bother to identify themselves (in *R. v. Findlay*, 1987 CarswellOnt 2565, para. 11; emphasis added).

As a consequence of such a shift in judicial rulings, the notion that we should be spending time considering the negative consequences and effects of the pornographic industry declines – and the idea that women are now enjoying the industry and choosing to be involved in it emerges as a powerful discourse, that needs more in-depth understanding.

The (in)visibility of discourse
By building on this earlier work, the current research develops the concept of the postfeminist porn star and discusses its role within "current representations of celebrity" (Evans & Riley, 2013, p. 2). To assist in this, it is helpful to adopt some ideas from the work of Michel Foucault to form a theoretical lens, in particular, his work on discursive analysis and power/knowledge. For Foucault (1972), discourse can be defined as, "a certain 'way of speaking'" (p. 193) and as "the group of statements that belong to a single system of formation" (p. 107). This formation is where power and knowledge are fused together, "which may be manifested in language (or other

symbolic forms)" (Yell, 2005, p. 15). By identifying the ways in which discourses operate, we are able to make them *'visible'* and to reduce their degree of control" (Yell, 2005, p. 16; emphasis added). Discourse can gain power through its dispersion and perpetuation and can lose power through resistance and challenges to its nature.

Contemplating power relations and sites of resistance, Foucault, "invites us to pay attention to the past and ongoing epistemic battles among competing power/knowledge frameworks that try to control a given field" (Medina, 2011, p. 10). And in so doing, pushes us to seek out the hegemonic discourse(s) and what Foucault calls, subjugated knowledges. These are, "forms of experiencing and remembering that are pushed to the margins and rendered unqualified and unworthy of epistemic respect by prevailing and hegemonic discourses" (Medina, 2011, p. 11). They often remain invisible to mainstream perspectives, and "have a precarious subterranean existence that renders them unnoticed by most people and impossible to detect by those whose perspective has already internalized certain epistemic exclusions" (Medina, 2011, p. 11). Therefore, research, such as this, aims to contribute to this process of making discourse visible so that we might determine its power and control and decipher how sex and sexuality are delineated within society.

Paratext and the pornographic
To examine discourse within the current research, a close discursive analysis was conducted of interviews undertaken by others, with female adult performers (available through various online publications and sites). When thinking about the discursive positioning of female celebrities, Nikunen and Paasonen (2007) state that interviews are pivotal in the construction of star image – and thus, have the potential to illuminate the processes and practices of stardom and

celebrification as they are played out in the modern world today. Further, what will be argued in this chapter, is that interviews such as this, provide an increasingly powerful paratext of the pornographic text (or film).

Paratext, as initially developed by Gérard Genette, is valuable to consider, because, "text rarely appears in its naked state, without the reinforcement and accompaniment of a certain number of productions" (Genette, 1991, p. 261). Paratextual elements (inside and outside of the text) have power to frame and shape our interpretations of texts, and through this, can offer to the reader, "the possibility either of entering or of turning back" (Genette, 1991, p. 261). Since Genette's development of the concept of 'paratext' in relation to the literary text, it has been increasingly applied to other forms of media, especially audiovisual forms, such as film and television (Birke & Christ, 2013). Various scholars have worked on understanding the role of paratext in the digital age. For example, Birke and Christ (2013) argue that paratext, "manages the reader's purchase, navigation, and interpretation of the text in its specific mediation" (p. 68). Further, when thinking about television, Jonathan Gray (2010) contends that paratexts have, "considerable power to amplify, reduce, erase, or add meaning" to texts (p. 46). In this case, interviews may have the power to shape how a pornographic film is to be read, and more specifically, "how the performance is to be read" (Webber, 2012, p. 218). This will be examined as we negotiate the women's responses to the interviewers' questions – and although, "we can rarely assume that any given paratext will be known to all audiences" (Gray & Lotz, 2012, p. 134), for those who are aware of it and have read the paratext, it is important to think about what power it might have in shaping an understanding of the pornographic filmic genre, and ultimately, through this, the adult industry.

Therefore, for this research, interviews were selected to decipher how they contribute to our understandings of pornography and the industry, and to delineate what the hegemonic discourse is regarding the women's own participation in such films. In order to do this, an online search was conducted on Google to identify a sample of interviews with female porn stars. Results responding to the search terms, "female" and "porn stars" were examined in order to put together a list of interviews. After the results were exhaustively checked, a total of thirty-five interviews, were collated, that represented the voices of forty-four women. The interviews were collected from a variety of online platforms that ranged from online periodicals to popular blog sites (e.g. Bitchtopia, BuzzFeed, *The Globe and Mail*, *Rolling Stone*, *Huffington Post*, Total Frat Move, Bro Bible, Adult DVD Talk, Slutever.com, *The Daily Beast*, Vice.com, The Fanzine.com and *Christian Post*). Their publication dates ranged from 1987 to 2015 (with two-thirds of the interviews being posted between 2012 and 2015). Although the questions asked of the performers varied, depending on the source, there were a number of similarities across the sample:

- Why did you choose this line of work?
- What is a regular day for you?
- Describe your experience in porn?
- What is your response to conceptions of the industry as abusive, oppressive?
- What is the (potential) impact of the Internet on the industry?
- When did you lose your virginity?
- When was your first girl-on-girl experience?
- What is your favourite position?

Drawing from the work of Jäger (2001), the tools of discourse analysis were used to tease out the various discourse strands within the interviews. Jäger (2001) argues that, "in a given society discourse strands form the overall societal discourse in a state of entanglement" (p. 50) and it is the role of the researcher to untangle this net and understand how the various discourse strands relate to each other. Through using such a concept, this chapter investigates the effects that the many discourse strands have on the construction and constitution of female celebrity and sexuality.

New wave of porn stars

As noted by Medina (2011), "in the battle among power/knowledge frameworks, some discourses come out on top and become dominant while others are displaced and become *subjugated*" (p. 11; emphasis in original). Through the discursive analysis of the interviews, rather than adopting the role of the victim, female porn stars are presented as the ultimate embodiment of the postfeminist subject – empowered, agentic, and successful. In such a way, this becomes the hegemonic discourse about the industry, displacing discussions about the dangers, harms and risks of being involved in the pornographic film genre. It was found that the postfeminist porn star was supported by various discourse strands, which can be organised into the following areas: (1) The Happy Porn Star; (2) The (Missing) Discourse of Female Desire; (3) Degradation as Sexy; and (4) Porn Entrepreneurs. These strands, both implicit and explicit, combine to illustrate what Beeche (2013) calls the "new wave of pornstars" (para. 5) and Breslin's (2013) discussion of "porn's enterprising female performers" (para. 7).

The happy porn star

Through an analysis of the interviews, what became evident was that, previous to this 'new wave', there was an explicit focus in mainstream representations of the adult industry as harmful and oppressive to women. Negative characterisations of women in the adult entertainment industry were prominent and on responding to why there was this focus, porn performer Christi Lake states,

> You saw the other girl on Nightline because that's what the news people want[ed] to talk about. Who wants to see a happy porn star? It's like a car accident. No one wants to pay attention to traffic; they'd rather stare at the wreckage (Nathan, 2004, para. 29).

However, a majority of the interviews illustrate a transition away from these representations towards an image of the 'happy porn star' that was invisible in earlier media depictions. Similar to what Evans & Riley (2013) call, "a confident 'up for it' femininity" (p. 269), interviewees demonstrate this, through such expressions as, "my passion is pornography" (James, 2014, para. 16); "I can never get enough of it" (Wyatt, 2002, para. 6); and "I'm so grateful to be here. I love being in porn" (Morris, 2014, para. 33). Further, interviewees highlight the positivity that they experience within the industry and make a point of separating themselves from being viewed as subjects of degradation. For example, Kimberley Kane comments that, "there are people that are educated and happy and healthy in this business, and *I am one of them*" (Benger, 2009, para. 7; emphasis added). And Siri, who presents herself as an advocate for change in the sex industry, particularly through her contribution to the The Unslut Project, states, "there's so much love and positivity in this industry, among its people, and in the work itself" (Tenreyro, 2014, para. 3). What these statements exemplify is a larger trend in the interviews celebrating female sexual agency and the women's *own* empowered choices to be involved in an industry that they love and enjoy. In such a way, these quotes seem to indicate what Nikunen and Paasonen (2007) call a discourse, "emphasizing the delights of pornography" (p. 33).

Consequently, instead of the industry being portrayed as a last resort, a choice made out of desperation, over two-thirds of the interviews tell a different story. In fact, the industry is now shown as a *viable* career choice. One of the most vocal performers to support this position is Asa Akira, who in both interviews included in the sample, illustrates her willingness to be involved in the industry, but also how it is viewed by her, as a dream occupation; a perfect career choice. In response to the interviewer's queries into how 'real' her statements are about her enjoyment of the industry, she responds, "the fact that I actually mean it makes me perfect for this job and this job perfect for me" (Bielski, 2014, para. 11).

Through "the act of repetition" (Webber, 2012, p. 218), these articulations gradually gain power as the 'happy porn star' becomes the most visible image, while the notion of a dangerous and oppressive industry is challenged by a majority of the female performers. In fact, a number of the women actively resist the prevailing narratives that the industry oppresses them and that female porn stars are 'crazy, damaged, and addicted' with a history of abuse. Christi Lake states, "just because women have sex and do it for a living doesn't mean they're oppressed" (Nathan, 2004, para. 3). And in response to the question, 'were you ever abused?' Joanna Angel almost responds in jest to showcase what she believes is a ridiculous misperception of the industry:

> When I was in the 4th grade I really wanted to go see Bon Jovi on a Friday night. My mother said no, because it was the Sabbath. I think that was total religious abuse. But other than that misfortune, no, I wasn't. And 3 out of 5 women EVERYWHERE were abused, not just in porn. The ratio of abused women to not abused women is pretty similar in porn as it is anywhere else. (Hodin, 2013, para. 9; emphasis in original)

Asa Akira also plays a role in this form of resistance by articulating that there are two types of women in the industry, those that fit the stereotype of the 'crazy, damaged, and addicted' porn star, and those that do not, such as herself. She states,

> There are definitely girls hooked on drugs, girls who have been abused by family members, girls who got into the business because their boyfriend – aka 'suitcase pimps' wanted them to. But that's only about half of them. There are also girls with college degrees, girls who are feminists, and girls who come from completely normal backgrounds. My agent told me the former group won't last long; the latter is the kind that will be around in a few years. (Thomas, 2014a, para. 4)

Furthermore, some of the women find it, at times, offensive to have what they clearly identify as authentic choices to be involved in the industry questioned. For example, Siri states, "I find it quite patronizing and insulting for someone else to tell me that it is degrading, when it was my choice to begin with" (Tenreyro, 2014, para. 4). And Asa Akira asks,

> is it so impossible for you to believe that a woman *enjoys* being a sexual being, to the point where she *wants to do it* for a living? Why is it that hard to believe? If it were a man, you wouldn't think twice. I find it offensive when people say, 'you're in denial.' I think society needs an answer for how someone like me exists. They need a reason for a woman to be so sexual. (Bielski, 2014, para. 10; emphasis added)

All of these statements support what Rosalind Gill outlines as indicative of a postfeminist media culture. Through these various articulations, the interviewees are presented as "active, desiring, sexual subjects" (Gill, 2007a, p. 151) who are "pleasing themselves" (Gill, 2007b, p. 91), through their choices to be involved in the pornographic film industry. In such a way, there is a dispersion of a particular image of womanhood that suggests a certain liberty in the presentation of self, one which is also achieved through a greater recognition and vocalisation of female sexual desire.

The (missing) discourse of female desire
A central feature of postfeminist discourse is this visibility and representation of female desire in the social and cultural landscape. Michelle Fine's (1988) influential article set the groundwork for a growing discussion on this topic as she brought to light 'the *missing* discourse of female desire'. Her focus was primarily on the educational system and sex education curricula – where she felt that there was a significant lack of recognition of female sexual desire. She maintains that,

> within today's standard sex education curricula and many public school classrooms, we find: (1) the authorized suppression of a discourse of female sexual desire; (2) the promotion of a discourse of female sexual victimization; and (3) the explicit privileging of married heterosexuality over other practices of sexuality. (Fine, 1988, p. 30)

Fine (1988) demarcates this absence and asserts that, "a discourse of desire, though absent in the "official" curriculum, is by no means missing from the lived experiences or commentaries of young women" (p. 35). Therefore, she advocates for such a dearth to be rectified through recognition of female sexuality, particularly through a discussion of desire and pleasure, and she argues that such discussion needs to go beyond the "official discourses of sexuality" (Fine, 1988, p. 40), that are continually promoted in curricula and beyond.

Within the interviews, there is an explosion of representations of female desire and sexual agency seemingly filling in this gap identified originally by Fine (1988). For example, the interviewees demonstrate this, through such expressions as, "I love sex. I love masturbating. I want every girl to love sex as much as I do" (Moneybags, 2015, para. 7); "I love having sex in any position" (Camm, 2015, para. 15); and "what most performers do and say on camera is a matter of what turns them on" (Tenreyro, 2014, para. 4). In this regard, women are presented as "knowingly and deliberately" playing with their own sexual desires, suggesting powerfully through their own voices, that they are "always 'up for it' (that is, sex)" (Gill, 2008, p. 41).

Degradation as sexy

In Canadian case law, particularly since the 1980s, there was a growing recognition given to whether pornographic material exploits sex in a 'degrading or dehumanising' manner. Such a concern started to arise, where cases began to deliberate and assess whether a film, for example, included content that degraded women (and sometimes men), to a point where they were portrayed "in positions of subordination, servile submission or humiliation" (Justice Sopinka, cited in *R. v. Butler*, [1992] 1 S.C.R. 452, para. 49). If this was deemed to be present, the courts started to consider this as a reason for a determination of obscenity. In such a way, this led to the creation of the 'degradation or dehumanisation' test. For example, County Court judge Borins contended,

> [i]n my opinion many of the films are exploitive of women, portraying them as passive victims who derive limitless pleasure from inflicted pain and from subjugation to acts of violence, humiliation and degradation. Women are depicted as sexual objects whose only redeeming features are their genital and erotic zones, which are prominently displayed in clinical detail. (in *R. v. Doug Rankine Company Ltd. And Act III Video Productions Ltd.*, [1983] O.J. No. 3339, para. 31)

These words were representative of a more protectionist approach to women in pornography in the legal realm. Women were seen as sexual objects and, as Provincial Court judge Harris ruled, content was to be viewed as obscene "when their humanity is removed and their automatonlike bodies are manipulated as they are" (in *R. v. Beeston*, [1987] O.J. No. 1932, para. 23).

In contrast to this, and in line with the emergence of 'the postfeminist porn star', is the reframing of this degradation and dehumanisation as sexual perversion or paraphilia. Instead of the women being passive victims, they are "active desiring sexual subjects" (Gill, 2007a; p. 151) who "derive limitless pleasure from inflicted pain" (County Court judge Borins, cited in *R. v. Doug Rankine Company Ltd. And Act III Video Productions Ltd.*, [1983] O.J. No. 3339, para. 31). In fact, such acts now are perceived of as satisfying the women's *own* fantasies and desires, as noted above. For example, at the age of nineteen, when responding to the question, 'what have you learned about yourself sexually since joining porn?', performer Kasey Warner replies, "I learned I like getting punched" (Jack, 2015, para. 47). At the age of eighteen, the successful Sasha Grey states, "I can't get off unless there is shit-talking involved. I don't want to hear sexy moans, I want to hear degradation, grunting, hyperventilating. It stimulates your psyche as well as your libido, allowing for a more intense scene" (Stosuy, 2006, para. 41). When asked about the implications of this trend, Asa Akira, who is known for engaging in extreme acts, that are often violent, responds, "I see how it could be troubling. I can see how a lot of people would see that kind of rough sex as degrading to women. For me, though, if that's my fantasy and I'm living it out, how is that degrading?" (Bielski, 2014, para. 20). From these responses, what emerges is a growing distinction between perversion and actual violence, in a sense, making degradation sexy.

Porn entrepreneurs
The final discourse strand of the postfeminist porn star is the emergence of the industry's wave of enterprising female performers. In line with a neoliberal governmental rationality, the image of the enterprising self (Rose, 1992), surfaces as a tenet of the ideal self, the good citizen. We conceive of the ideal citizen as one who is resourceful, energetic and willing to display initiative and take on new projects, such as transforming the self. Thus, the well-being of society is seen to be achieved, "not by centralized planning and bureaucracy, but through the *'enterprising'* activities and choices of autonomous entities" (Rose, 1992, p. 142; emphasis added).

In efforts to achieve success, it is evident from a majority of the interviewees' responses, that the women are making these attempts to show initiative, to be resourceful and be energetic in their chosen industry. Through the use of innovative measures, there is a consistent message that it can lead to more success for the women in the realm of sexual commerce. For example, Belle Knox is a student, while also engaging in various other endeavours, such as porn shoots, hosting a new reality series, and creating a new Doc Johnson sex toy line. Furthermore, she states herself in the interview, "the other thing you can do is sell clothes you wore on shoots and get a lot of money from that" (Morris, 2014, para. 25). Other examples include, Veronica Vain, the Wall Street Porn Star, who states, "perhaps one day I'll start an adult industry-centred venture capital fund. I've talked to numerous investors in the past who would love a piece of that business. Most people watch porn and buy sex products no matter the economic climate. It's a great market" (Camm, 2015, para. 11). And what is a consistent theme through a number of the interviews is the impact of the Internet on the industry. Women are asked about how they respond to some of the challenges accompanying the rise of amateur porn and piracy. A number of the interviewees talk about their solo work using webcams that serves to bring in some additional income. Because of the constant relativity of the technological landscape, the women develop a set of practices to refashion themselves as entrepreneurs (Besley & Peters, 2007). When talking about Jelena Jensen, the interviewer states,

> A film school graduate, Jensen runs her own website, manages other performers' sites, shoots videos, and hosts *The J Spot*, a radio show on Vivid radio. Working at home most days in front of a computer, she resembles your average one-person web entrepreneur – albeit one who works with titties and dicks. (Thomas, 2014b, para. 2; emphasis in original)

Jensen as well as other female performers engaging in this type of re-fashioning, are said to represent, "the rise of Gen Y, Pornstars turned entrepreneurs", who are "deliberate, calculated, and fiercely ambitious people, who know they can build massive engaged fan bases fast" (Beeche, 2013, para. 2).

Risky business

This concept of the postfeminist porn star emerges as the hegemonic discourse in such a way that it displaces and subjugates a counter discourse of 'risky business'. Just as the women above challenge the prevailing narratives of oppression and abuse, there are other points of resistance within the interviews, but these no longer have the power that they once did. What emerges in a minority of the interviews (less than one-third) are the voices of women who do see themselves more as victims of an oppressive and abusive system, and challenge the authenticity of the postfeminist porn stars. For example, through her interview, retired porn performer Carol Smith questions the words of women who say they love being in pornography by stating, "when you suffer from childhood sexual abuse or were severely abused as a child, you usually *repress those memories*. You are unable to say, I am doing this because I was abused as a child and this is all I know how to do. This is all I know how to feel" (Simonton, 2014, para. 18; emphasis added). Furthermore, she adds,

> They think it's great. They think it's wonderful. I could have looked you in the eye ten years ago and told you that I loved being in pornography, was proud of what I was doing and that I was having a great time. But now I can tell you that it's so far from the truth. I was very convincing. I could convince you. I mean, I could walk up to a porn star today and she could tell me the same story and I can remember being in her place. (Simonton, 2014, para. 16)

In contrast to the discourse strand of the 'happy porn star', these interviews highlight, at times, a history of extreme abuse in life before pornography, and also during it. Tori Black details numerous experiences of horrific abuse to the point where her response to dealing with it was to become involved in the adult industry. She states, "I just decided that I was here for somebody else's pleasure, that I existed to be whatever they wanted, to become their fantasy" (Sciortino, 2013, para. 67). While Elizabeth Rollings said after making a '25 guy' movie, that she, "mentally and emotionally checked out and ... felt like [she] died" (Lubben, 2013, para. 17), leading her to the "verge of suicide" (para. 28). These interviews talk about how they got out, their exit strategy, and their life after porn. Despite the power of some of these voices, detailing their experiences in the pornographic industry, they become subjugated, invisible to mainstream perspectives, and as Medina (2011) states, they represent, "forms of experiencing and remembering that are pushed to the margins and rendered unqualified and unworthy of epistemic respect by prevailing and hegemonic discourses" (p. 11).

Concluding remarks

Linda Williams (1993) asks, how "shall we interpret this postfeminist sensibility emerging so agreeably from the 'depths' of a misogynistic mass culture?" (p. 118). Through the paratextual elements discussed, does the presentation of the postfeminist porn star affirm the performance of authentic sexuality and a discourse of female desire? Or does it rather continue to privilege certain norms and ideals of femininity and sexuality? We are left in a position to ask, how do you get behind the self-fashioning evident in the interviews? And how can we validate the postfeminist porn star more? As Webber (2012) argues, "we must be cautious of applying the term 'authentic' (or 'inauthentic') to any particular representation of desire" (p. 232). Similar to Mason-Grant (2002) who, in response to Sabrina Johnson's interview (included in the sample), argues that,

> it is tempting to openly doubt that Sabrina Johnson is as thrilled as she claims to be in her "dream occupation." There is plenty of evidence from workers in the industry that conditions are often rotten. But it is a mistake to venture down this path – it would be inappropriately psychologizing Johnson without knowing her story. However, it is appropriate to ask what role such a published interview plays in the normalization of gender roles and sexual expectations among readers of *The Gazette*. (para. 1–2)

Although not that easy to critique post-feminism and its celebration of equality and female choice, the discourse of the postfeminist porn star in the interviews errs towards a misplaced optimism that *all* women are able to 'have it all' and make choices to be 'sexy' within ideal notions of femininity. It can be argued that there is a sense of conformity, which is definitely emergent in the interviews discussed, and consequent "exclusions of this representational practice" (Gill,

2003, p. 103). Power, sexuality and gender related to the production and consumption of pornography are simplified, covering over subjectivities in need of recognition. As Keller (2012) notes, a new conceptualisation of female celebrity, "privileges female celebrity subjectivities that can be read as real and authentic, yet unable to disrupt the dominance of hegemonic, white femininity" (p. 14). In this way, successful femininity (Ringrose & Walkerdine, 2008), as demonstrated by the concept of the postfeminist porn star, is coded as normal and universal; even though it is not likely to contribute to *all* women's sexual agency.

To disrupt this, Saunders (2014), in her examination of the site Pornhub, explores the potential power of the paratext. She argues,

> changing the paratext by allowing more unfettered input from users and female performers and by reducing the misogynistic and heteronormative frames which define all this porn site's textual offerings would begin to reveal the richness in what the porn genre already offers. Appreciating the new ways in which the paratext works online creates the possibility that the pornographic genre, what is expected of it and what it can potentially offer, can be redefined. (Saunders, 2014, p. 249)

I would agree with her sentiments, but add that these changes need to recognise the diversity of women's experiences in order to challenge effectively "the misogynistic and heteronormative frames" (Saunders, 2014, p. 249). By moving away from an erasure of difference and an assumption that there is a level playing field, it might go some way to understand the input of female performers on their experiences in the pornographic industry. Furthermore, Medina (2011) argues that the critical task of the scholar should be, "to resurrect subjugated knowledges – that is, to revive hidden or forgotten bodies of experiences and memories" (p. 11). A recognition that 'the happy porn star' who finds degradation sexy is not the experience for all women in the pornographic industry needs to be remembered, even within a socio-cultural landscape that celebrates the notion of the "active, desiring sexual subject" (Gill, 2007a, p. 151) who loves the pornography industry and would not want to be doing anything else.

References

Antiporngraphy.org. (n.d.). Ex-porn stars exposing the truth about the harms of the industry. Interviews with Traci Lords, Vanessa B., and Montana Fishburne. Retrieved from http://www.antipornography.org/ex_porn_stars_expose_truth.html

Attwood, F. (2009). Intimate adventures: Sex blogs, sex 'blooks' and women's sexual narration. *European Journal of Cultural Studies, 12*(1), 5–20.

Beeche, M. (2013). Young, focused & ambitious: The rise of Gen Y pornstars turned entrepreneurs. *Startup Daily*. Retrieved from http://www.startupdaily.net/2013/10/young-focused-ambitious-rise-gen-y-pornstars-turned-entrepreneurs/

Benger, R. (2009). Interview with Kimberley Kane. *Cogentbenger.com*. Retrieved from http://cogentbenger.com/porndemic/interviews/interview-with-kimberley-lane/

Besley, T. (A. C.), & Peters, M. A. (2007). *Subjectivity & truth: Foucault, education and the culture of self.* New York, NY: Peter Lang Publishing, Inc.

Bielski, Z. (2014). 'I'm an exhibitionist, I'm hypersexual': Porn star Asa Akira on why she loves her job. *The Globe and Mail*. Retrieved from http://www.theglobeandmail.com/life/relationships/im-an-exhibitionist-im-hypersexual-porn-star-asa-akira-on-why-she-loves-her-job/article18826704/

Birke, D., & Christ, B. (2013). Paratext and digitized narrative: Mapping the field. *Narrative, 21*(1), 65–87.

Breslin, S. (2013). What porn stars do when the porn industry shuts down. *Forbes*. Retrieved from http://forbes.com/sites/susannahbreslin/2013/12/20/what-porn-stars-do/

Brink, R. (2012). An interview with Stoya... The Porn Star. *Jenkemmag.com*. Retrieved from http://www.jenkemmag.com/home/2012/10/18/an-interview-with-stoya-the-porn-star/

Camm, J. (2015). Meet Veronica Vain, a hot redhead who just left her job on Wall Street to become a porn star. *Brobible.com*. Retrieved from http://www.brobible.com/life/article/veronica-vain-wall-street-porn-star/

Duggan, L. (2003). *The twilight of equality? Neo-liberalism, cultural politics, and the attack on democracy*. Boston, MA: Beacon Press.

Evans, A., & Riley, S. (2013). Immaculate consumption: Negotiating the sex symbol in postfeminist celebrity culture. *Journal of Gender Studies, 22*(3), 1–24. Retrieved from: www.researchgate.net/publication/235409070_Immaculate_consumption_negotiating_the_sex_symbol_in_postfeminist_ celebrity_culture

Fine, M. (1988). Sexuality, schooling, and adolescent females: The missing discourse of desire. *Harvard Educational Review, 58*(1), 29–53.

Foucault, M. (1972). *The archaeology of knowledge and the discourse on language*. New York, NY: Pantheon Books.

Genette, G. (1991). Introduction to paratext. *New Literary History, 22*(2), 261–272.

Gill, R. (2003). From sexual objectification to sexual subjectification: The resexualisation of women's bodies in the media. *Feminist Media Studies, 3*(1), 100–106.

Gill, R. (2007a). Post-feminist media culture: Elements of a sensibility. *European Journal of Cultural Studies, 10*(2), 147–166.

Gill, R. (2007b). *Gender and the media*. Cambridge, United Kingdom; Malden, MA: Polity Press.

Gill, R. (2008). Empowerment/sexism: figuring female sexual agency in contemporary advertising. *Feminism & Psychology, 18*(1), 35–60.

Gray, J. (2010). *Show sold separately: Promos, spoilers, and other media paratexts*. New York, NY; London, United Kingdom: New York University Press.

Gray, J., & Lotz, A. (2012). *Television studies*. Cambridge, United Kingdom: Polity Press.

Hodin, R. (2013). Porn star extraordinaire Joanna Angel talks To US about gang bangs with 8 dudes and other things. Thoughtcatalog.com. Retrieved from http://thought catalog.com/rachel-hodin/2013/09/porn-star-extraordinaire-joanna-angel-talks-to-us-about-gang-bangs-with-8-dudes-and-other-things/

Jack, Captain. (2015). Kasey Warner Interview. *Adultdvdtalk.com*. Retrieved from http://interviews.adultdvdtalk.com/kasey-warner/

Jäger, S. (2001). Discourse and knowledge: Theoretical and methodological aspects of a critical discourse and dispositive analysis. In R. Wodak & M. Meyer (Eds.), *Methods of critical discourse analysis* (pp. 32–62). London, United Kingdom: Sage Publications.

James, R. (2014). This is what it's actually like to work as a female porn star. Interview with Angela White, Tasha Reign, Little Red Bunny, Jessica Drake, & Kelly Madison. *BuzzFeed*. Retrieved from http://www.buzzfeed.com/richardhjames/this-is-what-its-actually-like-to-work-as-a-female-porn-star

Keller, J. M. (2012). Fiercely real? *Feminist Media Studies*. DOI: 10.1080/14680777.2012.740490.

Ken. (2013). Respect the ass: An interview with porn star MaryJean. *Kenandariel.com*. Retrieved from http://kenandariel.com/respect-ass-interview-porn-star-maryjean/

Lubben, S. (2013). Former porn star Elizabeth Rollings interview. *ShelleyLubben.com*. Retrieved from https://www.shelleylubben.com/shelleys-articles/former-porn-star-elizabeth-rollings-interview [source no longer available].

Malcolm, S. (2007). Interview with porn star Trina Michaels. *Pornstarcenter.com*. Retrieved from http://pornstarscenter.com/star.asp?id=309

Mason-Grant, J. (2002, 11 January). Pornstar interview analysis. *Gazette*, *95*(56). Retrieved from http://www.uwo.ca/media watch/pornstar.htm

McRobbie, A. (2004, 2 January). The rise and rise of porn chic. *Times Higher Education*. Retrieved from www.timeshighereducation.co.uk/182087.article

McRobbie, A. (2007). TOP GIRLS? Young women and the post-feminist sexual contract. *Cultural Studies, 21*(4–5), 718–737.

Medina, J. (2011). Toward a Foucaultian epistemology of resistance: Counter-memory, epistemic friction, and *guerilla* pluralism. *Foucault Studies, 12,* 9–35.

Miller, P., & Rose, N. (2008). *Governing the present: Administering economic, social and personal life.* Cambridge, United Kingdom & Malden, MA: Polity Press.

Moneybags, Rich Uncle. (2015). An interview with Carter Cruise, sorority girl turned porn star. *Totalfratmove.com.* Retrieved from http://totalfratmove.com/an-interview-with-carter-cruise-sorority-girl-turned-porn-star/

Morris, A. (2014). The blue devil in Miss Belle Knox: Meet Duke porn star Miriam Weeks. *Rolling Stone.* Retrieved from http://www.rollingstone.com/culture/news/the-blue-devil-in-miss-belle-knox-meet-duke-porn-star-miriam-weeks-20140423

Nathan, L. (2004). An interview with Christi Lake. *Counterpunch.org.* Retrieved from http://www.counterpunch.org/2004/12/11/an-interview-with-christi-lake/

Nikunen, K., & Paasonen, S. (2007). Porn star as brand: Pornification and the intermedia career of Rakel Liekki. *The Velvet Light Trap, 59,* 30–41.

R. v. Beeston, [1987] O.J. No. 1932

R. v. Butler, [1992] 1 S.C.R. 452

R. v. Doug Rankine Company Ltd. and Act III Video Productions Ltd., [1983] O.J. No. 3339

R. v. Findlay, 1987 CarswellOnt 2565 (Ontario Provincial Court, 1987)

Ringrose, J., & Walkerdine, V. (2008). Regulating the abject: The TV make-over as site of neo-liberal reinvention toward bourgeois femininity. *Feminist Media Studies, 8*(3), 227–246.

Rose, N. (1992). Governing the enterprising self. In P. Heelas & P. Morris (Eds.), *The values of the enterprise culture* (pp. 141–164). London, United Kingdom; New York, NY: Routledge.

Saunders, R. I. (2014). The pornographic paratexts of Pornhub. In N. Desrochers & D. Apollon (Eds.), *Examining paratextual theory and its application in digital culture* (pp. 235–251). Hershey, PA: Information Science Reference.

Sciortino, K. (2013). Bad girls do it well: A chat with porn icon tori black. *Slutever.com*. Retrieved from http://slutever.com/bad-girls-do-it-well-a-chat-with-porn-icon-tori-black/

Sears, C. A. (2014). "Flattening our opposition": Neoliberal governance and the (de)regulation of adult pornography in Canada. In J. Kilty (Ed.), *Within the confines: Women and the law in Canada* (pp. 456–493). Toronto, ON: Canadian Scholars Press Inc.

Simonton, A. (2014). Ann Simonton interviews ex-model and porn actress Carol Smith (Trigger Warning. HoF thread). *Democratic Underground*. Retrieved from http://www.democraticunderground.com/125535456

Snow, A. (2013). How a porn star retires: Aurora Snow on life after porn. *Thedailybeast.com*. Retrieved from http://www.thedailybeast.com/articles/2013/06/18/how-a-porn-star-retires-aurora-snow-on-life-after-porn.html#

Stosuy, B. (2006). Sasha Grey: Dawn of porn star (interview). *Thefanzine.com*. Retrieved from http://thefanzine.com/sasha-grey-dawn-of-porn-star-interview-2/

Tenreyro, T. (2014). Bitchtopia's interview with Siri, the feminist porn star. *Bitchtopia.com*. Retrieved from http://bitchtopia.com/2014/05/30/bitchtopias-interview-with-siri-the-feminist-porn-star/

Thomas, S. (2014a). Insatiable: An interview with porn star Asa Akira. *Thestylecon*. Retrieved from http://www.thestylecon.com/2014/04/14/insatiable-interview-asa-akira/

Thomas, S. (2014b). The Internet turned porn star Jelena Jensen into an Entrepreneur. *Vice.com*. Retrieved from http://www.vice.com/read/the-internet-turned-porn-star-jelena-jensen-into-an-entrepreneur-987

Webber, V. (2012). Shades of gay: Performance of girl-on-girl pornography and mobile authenticities. *Sexualities, 16*(1/2), 217–235.

Williams, L. (1993). A provoking agent: The pornography and performance art of Annie Sprinkle. *Social Text, 37*, 117–133.

Wyatt, D. (2002). "I can never get enough of it" Sabrina Johnson explains why she loves her job as a porn star. *The Gazette*. Retrieved from http://www.uwo.ca/mediwatch/pornstar.htm

Yell, S. (2005). Critical discourse analysis and social semiotics: Rethinking text and discourse in media and communication research. In K. Kwansah-Aidoo (Ed.), *Topical Issues in Communications and Media Research* (pp. 9–23). New York, NY: Nova Science Publishers, Inc.

CHAPTER SIX

SEXING UP POST-WAR JAPANESE CINEMA: LOOKING AT 1960s/1970s 'PINKY VIOLENCE' FILMS

Laura Treglia

In this chapter, I focus on a sub-set of Japanese exploitation films dating from the late 1960s and early 1970s known as 'pinky violence' (*pinkī baiorensu*). I propose a multi-layered investigation that, while enriching a classic textual analysis approach, considers the contexts of Japanese cinematic and cultural history, the local movie industry shifts and socio-political changes that Japan underwent during the post-war era. I show that from such a perspective we can see more in pinky violence than just low-budget titillation. In fact, these films may be seen to tackle new configurations of gender, sexuality and violence in a period of cultural and social turmoil, with the emergence in Japan of new political subjects such as students and radical feminists. The films give prominence to bold configurations of femininity – rebel, gutsy, resilient and assertive – although at the same time offering them up to the altar of sadistic fantasies and containment strategies. However, even when understood in exploitative and cautionary terms, the films may be seen at least to point to the anxiety generated by new discourses about womanhood, female sexuality and desires, which openly diverged from the conservative standpoints and policies promoted within dominant Japanese institutions of the time. From this perspective, the study of pinky violence films, while adding to recent research into Japanese adult cinema, intersects with the developing field of interdisciplinary and critical work on pornographies within

Anglo-American scholarship (Williams, 2014). Specifically, the multi-dimensional approach I suggest is in line with new research into pornography that "intends to investigate intersections between sexually explicit media and current social and political mores" (Attwood & Smith, 2014, p. 5). This study thus moves beyond commonplace assumptions that pornography and other material cultures dealing with sex and pleasure – and therefore perceived as 'trivial', if not offensive – are disconnected from more 'serious' facets of society.

The last decade has seen an increase in research dedicated to mapping a Japanese cinematic genre that has long been overlooked, especially outside Japan. This is the world of Japanese soft-core pornographic films, also known as 'pink films' (*pinku eiga*). However, independent pink cinema has received proportionally more attention than studio-made erotic films, not least for the ostensible political meaning of some work, such as that of director Wakamatsu Koji (Domenig, 2002; Sharp, 2008; Standish, 2011; Nornes, 2014). Even with respect to Nikkatsu film company's high-budget soft-core 'romantic pornography' (*romanporuno*, a variation of studio-made pink films), its pinky violence competitors are so far underexplored. It is to this group of films that I turn, in order to first frame their emergence within Japanese late post-war cultural and film industry settings and then to show how they constructed bolder articulations of femininity, pointing (at least in their best examples) to cultural anxieties of the time.

A typical storyline of a pinky violence film centres on unruly young women resisting social conventions and fighting against the injustices perpetrated by powerful male villains. Rape and S/M-style torture of women as well as 'strip-down' catfights and lesbian lovemaking scenes are conventional here. In this chapter, I show how the combination of revenge plots, cinematography and violent action enhances the conjuring up of feisty, non-normative configurations of femininity, emphasising a rebellious and violent agency.

Pink films and pinky violence: a new lucrative business

Pinky violence films fit into discussions around pornography and erotica since their main draw for contemporary audiences were the scenes of (partial) female nudity and suggestive erotic scenarios. The films are often part of different thematic cycles and may have period or contemporary settings. The expression *pinkī baiorensu* was coined in Japan during the 1990s (Mana, 2009, p. 215 note 2) and technically refers to the erotic programme fillers that Tōei film company produced approximately between 1968 and 1975. The films were usually shown together with a main feature (typically a gangster film) in multiple bill programmes at studio-owned and sub-run suburban cinemas. A broader interpretation of pinky violence would encompass films featuring similar material produced by other Japanese studios, such as Nikkatsu's 'new action' *Stray Cat Rock* series (1970–1971) and Tōhō's *Lady Snowblood* (1973–1974) or *Rika* (1972–1973) films. In this chapter, I will focus on Tōei films that were released during the golden era of pinky violence, which lasted until the mid- to late 1970s.

The word 'pinky' echoes the Japanese independent adult films (pink films), which appeared at the beginning of the 1960s. Originally named 'eroduction' (*erodakushon*) or 'three-million-yen' films (*sanbyakumanen eiga*), pink films were low-budget soft-core films that by the end of the 1960s had developed into a thriving business led by a few small, independent film companies (see Richie, 1991; Domenig, 2002, 2011; Sharp, 2008; Suzuki, 2011; Nornes, 2014).

During the 1960s, the big corporations that had long dominated the cinema industry in Japan underwent a major crisis, mainly due to competition with television. To revive box office revenues and stave off bankruptcy, around the beginning of the 1970s some of these majors, such as Tōei and Nikkatsu, started to produce films with a strong erotic charge, trying to emulate the success of the independent *pinku eiga* business model. While Nikkatsu launched soft-core romantic pornography, Tōei's hallmark contributions to this field were cycles featuring peculiar mixes of eroticism and action, horror, violence and comedy as the main sensational ingredients. For the topics addressed, their production and advertising styles, pinky violence films may be compared to American and European exploitation cinema (see Mathijs & Sexton, 2011).

Initially, pinky violence films were called by different names, such as 'erotic films' (*eroeiga*), 'porno action' (*porunoakushon*) or 'Tōei porno' (*Tōei poruno*). These and similar expressions appeared within titles, trailers and lurid poster art that promised racy content and pointed to the films' thematic cycle. Although the bawdy spectacles anticipated in the trailers often fell below expectations, the films were conceived to entertain and titillate an audience presumably made up of mainly young heterosexual men. Mixing eroticism with violence, action and coarse humour to degrees that were taboo in more mainstream cinema or television of the time, pinky violence films are characterised by distinct thematic strands. Tōei production planning managers devised evocative cycle concepts such as 'abnormal love' (*ijōseiai*), 'shameless' (*harenchi*) and 'shocking' (*shōgeki*) (Macias, 2000, p. 176; Mana, 2009, p. 182). The 'female delinquent boss' films (*zubekō banchō* or *sukeban*) feature tales of delinquent youth such as all-girl gangs. Popular films in this vein include the *Delinquent Girl Boss* series (dir. Yamaguchi Kazuhiko, 1970–1971), starring Oshida Reiko and the *Girl Boss Blues* (dir. Suzuki Norifumi, 1971–1972) series, with Ike Reiko and Sugimoto Miki. The *Terrifying Girls' High School* (1972–1973) series – one example of which is discussed in further detail below – set in repressive girls' schools, may also be listed under the *sukeban* film rubric. Other films revolve around spring resort geisha (*onsen geisha*), female gamblers/lone swordswomen and female prison inmates, with the *Lady Snowblood* (1973–1974) and *Female Prisoner Scorpion* (1972–1973) series – both inspired by adult comic strips (*manga*) – representing the latter two types.

Pinky violence and the circulation of the gaze

In pinky violence films enforced sex is frequently eroticised and female bodies are segmented and fetishised, either via bondage setups or filming techniques such as close-ups or low-angle shots. Cameras zoom in or pan over half-open mouths, breasts, napes, feet, women's faces writhing in pleasure (or pain during S/M-style tortures). Furthermore, many scenes suggest the characters are undressing, bathing or engaging in sexual activities oblivious to men who spy on them. Considering the above, these films substantiate Laura Mulvey's (1989) argument of the male scopophilic gaze as objectifying, fetishistic and voyeuristic. At the same time, however, pinky violence films also feature sequences in which heroines look back at their attackers with fiery, menacing gazes that terrify and act as preludes to revenge. They look into the camera, sometimes holding a blade or pointing a gun, not just at male characters, therefore, but also at complicit spectators. Female gambler and swordswoman Ochō (Ike Reiko) is often shown in this way in Suzuki's *Sex and Fury* (1973). In a memorable sequence, Ochō is bathing (with her back to the camera) when, glancing over her shoulder, she spots her enemies spying on her. With a swift move, Ochō hits a man's eye with a razor-sharp playing card. A showdown ensues, in which she swirls around naked with nothing but her sword. This is one of the instances in pinky violence films where lecherous men's ogling or unsolicited sexual advances are frustrated or blocked by women, and middle-aged men's sexual prowess derided in comic skits.

Pornographies

The close-ups on Sasori's piercing glares before she strikes back in Itō Shun'ya's *Female Prisoner Scorpion* (1972–1973) series are also emblematic of a circulating, 'counter-gaze' in pinky violence films. During a rape scene in the second instalment, when Sasori is abused by male guards in front of other female inmates, the camera shows her fiery stares at her attackers and depicts the latter as extremely grotesque. If the representation of female violent agency, resilience and will to overpower male antagonists does not obliterate the types of sexual objectification described in the above paragraphs, it certainly takes on (thanks to the hybridisation with horror and crime-action films) an unusual dimension and dynamism compared to the more stereotypical representations of celluloid heroines as enduring, sexually passive and meek.

Pinky violence, regulation and Japan's 'pornographic culture'
The depiction of genitalia (as well as pubic hair) and sexual intercourse has been subject to charges of obscenity in Japan under article 175 of the Penal Code. For this reason, erotic films legally produced within the country (including *pinku eiga*), while often raising calls for restriction, have never amounted to hard-core pornography. Censorship policies have been implemented through the combined action of the police, customs (for imported films) and a non-governmental self-regulatory body within the cinema industry known by its abbreviated name, *Eirin*. Therefore, while actresses frequently disrobe in pinky violence films, not just in bed scenes, but also while fighting or bathing, often by a seemingly casual unveiling of breasts and buttocks, there is never full frontal nudity; genital areas were covered or concealed in long- and medium-shots through the interposition of clothed characters, film props (e.g. umbrellas, foam) or clever use of perspective. Moreover, *pinku eiga* actresses used *maebari*, a minimal, nude coloured piece of

cloth or other material that covered the crotch area during shooting.

Japanese feminist authors Funabashi Kuniko (1995) and Yunomae Tomoko (1996)[3] critically analysed Japan's 'pornographic culture' in two well-known essays. They criticise a wide spectrum of Japanese popular and consumer culture, which pivots on the ubiquitous sexualisation of female bodies, the commodification of sex and, often, the eroticisation of sexual violence. This encompasses TV shows, magazines, pornographic comics or *eromanga*, advertising, cinema and video games, and a diverse sex entertainment industry (*mizushōbai*), which includes a rich range of sexual commodification and consumption practices (Allison, 1994; Buckley, 2002). One peculiarity of pornography in Japan has been its relative accessibility and visibility (X-rated material could be sold in convenience stores and vending machines). This has led to moral panics and media hypes, such as the 'wars' on *eromanga* first between 1965 and 1975 and then in the early 1990s (Kinsella, 2000; Buckley, 2002; McLelland, 2015). Women's groups such as housewives' and mothers' leagues, the Parent-Teacher Association (PTA) and the police called for a ban on pornographic comics based on the need to protect youths from *pornomanga*, believed to lead youngsters into deviancy (Kinsella, 2000; McLelland, 2015). The argument against pornography, as it had been in the 1980s in the USA, mainly adopted two frames: the alleged existence of a causal link between pornography and sexual crimes, and pornography promoting discrimination against women (Suzuki, 2001). Funabashi (1995) and Yunomae's (1996) critiques may also be seen as couched within the context of that period's debates.

---

[3] Due to the format of Japanese names these appear in the references as Funabashi, K. (1995) and Yunomae, T. (1996).

Pornographies

Since the 1970s, Japanese feminist groups such as the Women's Action Group have protested against the sexual objectification of women in the mass media by promoting pickets, petitions and sticker campaigns targeting offending advertising (Yunomae, 1996; Funabashi, 1995; Dales, 2009). However, Japanese feminists have been divided over censorship and the subject of pornography, with substantial anti-censorship endorsement (Suzuki, 2001; Buckley, 2002; McLelland, 2015).

It is undeniable that Japanese sexual entertainment industries and cultures of commodified sex reproduce sexist stereotypes about women, gender relationships and sexuality. Moreover, they often imply an underside of labour exploitation, criminal activities and racism that needs further investigation beyond the scope of this chapter. Nonetheless, I tend to dispute a definition of 'pornographic culture' that singles out Japan as a wonderland for porn consumers. This is an Orientalist misconception that even assumes a misleading and hierarchical notion of 'culture'. Although agreeing that pornography, as other cultural expressions, is part of a system of power relations and capitalist economic logics that may also be overwhelmingly sexist, I do not share the pro-censorship, causal nexus and protection-driven standpoints from which porn cultures are being contrasted. Too often such premises have been used within conservative, nationalist and moralistic agendas. Instead, as Feona Attwood and Clarissa Smith (2014) point out: "to pursue the study of pornography in a meaningful way requires the close and contextualized study of different facets and aspects of specific pornographies. In this way, it becomes possible to understand a variety of porn practices in their particularity" (p. 2). If the pervasiveness of rape and torture fantasies in Japanese pornography may be dispiriting (Shigematsu, 1997), it is however important to highlight increasing consumption patterns that fall outside those of the strictly heterosexual (and often heterosexist) genres produced by and for male consumers. These include: pornographic comics targeting adult women (*redisu manga*), male homoerotic fantasies authored and consumed by girls (*yaoi manga*), and self-proclaimed feminist erotic performances by female artists (see Shigematsu, 1997 and 1999; Nagaike, 2003; Shamoon, 2004; Mezur, 2005). Contextualised studies are therefore necessary. In order to frame pinky violence films along the lines proposed by Attwood and Smith (2014), I now proceed to frame their emergence historically within a wider view of Japanese popular culture and the 'sex hype' phenomenon that developed in the country immediately after the Second World War. From such view, it will be clearer how pinky violence, like "(p)ornography, then, is profoundly and paradoxically social, but even more than that, it's acutely historical" (Kipnis, 2006, p. 122).

Japan's historical erotica and the post-war sexualisation of culture

The appreciation and consumption of erotic artefacts, literary works and performances containing sexual references or explicit depictions of sexual rendezvous are part and parcel of much Japanese artistic heritage. In the foundational myths of Japan it is described how a strip dance performed by the goddess Ame no Uzume resolved a crisis by provoking the laughter of all attending deities. Allusions to sexual encounters can be found in the eleventh-century Japanese literary classic *The Tale of Genji*, as well as in salacious folktales of medieval itinerant storytellers. The most popular example is however that of erotic woodblock prints (*shunga*, literally 'spring images'), the production of which flourished during the Tokugawa period (1603–1867). The origins of kabuki theatre also involve sexually charged dances and the sexual availability of performers to their patrons. More recently, there are records of the existence of peep shows between the pre-modern and Meiji (1868–1912) periods (Buckley, 2002, p. 386), while eroticism pervaded many pastimes and leisure activities of Japan's mass culture from the 1920s through the early 1930s (Silverberg, 2007). In general, before Western morality and sense of decency started to influence Japanese policy makers and intellectuals towards the second half of the nineteenth century, unclothed body parts were not necessarily attributed sexual meanings and sex was considered a natural part of life insofar as relationships did not upset the reigning social order (McLelland, 2015; Burns, 2005).

Japan's history offers many different cultural expressions that emphasise a mix of eroticism and gloomy, grisly tinges. Some aspects of popular culture between the latter half of the nineteenth and the early twentieth centuries are exemplary in this respect. Woodblock print artist Yoshitoshi Tsukioka produced a print series graphically depicting famous violent murders and including scenes of bondage, decapitations, and tortures perpetrated upon pregnant women. A few decades before, the kabuki theatre playwright Tsuruya Namboku IV launched a new genre of plays centred on lowlifes' stories (*kizewamono*), which often featured violence and the supernatural (McDonald, 1994). A now classic study by Miriam Silverberg (2007) brilliantly illustrates the peculiar aesthetics referred to by the phrase 'erotic-grotesque-nonsense' (*ero-guro-nansensu*) that pervaded Japanese mass culture in the 1920s and 1930s (see also Driscoll, 2010). Such sensibility was based on the marketing and enjoyment of things erotic, grotesque and nonsensical, as the above-mentioned Japanese phrase indicates. The writer Edogawa Ranpo's mystery novels epitomise the *ero-guro* taste (see Kawana, 2008) and later inspired many of director Ishii Teruo's films, some of which enlisted dancer and choreographer Hijikata Tatsumi, who, in the 1960s, developed stage performances with similar aesthetics and themes (*ankoku butō*, literally 'dance of darkness').

Since the early years of Japan's Occupation (1946–1952) by the Allied forces after the Second World War, there was in the country an upsurge in the production of discourses and practices about bodies and sensual pleasures, which emerged also in connection with the occupiers' plans for Japan's 'democratisation' (McLelland, 2012). Igarashi Yoshikuni (2000) aptly defines the period spanning from 1945 to 1970 as "the age of the body" (pp. 47–72), that is, a time when the body came to symbolise liberation from wartime restrictions. The novels of authors such as Tamura Tajirō and Sakaguchi Ango printed in the immediate post-war period are associated with the birth of the 'literature of the flesh' (*nikutai bungaku*) (Marran, 2007, pp. 138–143; Slaymaker, 2004, pp. 8–30). Within Tamura's novels, the depiction of eroticism and the body carried precise political and philosophical meanings, signifying an invitation to trust only the senses at the expense of thought, in open rebellion against wartime ideologies and disciplinary regimes (Igarashi, 2000).

Other areas that between the late 1940s and the 1950s relayed and exploited the post-war discursive celebration of carnal pleasures include the *kasutori* (dregs) press – pulp magazines that dealt with sensational and titillating material and continued the pre-war *ero-guro* aesthetics (Marran 2007; McLelland, 2012) – and a variety of film genres such as sex education films (intended to teach physical and moral hygiene but bordering on sexploitation, see Domenig, 2007), Shintōhō studio's exploitation films (Schilling, 2010) and Nikkatsu studio's 'sun tribe' (*taiyōzoku*) films, which visualised a post-war decadent youth indulging in sex and violence.

The world of Japanese independent cinema during the 1960s and the 1970s forms another significant and more immediate context within which to consider pinky violence films. In fact, during the 1960s and early 1970s, there was significant overlapping between the world of pink films and another sector of independent cinema developed at the end of the 1960s: avant-garde films. A few small labels produced and distributed experimental films made by directors who are now considered the innovators of Japan's New Wave – Ōshima Nagisa and Imamura Shōei among others. Pink and avant-garde films may be seen to overlap in their consistent use of the naked female body and sex as the privileged means of expression. Sex and bodies were politicised by New Wave filmmakers, who used sexual relationships as allegories for power relations and thematic conduits for socio-political commentaries (Desser, 1988; Satō, 1982; Standish, 2011). In line with the whole cultural context, post-war cinema increasingly lent sexualised (female) bodies a political significance: endowed with sexual agency, they stood to signify the reaffirmation of the individual desires and freedom over war-time ideologies of self-sacrifice (Standish, 2007, p. 218).

Pinky violence exploitation and the construction of non-normative subjects

For the influence they have on Japanese cinema and in terms of numerical output, pink films represent an important part of the country's film industry and culture (Domenig, 2002). As mentioned above, there has been a growing interest in this field since the early 2000s, jointly with burgeoning research into the wider political and cultural landscapes of 1960s–1970s Japan that focus especially on the artistic avant-gardes (Standish, 2011; Eckersall, 2013; Shigematsu, 2012). Pinky violence films were also the product of independent cinema's innovations and wider socio-cultural shifts; nevertheless, although information about Tōei studio's sexploitation is growing on the Internet (even Wikipedia and Urban Dictionary have dedicated entries), material is still scattered and mostly informative, without much analytical depth or scope (e.g. Macias, 2000; D., 2005; Yamane, 2008), except for some more substantial research in Japanese (Yomota & Washitani, 2009; Suzuki, 2011). Interest in these films was revived also thanks to the success of Quentin Tarantino's *Kill Bill Vol. 1* (2003), which is clearly inspired by *Lady Snowblood* (1973–1974). Distribution companies such as Panik House, Eureka! and Synapse started providing non-Japanese audiences with subtitled films in DVD format, thus engendering growing curiosity and knowledge about this material. The same can be said of festivals and retrospectives screening pinky violence films and thus disclosing less known aspects of Japanese cinema to a global audience.

Concurring with Kipnis (2006) that pornography foregrounds cultural politics of exclusion, I argue that it is possible to see several interconnected dimensions in pinky violence films, especially considering the industrial shifts and socio-political struggles within which they appeared. Indeed, they can be seen to make sense (albeit within a framework of commercial exploitation) of shifting socio-cultural configurations of heterosexual femininity in the wake of the 1960s/1970s socio-political unrest that saw the emergence of countercultural and new feminist movements in Japan. This approach may help to challenge *a priori* assumptions that exploitation cinema (as well as other streams of pornographic work and erotica) is less conducive than politically committed 'art' to discussions about (sexual and other) politics. Pinky violence movies are worthy of closer investigation not *despite* but *because* of their taboo subject matter and the way this is handled within them. As can be said of pornography more generally, they put at centre stage notions of gender, sexuality and power relationships.

Pinky violence films put their female protagonists at centre stage, highlighting their violent, rebellious behaviour and expression of desire in a manner that is startling when compared to the gender ideology of official discourses, mainstream media and cinema of the time. Japanese television dramas for example (directed to an audience largely made up of housewives) offered stories centred upon relationships within the family, especially those between parent and child, and often featuring enduring women (Gössman, 2000). Thus, while television programmes kept reproducing traditional values and official articulations of mainly domestic femininities, movie theatre screens were crowded with personages, both male and female, breaking every possible social norm and blurring class, gender and racialised boundaries.

Post-war legislative measures in Japan provided women with a platform from which to claim equal treatment within the family, the workplace and public institutions. However, decades after the promulgation of the new Japanese Constitution (1947), discrimination based on sex difference in many life spheres was far from being overcome. From the 1950s, Japan experienced outstanding economic growth coupled with an overall restructuring of the industrial system. This period represented for women the chance to pursue education to higher levels and a career outside the domestic sphere, also thanks to a labour market expansion connected with this growth (see Tanaka, 1995). Unfortunately, however, cultural expectations about women's roles as the primary caretakers within the home persisted, becoming *de facto* one of the central assets that made national economic growth possible. As Kathleen Uno (1993) has shown, the pre-war ideology of 'good wife, wise mother' (*ryōsai kenbo*) was 're-packaged' and promoted in post-war Japan mainly through governmental and corporate policies, which in turn fostered women's internalisation of the gendered identities it promoted. Julia Bullock (2010) also explains how the attempts at naturalising the gender binary of masculine and feminine as complementary and mutually exclusive roles underpinned the national project of economic growth.

Women's direct experience of the contradiction existing between constitutional rights and everyday life (Matsui, 1990) contributed to the rise of the Japanese Women's Liberation Movement (*ūman ribu*), born out of the first student and civil protest movements of the 1960s. This is a radical feminist movement that is often referenced in relation to the birth of 'second-wave' feminism in Japan (Shigematsu, 2012). *Ribu*'s strong anti-family stance and aversion to women's established roles within the family marked its radically new perspective and comprehensive critique of Japanese post-war society. Bullock points this out clearly: "Challenging these models of normative gender effectively meant challenging the very basis of prosperity itself, something that violated contemporary common sense and rendered the challenger a subversive threat to the integrity of a newly stabilized Japanese society" (2010, p. 6). Moreover, biological sex was re-conceived by *ribu* feminists as the fundamental basis of oppression for women as class was for workers in classic Marxist terms. Therefore, according to radical Japanese feminists, sex constituted a potentially liberating force not just for women but to up-end and disrupt an entire capitalist-imperialist social system based on such oppression – disciplined sex was actually the key to the reproduction of that system. The subordination of women's desires as individuals to state- and corporate-driven policies for regulating their lives (e.g. work path, marriage, access to abortion) according to plans for economic growth (through the reproduction of labour force and procurement of a pool of cheap, unskilled labour and family welfare) was the continuation of the interwar regimentation of sexuality and gender roles serving the colonial ambitions of Imperial Japan (see Frühstück, 2003). It is therefore clear why the movement considered claiming back women's autonomy over their own bodies and sexuality a fundamental political step.

The female characters populating pinky violence films may be seen to conjure up and negotiate such new ideas, even if in highly ambivalent and sensationalist fashion. The wayward heroines of the films typically lead a nomadic, reckless life, often ending up receiving unwanted sexual attentions from men or suffering violent assaults; however, they defy any attempt to control them even by engaging in violent retaliations. Quite often a revenge narrative structure, which is a genre-crossing leitmotif in Japanese cinema, underpins the main story. This gives female protagonists violent agency and empowerment (even though temporarily and with many caveats) that is not easy to find in mainstream Japanese cinema up to the 1960s – perhaps with the exception of ghost and horror films. In this sense, these films transgress stereotypical media images of women of the time in at least two important respects: young girls are portrayed as rebellious, desiring subjects and are capable of returning violence, thus rejecting the position of passive compliance associated with women and femininity in Japanese conservative gender ideologies.

Furthermore, class, status, generational and racialised conflicts are brought to the fore, which are crucially articulated with, and enhance the scope of, an analysis solely informed by gender considerations. Pinky violence films' protagonists are socially marginal and economically deprived subjects who often side with figures in analogous positions of exploitation or discrimination such as boys of Afro-American and Japanese descent, outcasts, underprivileged or nonconformist people. Especially in the 'girl boss' films directed by Suzuki Norifumi, young women rebel against the men – often middle-aged and powerful – who prey upon them. Thus the films literalise and exploit the radical feminists' claim of sex being the basis of women's oppression by male power, which is personified as the girls' enemies: gangsters, representatives of state authority and coercive power (policemen, wardens, teachers) and figures endowed with high social, political and economic capital (politicians, bureaucrats). Young female avengers may therefore represent the violent, insurgent potential of interconnected subaltern positions. This allows us to draw out a more complex allegory of their struggle in the stories, which then appears to have more dimensions than just erotic appeal.

The difference that pinky violence films highlight in the construction of their female protagonists can readily be understood as aberrance and excess in respect to state-sanctioned official ideologies of gender propriety, the regulatory power of which is cyclically sustained by precise institutional policies and corporate business practices, and reproduced in mainstream cinema.

The *Girl Boss Blues* (1971–1972) films' opening sequences present the delinquent girl gangs dressed in trendy outfits and strutting around the entertainment quarters while smoking cigarettes, dancing in clubs, sniffing glue, picking fights or eluding policemen. This model of nonconforming femininity is further highlighted when juxtaposed within the same sequences with real-life scenes of diligent schoolgirls commuting and factory workers toiling at their posts. The second film in director Suzuki's *Terrifying Girls' High School* series, *Lynch Law Classroom* (1973), connects girls' rebellion against traditional gender roles with the student protests' anti-establishment spirit. During the late 1960s occupation of Japanese university campuses, students protested against conservative administrations and the academic establishment, building barricades and fighting against the riot police. The opening and closing sequences of this film suggest these connections. In the establishing shots of the 'Hope' girls' high school's premises, the camera zooms in on a plaque placed at the entrance, which has the school's name and the phrase 'good wife, wise mother' carved on it. The latter encapsulates the school's mission, which, as the headteacher's welcoming speech clarifies, is to provide Japanese society with reformed young women ready to perform their roles of good wives and wise mothers – a close-up of the plaque with the inscription is then interjected. Good wives and wise mothers, he goes on, are the foundation of society, and therefore what the country would most benefit from. The speech reiterates Meiji-era national policies on women's education being geared toward nurturing and home management roles, the importance of which was linked to national tranquillity (see Mackie, 2003). The film features nudity, female homoeroticism and other material for titillation inserted in both dramatic and comic scenes. In the final sequences, the schoolgirls unite to rebel against the school – whose bedrock of hypocrisy, violence and corruption is exposed – and consequently against the feminine roles they are pressurised to take up. A full-scale mutiny ensues; the students devastate the school facilities and resist the police in riot gear with a barricade, wooden poles and a water cannon. The film thus evokes real-life clashes between the police and university students, the feel made vivid through the use of a hand-held camera and bird's-eye shots. The girls overturn and set fire to the chairman's car and an image of the Japanese flag enveloped by the flames cuts to an upside-down shot of the plaque reading 'good wife, wise mother', which had appeared in the beginning. Even though the film ends with the girls responsible being hauled away in the police van, they accomplish their mission of destroying the school and exposing its (male) administrators' sexual depravity.

Conclusion

As Peter Alilunas (2014) points out, the study of pink films makes a fitting and timely contribution to the larger field of pornography studies. As a yet understudied segment of pink films and Japanese cinema history, a critical evaluation of pinky violence films intersects both areas of research. In line with intellectual approaches to pornography that see such material as having a complexity of its own and thus justify critical and interdisciplinary enquiries, I have shown how an examination of socio-historical, cultural and industrial contexts for the emergence of pinky violence films illuminates multiple dimensions to explore, moving past moral panics or taste-based dismissals. This way, the films may be seen to address and allegorise the inadequacy of cultural myths about femininity that much of earlier and contemporaneous mainstream Japanese visual culture tended to naturalise and reproduce. These are part of a discourse that normalises a conflict-free complementarity of gender roles where women are primarily construed as home-bound caretakers, constitutionally incapable of violence. As pointed out above, the notion of masculine and feminine gender roles' complementarity is central to official, corporate and mainstream media discourses that articulate domestic and nurturing aspects of femininity as constituting women's principal identities (wife and mother). Such gender ideology was promoted in support of new economic imperialist, national(ist) endeavours operating during the period of high economic growth in post-war Japan, through the revival, for example, of the 'good wife, wise mother' pre-war discourse. As shown especially through the *sukeban* cycle, pinky violence films point to cultural anxieties of the time and even converge (although in an exploitative mode) with contemporaneous countercultural and feminist claims, thereby revealing something *besides* semi-naked chicks wreaking havoc to titillate heterosexual male audiences.

As exploitation films, pinky violence movies display women's bodies for the pleasure of viewers and often eroticise action and violence. However, even the exhibition of their semi-naked bodies can be seen to serve as a prelude to the women's violent reactions to men's offences as well as erotic spectacles for the audiences. Rather than being the exclusive premise of male voyeuristic and fetishistic desire, the gaze in pinky violence cinema circulates and may be returned by women to frustrate men's sexual advances, intimidate attackers and anticipate counter-violence. And if pinky violence heroines' non-normative articulation is contained by narrative and visual strategies that clearly criminalise them (e.g. via a cautionary tale pattern) or make them abject (through horror-like depictions of their violence), nonetheless the films champion these characters' exercise of a retributive, violent agency. In fact, these films articulate narratives of personal redemption outside of the conventional patterns of romance or melodrama, in which underprivileged but undaunted young women are given prominence as rebellious and non-domestic subjects who may subvert (even if temporarily) hierarchies of (male) power and violence.

References

Alexander, J. R. (2003). Obscenity, pornography, and the law in Japan: Reconsidering Oshima's In the Realm of the Senses. *Asian-Pacific Law & Policy Journal*, 4(1 Winter), 148–168.

Alilunas, P. (2014). Afterword: Pink film and porn studies. In M. A. Nornes (Ed.), *The pink book. The Japanese eroduction and its contexts* (2nd ed., pp. 393–403). Kinema Club. Retrieved from http://kinemaclub.org/pink-book-japanese-eroduction-and-its-contexts

Allison, A. (1994). *Nightwork: Sexuality, pleasure, and corporate masculinity in a Tokyo hostess club*. Chicago, IL: The University of Chicago Press.

Attwood, F., & Smith, C. (2014). Porn studies: An introduction. *Porn Studies*, *1*(1–2), 1–6. Retrieved from http://dx.doi.org/10.1080/23268743.2014.887308

Buckley, S. (2002). *Encyclopedia of contemporary Japanese culture*. London, United Kingdom: Routledge.

Bullock, J. C. (2010). *The other Women's Lib: Gender and body in Japanese women's fiction*. Honolulu, HI: University of Hawai'i Press.

Burns, C. (2005). *Sexual violence and the law in Japan*. Richmond, United Kingdom: Curzon Press Limited.

Cather, K. (2014). Policing the pinks. In M. A. Nornes (Ed.), *The pink book. The Japanese Eroduction and its Contexts* (2nd ed., pp. 93–147). Kinema Club. Retrieved from http://kinemaclub.org/pink-book-japanese-eroduction-and-its-contexts

Dales, L. (2009). *Feminist movements in contemporary Japan*. Abingdon, UK: Routledge.

D. [Desjardins], C. (2005). *Outlaw masters of Japanese film*. London, United Kingdom: I. B. Tauris.

Desser, D. (1988). *Eros plus massacre: An introduction to the Japanese New Wave cinema*. Bloomington, IN: Indiana University Press.

Domenig, R. (2002). *Vital flesh: The mysterious world of Pink Eiga*. Retrieved from http://194.21.179.166/cecudine/fe_2002/eng/PinkEiga2002.htm

Domenig, R. (2007). *A history of sex education films in Japan Part 2: The post-war years and the Basukon Eiga*. Retrieved from http://www.midnighteye.com/features/a-history-of-sex-education-films-in-japan-part-2-the-post-war-years-and-the-basukon-eiga/

Domenig, R. (2011). *Proud to be pink: A brief history of Kokuei*. Retrieved from http://www.fareastfilm.com/easyne2/lyt.aspx?idlyt=7803&code=fefj&st=sql&sql=id_documento%3d3064

Driscoll, M. (2010). *Absolute erotic, absolute grotesque: The living, dead, and undead in Japan's Imperialism, 1895–1945*. Durham, NC: Duke University Press.

Eckersall, P. (2013). *Performativity and event in 1960s Japan: City, body, memory*. Basingstoke, United Kingdom: Palgrave Macmillan.

Fujita, T., & Hasebe, Y. (Directors). (1970–1971). *Stray Cat Rock* [Nora Neko Rokku] [Film series]. Japan: Nikkatsu.

Fujita, T. (Director). (1973–1974). *Lady Snowblood* [Shūrayuki Hime] [Film series]. Japan: Tōhō.

Funabashi, K. (1995). Pornographic culture and sexual violence. In K. Fujimura-Fanselow & A. Kameda (Eds.), *Japanese Women: New feminist perspectives on the past, present, and future* (pp. 255–263). New York, NY: Feminist Press at CUNY.

Frühstück, S. (2003). *Colonizing sex: Sexology and social control in modern Japan*. Berkeley, CA: University of California Press.

Gössman, H., M. (2000). New role models for men and women? Gender in Japanese TV dramas. In T. J. Craig (Ed.), *Japan Pop!: Inside the world of Japanese popular culture* (pp. 207–221). Armonk, NY: M. E. Sharpe.

Igarashi, Y. (2000). *Bodies of memory: Narratives of war in postwar Japanese culture, 1945–1970*. Princeton, NJ: Princeton University Press.

Itō, S., & Hasebe, Y. (Directors). (1972–1973). *Female prisoner scorpion* [Joshū Sasori] [Film series]. Japan: Tōei.

Jackson, B. (1999). Ishii Teruo kantoku vs seken no jōshiki. In J. T. Sugisaku & T. Uechi (Eds.), *Tōei pinkī baiorensu rōman arubamu* (pp. 220–221). Tokyo, Japan: Tokuma Shoten.

Kawana, S. (2008). *Murder most modern: Detective fiction and Japanese culture*. Minneapolis, MN: University of Minnesota Press.

Kinsella, S. (2000). *Adult manga: Culture and power in contemporary Japanese society*. London, United Kingdom: Routledge.

Kipnis, L. (2006) [1999]. How to look at pornography. In P. Lehman (Ed.), *Pornography: Film and culture* (pp. 118–129). New Brunswick, NJ: Rutgers University Press.

Macias, P. (2000). *Tokyoscope: The Japanese cult film companion*. San Francisco, CA: Cadence Books.

Mackie, V. C. (2003). *Feminism in modern Japan: Citizenship, embodiment, and sexuality*. Cambridge, United Kingdom: Cambridge University Press.

Mana, Y. (2009). Kedakaki rashin no musumetachi–Tōei pinkī baiorensu. In I. Yomota & H. Washitani (Eds.), *Tatakau onnatachi: Nihon eiga no josei akushon* (pp. 179–216). Tokyo, Japan: Sakuhinsha.

Marran, C. L. (2007). *Poison woman: Figuring female transgression in modern Japanese culture*. Minneapolis, MN: University of Minnesota Press.

Mathijs, E., & Sexton, J. (2011). *Cult cinema*. Malden, MA: Wiley-Blackwell.

Matsui, M. (1990). Evolution of the feminist movement in Japan. *NWSA Journal, 2*(3), 435–449.

McDonald, K. (1994). *Japanese classical theater in films*. Rutherford, NJ: Fairleigh Dickinson University Press.

McLelland, M. (2012). *Love, sex, and democracy in Japan during the American Occupation*. New York, NY: Palgrave Macmillan.

McLelland, M. (2015). Sex, censorship and media regulation in Japan: A historical overview. In M. McLelland & V. Mackie (Eds.), *Routledge handbook of sexuality studies in East Asia* (pp. 402–413). Oxford, United Kingdom: Routledge.

Mes, T. (2014). Kick out the jams! Nikkatsu's Stray Cat Rock series. *MidnightEye. Visions of Japanese Cinema*. Retrieved from http://www.midnighteye.com/features/kick-out-the-jams-nikkatsus-stray-cat-rock-series/

Mezur, K. (2005). Sex with nation: The OK (Bad) Girls Cabaret. In L. Miller & J. Bardsley (Eds.), *Bad girls of Japan* (pp. 175–196). New York, NY: Palgrave Macmillan.

Mulvey, L. (1989) [1975]. Visual pleasure and narrative cinema. In L. Mulvey (Ed.), *Visual and other pleasures* (pp. 14–26). Basingstoke, UK: Macmillan.

Nagaike, K. (2003). Perverse sexualities, perversive desires: Representations of female fantasies and "Yaoi Manga" as pornography directed at women. *U.S.-Japan Women's Journal. English Supplement, 25*, 76–103.

Nakahira, K., & Yoshimura, K. (Directors). (1972–1973). *Rika* [Rika] [Film series]. Japan: Tōhō.

Nornes, M. A. (Ed.). (2014). *The pink book: The Japanese eroduction and its contexts* (2nd ed.). Kinema Club. Retrieved from http://kinemaclub.org/pink-book-japanese-eroduction-and-its-contexts

Richie, D. (1991). *A lateral view: Essays on contemporary Japan*. Tokyo, Japan: *The Japan Times*.

Satō, T. (1982). *Currents in Japanese Cinema: Essays*. (G. Barrett, Trans.). Tokyo, Japan: Kodansha International.

Schilling, M. (2010). *Nudes! guns! ghosts! The sensational films of Shintoho*. Udine: Centro Espressioni Cinematografiche Udine.

Shamoon, D. (2004). Office sluts and rebel flowers: The pleasures of Japanese pornographic comics for women. In L. Williams (Ed.), *Porn Studies* (pp. 77–103). Durham, NC: Duke University Press.

Sharp, J. (2008). *Behind the pink curtain: The complete history of Japanese sex cinema*. Godalming, UK: FAB Press.

Shigematsu, S. (1997). "The law of the same" and other (non)-perversions: Woman's body as a "use-me/rape-me" signifier. *U.S.-Japan Women's Journal. English Supplement*, *12*, 154–177.

Shigematsu, S. (1999). Dimensions of desire: Sex, fantasy, and fetish in Japanese comics. In J. A. Lent (Ed.), *Themes and issues in Asian cartooning: Cute, cheap, mad, and sexy* (pp. 127–163). Bowling Green, OH: Bowling Green State University Popular Press.

Shigematsu, S. (2012). *Scream from the shadows: The Women's liberation movement in Japan*. Minneapolis, MN: University of Minnesota Press.

Silverberg, M. (2007). *Erotic grotesque nonsense: The mass culture of Japanese modern times*. Berkeley, CA: University of California Press.

Slaymaker, D. (2004). *The body in postwar Japanese fiction*. New York, NY: Routledge Curzon.

Standish, I. (2007). Transgression and the politics of porn. Ōshima Nagisa's In the Realm of the Senses (1976). In A. Phillips & J. Stringer (Eds.), *Japanese cinema: Texts and contexts* (pp. 217–228). Abingdon, UK: Taylor & Francis.

Standish, I. (2011). *Politics, porn, and protest: Japanese avant-garde cinema in the 1960s and 1970s*. New York, NY: Continuum.

Suzuki, N., & Shimura, M. (Directors). (1972–1973). *Terrifying girls' high school* [Kyōfu Joshi kōkō] [Film series]. Japan: Tōei.

Suzuki, N. (Director). (1973). *Terrifying girls' high school: Lynch law classroom* [Kyōfu Joshi Kōkō: Bōkō Rinchi Kyōshitsu] [Film series]. Japan: Tōei.

Suzuki, N. (Director). (1971–1972). *Girl boss blues* [Sukeban burūsu] [Film series]. Japan: Tōei.

Suzuki, N. (Director). (1973). *Sex and fury* [Furyō Anego Den: Inoshika Ochō]. Japan: Tōei.

Suzuki, N. (Director). (1974). *School of the Holy Beast* [Seijū Gakuen]. Japan: Tōei.

Suzuki, T. (2001). Frame diffusion from the U.S. to Japan: Japanese arguments against pornocomics, 1989–1992. In J. Best (Ed.), *How claims spread: Cross-national diffusion of social problems* (pp. 129–145). New York, NY: Aldine de Gruyter.

Suzuki, Y. (2011). *Shōwa pinku eigakan: Maboroshi no joyū, densetsu no seigō, yami no naka no katsudōyatachi*. Tokyo, Japan: Shakai Hyōronsha.

Tanaka, K. (1995). The new feminist movement in Japan, 1970–1990. In K. Fujimura-Fanselow & A. Kameda (Eds.), *Japanese women: New feminist perspectives on the past, present, and future* (pp. 343–352). New York, NY: Feminist Press at CUNY.

Tarantino, Q. (Director). (2003). *Kill Bill: Vol. 1*. [Motion pictue]. USA: Miramax.

Uno, K. S. (1993). The death of "good wife, wise mother"? In A. Gordon (Ed.), *Postwar Japan as history* (pp. 293–322). Berkeley, CA: University of California Press.

Williams, L. (2014). Pornography, porno, porn: Thoughts on a weedy field. *Porn Studies, 1*(1-2), 24–40. DOI: 10.1080/23268743.2013.863662

Yamaguchi, K. (Director). (1970–1971). *Delinquent girl boss* [Zubekō banchō] [Film series]. Japan: Tōei.

Yamane, S. (2008). Genealogía de las mujeres guerreras de Toei. In R. Cueto (Ed.), *Japón En Negro: Cine Policíaco Japonés/Japanese Film Noir* (pp. 87–103). Donostia-San Sebastián: Donostia zinemaldia-Festival de San Sebastián Filmoteca Española.

Yomota, I., & Washitani, H. (Eds.). (2009). *Tatakau onnatachi: Nihon eiga no josei akushon*. Tokyo, Japan: Sakuhinsha.

Yunomae, T. (1996). Commodified sex (sexism): Japan's pornographic culture. In J. A. Q. AMPO (Ed.), *Voices from the Japanese women's movement* (pp. 101–110). Armonk, NY; London, United Kingdom: M. E. Sharpe.

CHAPTER SEVEN

'SLUTBURGERS' AND SEXUAL SUBJECTS? THE RE-SEXUALISATION OF WOMEN IN FAST-FOOD ADVERTISING AND CULINARY CULTURE

Natalie Jovanovski

In her 2012 commercial for American fast-food giant Carl's Jr., *Sports Illustrated* model Kate Upton is shown carefully unwrapping the Southwest Patty Melt burger. As she takes her first bite, we watch her transform from sweet-looking girl-next-door into fiery vixen, following the sweat beads that run down her ample cleavage. The more she devours the burger, the more items of clothing she removes. As she writhes in ecstasy, blissfully unaware of her surroundings, the camera pans into the car next door, where a man is shown staring with his angry girlfriend sitting by his side. The male narrator interjects with, "the classic just got a whole lot hotter".

Away from the greasy marketplace of the fast-food industry and on to the glossy cover of UK magazine *Stylist*, another sexualised depiction of a female celebrity is taking place, once again involving food. Self-proclaimed domestic goddess Nigella Lawson is featured on the front cover of a special edition of *Stylist* (2011, December) next to the headline, "Nigella's Obsession: *Stylist's* Guest Editor on the Joys of Salted Caramel". Wearing dark heavy eye make-up with a seductive look on her face, Lawson is bathed in the sticky, sweet sauce, which drips off her eyelashes and onto her slightly parted lips.

These images of active, desiring female subjects, who revel in and conflate their sexual and gustatory appetites, are becoming increasingly visible in a postfeminist cultural climate (Magee, 2007). As Rosalind Gill (2008; 2009a; 2009b) explains in reference to postfeminist trends in advertising, images that were once perceived as offensive to women are now being read as subversive, empowering and even 'feminist'. This is increasingly becoming the case with contemporary fast-food advertising and culinary culture, where women's desires for food and sexuality are foregrounded as feminist and emancipatory, despite their reliance on the heterosexual male gaze. While some champion this rising trend, touting it as a welcome subversion of the sexless dieter of yesteryear (e.g. Neil, 2009), others see the sexual subjectification of women in advertising as a harmful cultural practice that may hold negative consequences for women's relationships with their bodies (Halliwell, Malson, & Tischner, 2011; Malson, Halliwell, Tischner, & Rudolfsdottir, 2011). Given the proliferation of these images throughout the United States and, to a much lesser extent, other Western countries such as Australia (Roper, 2015; Tankard-Reist, 2011), it is worth examining whether sexualised depictions of women and food are in fact subversions of harmful female stereotypes, recycled and objectified images of women that are typically found in pornography, or something new altogether. Drawing on the assertion that a tacit, disciplinary shift has occurred from sexual objectification to sexual subjectification, and that this shift has been informed by the growing influence of pornography on popular culture, this chapter will examine how contemporary fast-food advertisements and culinary culture depict women's relationships with food using soft-core pornographic tropes of femininity. While there is evidence that themes of self-sexualisation in fast-food advertising and culinary culture occur throughout the Western world, this chapter will only focus on the most prominent Western references, such as those found in the USA and UK. Rather than being counter-cultural, it is argued that these messages further complicate the associations between women, food and sexuality and reinforce the dominance of the heterosexual male gaze in media and advertising (Mulvey, 1975).

Tasty sexual subjects

Soft-core pornographic depictions of women in advertising and popular culture have been a much-contested topic in feminist literature for over three decades. While criticisms of sexualisation once focussed on the objectification of women and their treatment as 'meat' (e.g. Adams, 2010; Bartky, 1990; Dworkin, 1974; Jeffreys, 2005), increasingly, feminist researchers have focussed their attention on the harmful psychological effects of sexual subjectification narratives (Halliwell, Malson & Tischner, 2011; Malson, Halliwell, Tischner, & Rudolfsdottir, 2011). According to Dines (2010), messages of sexual empowerment have stemmed from an all-encompassing porn culture, one that has made the "soft-core pornography of ten years ago" (p. 26) into a mainstream cultural discourse. As Gill (2008; 2009a) explains, within this increasingly pornographised culture, passive depictions of women as sex objects have been replaced by narratives of active and desiring sexual subjects, complicating discussions on the harms and pervasiveness of sexualisation through the rebranding of soft-core pornography as a form of feminist empowerment. Angela McRobbie (2009) refers to this cultural shift as being part of a broader postfeminist cultural landscape, one that foregrounds liberal-individualist and capitalist sentiments over collective feminist politics (Chen, 2013; Gill, 2008). Rather than being politically empowering, however, the postfeminist messages generated in popular culture merely reiterate soft-core pornographic tropes of femininity and encourage women to internalise the heterosexual male gaze as a source of empowerment (Chen, 2013).

The sexual subjectification of women, as discussed by Gill (2008) and McRobbie (2009), coincides with the prevailing cultural tendency to sexualise all aspects of the marketplace.

Pornographies

According to Levy (2005), "sex appeal has become a synecdoche for all appeal ... The glossy, overheated thumping of sexuality in our culture is less about connection than consumption" (pp. 30–31). Rather than foregrounding women's sexual experiences, the appearance and promotion of sexual subjectification in advertising and popular culture simply aims to transform otherwise 'unsexy' consumer products into sexy and 'empowering' ones. Playing on cultural anxieties, such as women's relationships with food, eating and their bodies, advertisers capitalise on the sexualisation of women through the façade of feminist empowerment, operating largely under the guise of corporate social responsibility (McNally, 2015). While seemingly distinct, both the fast-food industry and mainstream culinary culture utilise the sexual subjectification of women in similar ways. The fast-food industry, and its negative associations with obesity and preventable illnesses, utilises supposedly 'empowering' pornographic tropes of women to cater to their predominantly heterosexual male audiences. Similarly, mainstream culinary culture, in an effort to shed the negative connotations of domesticity and traditional femininity, also focusses increasingly on the supposedly agentic and sexualised depiction of female food celebrities to entice both male and female audiences. The promotion of pornographic identities for women, thus, serves the dual function of capitalising on both men's and women's interests, whereby women are encouraged to enjoy self-sexualisation through food and eating, and men are encouraged to consume women visually as tasty sexual subjects.

The fast-food industry

The delineation between "junk food" (i.e. fast-food) and "junk sex" (i.e. pornography) is becoming increasingly blurred in contemporary Western culture. According to Eberstadt (2009), this blurring points to a cultural discourse that favours instant gratification over sustenance. Some fast-food companies rely on the notion of instant gratification to attract their heterosexual male customer-base; using the sexual subjectification of women as a way of achieving this. American fast-food chain Carl's Jr., in particular, is known for its sexually suggestive marketing and formulaic advertising campaigns. Made famous by its use of scantily clad female celebrities such as Paris Hilton, Kim Kardashian and Kate Upton, the Carl's Jr. franchise has received much attention by lay people and social commentators alike, and has colloquially been referred to as the home of the "slutburger" (O'Brien, 2014).

Carl's Jr.'s 2003 advertisement with *Playboy* founder Hugh Hefner was its first effort towards sexualising the brand, which sparked a backlash in the United States by various activist groups who called for a boycott of all Carl's Jr. products (Off Our Backs, 2004). In the offending advert, Hefner is shown surrounded by a group of *Playboy* bunny lookalikes, struggling to make a decision about which hamburger filling to choose. With a resolved look on his face he finally says, "It just depends what I'm in the mood for", prompting the male narrator to explain, "Because some guys don't like the same thing night after night". The double entendre, equating women with meat, led to criticisms that Carl's Jr. objectified women, which prompted representatives of the company to issue a series of statements both defending its advertisements and professing its respect for women (Off Our Backs, 2004). Perhaps in response to these complaints, Carl's Jr. advertisements in the US after 2003 took on a markedly postfeminist flavour, one that foregrounded women as hungry and lustful protagonists rather than passive sex objects awaiting visual consumption.

The hot lesbians
The 'hot lesbians' stereotype that dominates much of contemporary advertising and pornography, for example, is one of the

problematic ways that Carl's Jr. capitalises on the (self-) sexualisation of women. In its 2012 Memphis Barbecue Burger campaign advertised exclusively in the United States, model-turned-actress Emily Ratajkowski is shown standing over a sizzling barbecue at a county fair, wearing nothing but a patriotic stars and stripes bikini top and shorts that barely cover her buttocks. Former *Playboy* centrefold Sara Underwood enters the frame carrying a large tray of pulled pork. In a similarly skimpy outfit, she begins tussling with Ratajkowski over use of the grill. As the two struggle to claim dominance over the cooking space, their ingredients accidentally combine. With a look of excitement, both women start devouring the combination of beef and pulled pork; feeding it to each other enthusiastically and collapsing on to a nearby haystack in what seems to be both sexual and gustatory bliss. Two men are shown in the stall next door staring with their mouths ajar, filming the spectacle on their iPhones. The male narrator interjects with the phrase, "barbecue's best pair".

One of the key features of the postfeminist sexual subject is the emphasis on desire, consumption, and the notion that being sexually admired by men is a sign of female empowerment, regardless of one's sexual orientation (Chen, 2013; Halliwell, Malson, & Tischner, 2011). Unlike the passive and objectified *Playboy* bunnies that featured in Carl's Jr.'s 2003 advertising campaign, Ratajkowski and Underwood are depicted as *both* sexual objects and sexual subjects who revel unashamedly in their appetites for food and sex. Rather than being seen as victims of the heterosexual male gaze though, they are depicted as powerful, while the men are depicted as passive and somewhat desperate observers. According to Gill (2009a), the "sexual power to bring men to their knees" (p. 103) is part of a broader postfeminist discourse of female empowerment, where it suggested that women of all sexual orientations benefit from their ability to 'control' men through their sexual appetites. While their appetites for food and sex are exaggerated, however, the centrality of the heterosexual male gaze is a problematic narrative to reinforce, especially in the context of lesbian discourses.

One of the more dominant representations of the '173' stereotype – and the representation of Ratajkowski and Underwood in the aforementioned advert – involves two women who closely resemble each other engaging in sexual activity, a marketing technique known as 'doubling'. According to Gill (2009b), "doubling is ... [a] common male sexual fantasy which plays out in porn" (p. 152) and functions as an unthreatening portrayal of lesbianism marketed to an exclusively heterosexual, male audience. Rather than providing women with alternative sexual representations, 'doubling' serves the function of broadening men's sexual repertoires and, implicitly, erasing lesbian narratives from contemporary advertising altogether (Wirthlin, 2009). Wirthlin (2009) argues this sexualised depiction of 'lesbian' figures in popular culture is nothing more than a heteronormative appropriation of lesbian culture used to cater to the male gaze and, as such, serves no liberating purpose to lesbians themselves. Like the two men ogling Ratajkowski and Underwood in the advert and filming the spectacle on their phones, Wirthlin (2009) argues that men are said to "want two young, hot, *straight* girls to fondle each other in front of them, for their sexual pleasure. They really want a momentary appropriation of [lesbian] sexuality in order to contort it as a mere, fleeting sexual moment on which to get off" (pp. 108–109). Rather than being facets of female empowerment, then, the 'hot lesbian' trope in Carl's Jr.'s advert for the Memphis Barbecue Burger seems to reinforce pre-existing notions of the heterosexual male gaze and the heteronormative availability of the female body. The sexual and gustatory appetites of lesbians, from this perspective, become inconsequential, as the audience truly being fed is male. Indeed, the use of two heterosexual women emulating a pseudo-lesbian male fantasy is potentially harmful to women who identify as lesbians. In their study on the harmful effects of self-objectification in lesbians, Haines, Erchull, Liss, Turner, Nelson, Ramsay, & Hurt (2008) found that despite lacking sexual and romantic interest in men, some of the lesbians in their sample still internalised heterosexist attitudes and experienced higher levels of self-objectification and negative attitudes to food and eating (Haines et al., 2008). Similar findings were uncovered by Kozee and Tylka (2006), where they showed that the lesbians in their study experienced high levels of body surveillance, despite rejecting the heteronormative thin ideal propagated in Western culture. They suggested that even without acting on the cultural pressure to lose weight, and despite being exposed to a broader range of beauty standards, that lesbians are still subject to the heteronormative male gaze and the pressures associated with it. What Carl's Jr. depicts, then, is a heteronormative appropriation of lesbian women's sexual and gustatory appetites under the guise of female empowerment; an image that has potentially negative consequences for lesbians. Unsurprisingly, similar themes were found for other demographics of women, such as the newly celebrated 'older' woman.

The cougar
The role of the sexually voracious 'cougar' is another problematic, yet dominant soft-core pornographic stereotype used by Carl's Jr. to portray women as hungry, desiring sexual subjects. Cougars refer to "older, unmarried women who express their sexuality by publicly pursuing younger men for casual relationships or sexual encounters" (Montemurro & Siefkin, 2014, p. 35). Closely related to the 'MILF' (i.e. Mother I'd Like

to Fuck), the 'cougar' is used increasingly as a pornographic trope, and occupies a growing and profitable space within popular culture. Indeed, according to Vannier, Currie and O'Sullivan (2014), the caricature of the older, sexually uninhibited woman is quickly becoming one of the most widely searched categories on pornographic websites. While the 'cougar' remains a contentious figure within mainstream depictions of female sexuality, she is also being increasingly embraced by mainstream cultural discourses. German supermodel Heidi Klum features in the 2013 campaign for Carl's Jr. Jim Beam Bourbon Burger, which relies strongly on the notion of the sexually predatory older woman. In a parody of the 1967 classic film *The Graduate*, Klum plays a Mrs Robinson-type character, who tries to seduce a much younger Benjamin with the Jim Beam Bourbon Burger. Ordering Benjamin to "sit down", the former *Victoria's Secret* model is shown standing over the young man's body with one leg raised, widening the slit in her black dress and exposing her underwear outside of the camera's gaze. As she shoves the burger into his mouth, licking the barbecue sauce off her fingers, a very nervous Benjamin asks, "Mrs Robinson, you're trying to seduce me … aren't you?", at which point the male narrator announces, "it'll make a man out of you".

Like Klum's seemingly empowered, self-sexualised performance in the Carl's Jr. Jim Beam Bourbon Burger advert, some researchers suggest that the cougar stereotype can be seen as a progressive, 'feminist' depiction of female agency (Montemurro & Siefken, 2014; Vannier et al., 2014). According to Montemurro and Siefken (2014), the cougar stereotype enables women who otherwise fall outside of the young, ageist norms of female sexuality to be given a mainstream platform to express themselves. Rather than being perceived as asexual, these researchers argue that, through the cougar persona, older women are afforded new ways to assert their agency, and of seeing themselves as attractive, strong and confident. Vannier et al. (2014) reinforce this notion when they argue that 'older' women in mainstream pornography are more sexually dominant than their younger counterparts and male co-stars, and that this may be a progressive step for women in pornography and popular culture.

Far from being progressive, however, the cougar stereotype is also subject to the same objectifying male gaze that is cast on other demographics of women. While some describe the sexualised stereotype of the 'cougar' as being an empowering figure of female sexuality, others suggest that her hyper-sexualised and conventionally attractive persona merely reinforces the limited caricatures of idealised femininity already on offer to women (Montemurro & Siefkin, 2014). This notion is made obvious in Klum's portrayal of Mrs Robinson, which is highly sexualised and representative of ideal femininity, and an identity that is predicated upon the attention of a heterosexual male audience. As Grippo and Hill (2008) suggest, how women respond to the sexual scrutiny of their bodies depends, in part, on their internalisation of mainstream norms of youth, beauty and sexual availability. In their study looking at the harmful effects of self-objectification on middle-aged and older women, they found that their sample of older women who internalised culturally reinforced standards of beauty which favoured youthfulness and self-sexualisation experienced similar levels of self-objectification and habitual self-monitoring to their younger sample of women. Similarly, in their study on objectification theory and age, Augustus-Horvath and Tylka (2009) found that in their sample of 'older' women (i.e. women over the age of 25), those who reported increases in sexually objectifying experiences were more likely maladaptive eating behaviours. While these researchers do not explicitly argue that the cultural sexualisation of older women leads to disordered eating behaviour per se, they argue that the sexualisation of women may be internalised by some older women, and that this is potentially harmful to their physical and psychological well-being. Rather than serving as an empowering caricature of femininity, the sexualised depiction of the 'cougar' in Carl's Jr.'s Jim Beam Bourbon Burger advert reinforces the notion that women, regardless of their age or sexual orientation, need to be palatable to the heterosexual male gaze and that it is beneficial, rather than harmful, to their sense of self. Indeed, this theme extends into Carl's Jr.'s sexualised narratives involving ethnicity.

The spicy 'other'
Like the problematic narratives of sexual subjectification found in the appetites of 'hot lesbians' and 'cougars', Carl's Jr. also relies on the equally problematic and sexualised portrayal of the 'exotic Other' to market its products. In its television advert for the Big Western Bacon Burger (hereafter referred to as the 'Big Western'), former lingerie model and *Food Network* star Padma Lakshmi is shown walking through a crowded marketplace, sampling the food and spices on offer in a mock cooking show format. In a flowing dress with a plunging neckline, the model turned cooking-show host is heard describing her travels around the world, pointing to her preference for Carl's Jr.'s Big Western over "every flavour imaginable". In an overtly sexualised way, she takes a big bite out of the burger and spills some of the spicy sauce on to her leg. As the camera zooms into the sauce on her ankle, we watch her scooping it up and seductively sucking it off her finger. The male narrator has the final word, announcing that the burger – and, implicitly, Lakshmi – is "more than just a piece of meat".

The postfeminist flavour of Lakshmi's sexual and gustatory appreciation of the Big Western is one that, on the surface, appears to address feminist criticisms of sexual objectification by showing her embracing food that is typically perceived by women as 'bad'. Indeed, as Dan Neil (2009) explains in his article for the *Los Angeles Times*, the double entendre "more than just a piece of meat" strengthens feminist contentions rather than merely reiterating sexist attitudes towards women. He states,

> I can see neo-feminist subversion in these messages. Note the tagline of the ... commercial: "More than just a piece of meat". This was the cri de coeur of feminism back in the day, and though it refers to the burger, it is also a tweak of conscience to males slobbering over the accomplished actress-author-chef. Take that, you objectifying pig. ... Also, in a culture in which glamour and beauty have been so thoroughly yoked to anorexia, isn't it great to see a sexy woman eat like a stevedore? (n.p.)

From Neil's (2009) perspective, watching Lakshmi enjoy the Big Western and revel in her sexual subjectification is a victory for feminists, as it directly conflicts with the prevailing, and often restrictive, narratives of women's relationships with food and their sexuality. However, what is missing from Neil's (2009) fleeting analysis is that the male narrator, who serves as a metaphor for the male gaze, still refers to Lakshmi as 'meat', regardless of his suggestion that she is "*more than* just a piece of meat". Rather than drawing on feminist assertions that women are *not* pieces of meat awaiting the visual consumption of men (e.g. Adams, 2010; Dworkin, 1974), the tagline of the campaign in question emphasises that, in fact, they *are* meat and that they *enjoy* being seen as meat. This distinction is important, as it not only underscores the centrality of the heterosexual male gaze that features prominently in Carl's Jr. advertising campaigns, but also emphasises how women's sexual subjectification is explicitly tied to the embrace of their cultural objectification. As

'Slutburgers' and Sexual Subjects?

Gill (2009a) and Chen (2013) explain, one of the dominant features of postfeminist media culture is that experiencing sexual subjecthood involves playing with and, in some instances, embracing the sexual attention one receives from men. Like Carl's Jr.'s adverts with Ratajkowski, Underwood and Klum, the way that this is achieved is by reinforcing the traditionally subordinated and orientalised pornographic trope of the 'exotic' and 'ethnic' Other (e.g. Cowan & Campbell, 1994; Said, 2003) as a sign of empowerment.

The appropriation of a South Asian woman to market a burger with the words 'Big Western' in the title can be perceived as a deliberate attempt to foreground ethnicity as a marker of women's sexual subjectification (and, implicitly, objectification) within Western cultures. Some writers note that the sexualisation of South Asian women in popular culture serves as a juxtaposed reminder of colonialism, domination and exoticisation of the 'Other' (Durham, 2001; Mannur, 2005). In her article on the popularisation of Indian fashion in American culture, Durham (2001) argues that, like advertisers who capitalised on the allure of exotic "Oriental female sexuality" (p. 205) in Britain during the nineteenth century, advertisers in the twenty-first century use the eroticised Eastern 'Other' as a way of safely co-opting elements of their culture without directly including them in mainstream Western discourses. Rather than being progressive, Durham (2001) explains that "the fetishistic nature" of this discourse is "paradoxically infused with both erotic desire and racial contempt" (p. 206). When Lakshmi's exotically 'ethnic' features are juxtaposed against the patriotic Big Western burger, *she* becomes the 'spicy' ingredient that the heterosexual male viewer wishes to consume. Devouring the 'Big Western' feast, and foregrounding it as the most delicious meal she has had, becomes synonymous with devouring the supposedly 'Big

Western' male audience that is voyeuristically watching her. In a sense, the Big Western burger – like all of the burgers discussed in this chapter – becomes what Madeleine Davies (2013, n.p.) sarcastically refers to as a phallic symbol; as a depiction that is less about women's appetites and more about their ability to "fellatiate a sandwich" for the heterosexual male gaze. From this perspective, Lakshmi's conflation of eating and sexual expression is less about her own sexual subjectivity and more about her 'exotically ethnic' version of male sexual desire that is currently on offer. Despite being offered a platform to express her relationship with food and sexuality, the depiction on offer ultimately reverts back to heteronormative and Western depictions of female sexuality. Perhaps unsurprisingly, similar narratives are found in mainstream culinary depictions of women's relationships with food; a cultural discourse that is principally marketed to women.

Mainstream culinary culture
Coinciding with the sexualisation of women in fast-food advertising, representations of women in mainstream culinary culture have also been increasingly couched within the postfeminist language of sexual subjectification. Unlike fast-food advertisements, however, which are primarily directed towards heterosexual male audiences, culinary culture is perceived to be largely the domain of women and, thus, used as a way to socialise them into contemporary gender norms relating to food preparation (Mitchell, 2010). The traditionally "unsexy" connotations of the kitchen as a site of women's subordination (Friedan, 1963; Greer, 1971; Oakley, 1976), have been, in more recent times, replaced by narratives of the visually palatable role of the TV cook, and, as Magee (2007) explains, have aligned conveniently with pornographic tropes that depict cooking as a pleasurable, sensual and even empowering pursuit. As Christine Mitchell (2010) explains, this

is reflected in the historical changes associated with the female food celebrity, whose role has shifted from being largely educational (i.e. educating women on the fine art of domestic cooking and entertaining) to being predicated upon the notion of entertainment, or as she refers to it, as "glitter overwhelm[ing] substance" (p. 537). Rather than being informative, then, female food celebrities in the twenty-first century appeal to women's desire for subversive messages around food and cooking, which are often expressed through sexualised connotations and advice giving. Coupled with the notion of sexual subjectivity, the female food celebrity, in her conflated sexuality and appetite for food, becomes synonymous with the dishes she prepares, rather than their method of preparation. Prominent British and American female food celebrities Padma Lakshmi, Nigella Lawson and Rachael Ray all rely on elements of sexual subjectivity to reinforce their conflated relationships with food and eating.

Food-as-sex therapists
Arguably, the most famous food celebrity capitalising on the self-sexualisation trend is self-proclaimed domestic goddess Nigella Lawson (Hewer & Brownlie, 2009; Magee, 2007; Sanders, 2008). Described by some writers as being "as much a sex symbol as a cook" (Ellicott, 2014, n.p.), Nigella has built a name for herself by simultaneously titillating male audiences and posing as a "virtual girlfriend [and] confidante" to her female fans (Chan, 2003, p. 50). As Chan explains, Nigella's fame has been predicated upon her ability to "confidently dispens[e] advice and offer [opinions], but always with a recipe/prescription for every woe" (p. 50). This food-as-sex therapist stance, which is reinforced by her postfeminist cultural persona, underscores the importance of food in expressing sexual subjectification narratives. In her cookbook *Kitchen* (2010), for example, a modified recipe of the Italian dish 'Pasta

alla Puttanesca', or 'Slut's Spaghetti', is featured. Posing next to the recipe in a red silk robe with tousled hair, Nigella is shown tucking into the meal in her trademarked hedonistic style. In the recipe itself, Nigella goes to great lengths to describe herself as the anti-housewife, explaining that the recipe is "the sort of dish cooked by slatterns who don't go to the market to get their ingredients fresh" (p. 188) and that, in reference to serving the dish, that presentation should be done in a "slatternly style, predictably with an untipped cigarette clamped between crimson-painted lips" (p. 188).

Nigella's use of the term 'slattern' in this context, drawing reference to a dirty, unruly woman, coupled with the sexualised connotations of her photograph, point to what Winch (2011) refers to as the empowered discourse of postfeminist girlfriend culture. According to Winch (2011), postfeminist girlfriend culture celebrates the 'empowered' choices that women make, and their reclamation of traditionally sexist terms such as 'slut', 'bitch' and 'whore' (Kleinman, Ezzell, & Frost, 2009). When Nigella describes herself as a "slattern", and refers to her recipe as "whore's pasta", she is using the 're-claimed' terminology of postfeminist girlfriend culture to assert her empowered persona. This is also expressed in her book *Nigella Bites* (2001), where she dedicates an entire chapter to what she refers to as "trashy" foods, which draws reference to foods that contain a high fat, sugar and salt content. Holding a martini glass and wearing a T-shirt with the *Playboy* bunny logo emblazoned on it, Nigella paints her appetites for food and sex as being synonymously 'dirty', unruly and anti-puritanical (Magee, 2007). Far from being subversive, however, the food-as-sex advice that Nigella dispenses is predicated upon her sexual palatability, which is constantly reiterated in the sexual presentation of her appearance. Despite the intended irony of her culinary discourse, one that rejects puritanical notions of the ideal housewife, her expressive sexual subjectivity veers towards self-objectification.

Likewise, Padma Lakshmi utilises her persona as a sexual subject to bolster her culinary credibility. Other than appearing in fast-food advertising as an 'exotic' seductress, Lakshmi's role as a food celebrity is also dependent on her ability to both titillate male audiences and provide women with an empowered, anti-domestic template with which to refer to food (Mannur, 2005; e.g. Gallas, 2010). According to Mannur (2005), it is not so much her ability to cook that draws attention to her television show *Padma's Passport*, but rather, her ability to sexualise the cooking experience. This is reinforced by the "deliberately sexualised" presentation of her appearance, where she "wears revealing outfits, [such as] leather pants, short T-shirts exposing her midriff, tight sleeveless dresses [and] low-cut blouses ... [outfits that are] not typically associated with the "sensible clothing" of most Food Network stars" (p. 80). When coupled with her often clumsy and seemingly novice relationship with cooking, Lakshmi appeals to both female and male audiences alike and, specifically, gives women permission to be imperfect in the kitchen. While Lakshmi has a loyal female following, it is the sexualisation of her body – and her confident, sexualised persona – that draws heterosexual male audiences (Mannur, 2005).

Lakshmi's frequent involvement in men's magazines is evidence of blurring of her sexual and gustatory appetites. In a piece for *Men's Fitness*, Lakshmi adopts the role of a knowledgeable pseudo-food/sex therapist, informing men about the benefits of using food as a way to seduce women. In an excerpt from the article, Lakshmi explains that, "when you have sex, you consume another person. You're consumed. Food is like that" (as cited in Gallas, 2010, p. 76). Lakshmi's conflation of food with sex, and her suggestion that one "consumes" one's partner during sexual encounters, foregrounds her food-as-sex advice persona and, thus, her active sexual subjectivity. However, rather than merely asserting her proficiency in sexual and gustatory matters, Lakshmi is also served as a feast for the heteronormative male gaze. Indeed, the sexualisation of her features is a regular occurrence in men's magazines. In *Maxim*, for example, Lakshmi is depicted looking confident, wearing a tight blue bandage dress and enticingly holding a green apple. The caption next to the picture reads, "The adorably edible host of Top Chef is a feast for the eyes – and the spicy dish that makes Bravo's hit cooking show totally appetising" (2015, n.p.). The description of Lakshmi as "edible", "a feast for the eyes" and a "spicy dish" indicates that whatever power she elicits from her conflation of sex and food, she is still objectified by the male gaze and orientalised in the process. The image of female sexuality that she depicts is one that is more directed towards the appetites of heterosexual male audiences rather than working to empower women. While both Nigella and Lakshmi veer between sexual subjectification and sexual objectification narratives with a postfeminist sense of irony and playfulness, rejecting traditional notions of domesticity and subservience, sometimes – as will be discussed below – the association between food and sex is more literal.

The girl-next-door
In a 2003 edition of men's magazine *FHM*, *Food Network* star and wholesome 'girl-next-door', Rachael Ray, is featured in a series of photographs that cast domesticity and cooking as a playful sexual experience. Wearing nothing but a black brassiere, chequered mini skirt and spaghetti strap heels, Ray is shown pulling a glazed turkey out of the oven with a toothy grin on her face. In another shot, and in a similarly skimpy mini skirt and midriff revealing top, the glazed turkey is replaced by a cherry pie. The photographs depicting Ray eating are presented

in a similarly sexualised way. In one shot, Ray is shown licking chocolate sauce off a wooden spoon with nothing but a black brassiere on, and in another she is shown sucking seductively on a strawberry. In a way that is distinct from Nigella's ironic, tongue-in-cheek merging of her sexual and gustatory appetites, Ray's soft-core pornographic photographs seem to be more of a literal, rather than figurative, display of sexualised domesticity.

In an interview with Cynthia McFadden for *Nightline*, Ray defends her *FHM* photo shoot through a postfeminist narrative of choice, empowerment and agency:

> The PR person at Food Network said we actually have an unusual request from FHM magazine. And I thought about it – I think I was thirty-five at the time. Thirty-four or thirty-five. And I thought about it for a while, and I said, you know what? This magazine has as young as seventeen, eighteen-year-olds in hottie bikinis, and these are all actresses, models, pin-up girls. I don't belong to any, even remote, club of theirs. And I thought if I'm gutsy enough to do this, this is a good thing for everybody. This is the everywoman, here she is. And I thought, what the heck? I asked my husband what he thought of it and he said, [giggles] oh, kinda cool. And I did it and it was the most scared I've ever been and I wouldn't change a thing. I'd do it again tomorrow ... My mother was furious. Remains furious. You don't have to do that kind of trash, you don't need to sell yourself that way, blah blah blah. I was proud of it. And I would do it again, even though my mom would be mad at me. I know she still loves me. (Ray, as cited in Shea, 2009, n.p.)

Ray's emphatic assertions that she is "proud" of her decision, and that she is an "everywoman" who is "gutsy enough to do this", is evidence of a cultural narrative that features prominently in postfeminist discourses of female sexuality. Indeed, it can be argued that these messages reinforce the notion that a woman gains power and visibility through the sexualisation of her character, a phenomenon that has been referenced in feminist literature as 'raunch culture' (Chen, 2013; Levy, 2005). According to Levy (2005), raunch culture, or the mainstreaming of pornography, emerged several decades after the second-wave feminist revolution and during the height of conservative Western politics. Couching itself within the feminist language of 'empowerment' and 'agency', the main premise behind raunch culture was to emulate pornographic actresses, and to achieve cultural power and recognition in doing so. Ray's photographs, and her interview on *Nightline*, demonstrate the extent to which she speaks from an empowered narrative despite engaging in behaviours typically confined to soft-core pornographic actresses. Indeed, this notion is even more complicated by her sexualisation of domesticity.

The sexualisation of Ray's domestic role, where she is featured cooking in scanty attire, takes Levy's (2005) notion that postfeminist raunch culture has infiltrated all aspects of contemporary Western culture to another level. Seeing Ray find pleasure in both sexualising herself *and* cooking serves the function of merging the desiring, empowered sexual subject of contemporary advertising with the archaic and – as some would suggest – mythical caricature of the 'happy housewife' (Friedan, 1963; Oakley, 1976). Prominent figures in the second-wave feminist movement, such as Betty Friedan and Ann Oakley, defined domesticity – and by extension, women's relationships with food and cooking – as broader symptoms of women's inequality. Radical feminist writer Ann Oakley (1976) saw women's cooking responsibilities as anti-feminist actions and even went so far as to entertain the notion of the kitchenless home. Liberal feminist writer Betty Friedan (1963) made similar assertions in her text *The Feminine Mystique*. Interviewing women who classified themselves as 'housewives' in the 1960s, Friedan found that, regardless of the prevailing cultural narrative that domesticity was useful to women, the women in her study experienced an overarching sense of hopelessness in relation to being confined to selfless nurturing roles, such as cooking. The notion of the 'happy housewife', she argued, was one that was only found in furniture catalogues rather than reality. The domestic picture that Ray paints, however, is one that conflicts with second-wave feminist narratives of domestic servitude, and suggests that not only does the happy housewife exist, but she also exists in a pornographic realm. Ray's pride in merging the sexualisation of her body with the sexualisation of her role as a cook reiterates how postfeminist depictions of women's sexual and gustatory appetites are increasingly being mobilised for the heterosexual male gaze. Rather than being depicted in a professional kitchen, Ray is foregrounded in the narrative as a sexy girl-next-door, blissfully confined to the domestic kitchen and the sexualisation that comes along with it. Ultimately, and despite Ray's assertions that she is "proud" of her participation in the photo shoot, her actions in the *FHM* domestic kitchen serve the heteronormative male gaze, merging traditional, subordinated aspects of the 'happy housewife' with contemporary soft-core pornographic depictions of femininity.

Soft-core food pornography: sexual subjects, tasty objects or something else?

The sexualisation of women in fast-food advertising and mainstream culinary culture is depicted as a postfeminist victory and an expression of women's sexual subjectification. However, the soft-core pornographic tropes representing women's sexual subjectification ultimately rely on sexually objectifying narratives and, thus, are only affirmed and validated through the existence of the male gaze. Carl's Jr.'s advertising campaigns rely on formulaic, soft-core pornographic depictions of women; depictions where women relate to hamburgers as glorified phallic symbols. Despite drawing on 'empowering' postfeminist discourses that appear to foreground women's appetites for sex and food, Carl's Jr. merely reiterates that the male gaze is ever-present; both in the comments of its male narrator, and in the representation of women as glorified porn actresses. Mainstream culinary figures, while seemingly distinct, take the notion of sexual subjectification further by adding domesticity and advice giving as important ingredients. While Nigella Lawson and Padma Lakshmi play the empowered food-as-sex therapists, socialising women into untraditional, yet sexualised notions of domesticity, food celebrity and girl-next-door Rachael Ray takes her message further by explicitly sexualising the domestic sphere. Given the prevailing discourse of sexual subjectification in fast-food advertising and culinary culture, it is reasonable to conclude that women's relationships with food and their sexuality have been "ransacked, cannibalised, incorporated and 'domesticated'" (Gill, 2009a, p. 108) by this porn-inspired shift to 'empowerment'. The soft-core food pornographies available to women, thus, do nothing to emancipate women from the ever-present heterosexual male gaze. Instead, they destructively transform women into tasty morsels under the guise of female empowerment, and foreground men's sexual interests by doing so.

References

Adams, C. J. (2010). *The sexual politics of meat: A feminist-vegetarian critical theory (20th anniversary edition)*. New York, NY: Continuum.

Augustus-Horvath, C. L., & Tylka, T. L. (2009). A test and extension of objectification theory as it predicts disordered eating: Does women's age matter? *Journal of Counselling Psychology, 56*(2), 253–265.

Bartky, S. L. (1990). *Femininity and domination: Studies in the phenomenology of oppression.* New York, NY: Routledge.

Chan, A. (2003). 'La grand bouffe': Cooking shows as pornography. *Gastronomica: The Journal of Food and Culture, 3*(4), 46–53.

Chen, E. (2013). Neoliberalism and popular women's culture: Rethinking choice, freedom and agency. *European Journal of Cultural Studies, 16*(4), 440–452.

Cowan, G., & Campbell, R. R. (1994). Racism and sexism in interracial pornography. *Psychology of Women Quarterly, 18*, 323–338.

Davies, M. (2013). Put it in my mouth: A history of disgusting Carl's Jr. ads. Retrieved from http://jezebel.com/5990397/put-it-in-my-mouth-a-history-of-disgusting-carls-jr-ads

Dines, G. (2010). *Pornland: How porn has hijacked our sexuality.* Boston, MA: Beacon Press.

Durham, M. G. (2001). Displaced persons: Symbols of South Asian femininity and the returned gaze in U.S. media culture. *Communication Theory, 11*(2), 201–217.

Dworkin, A. (1974). Woman hating: A radical look at sexuality. New York, NY: E. P. Dutton.

Eberstadt, M. (2009). Is food the new sex? *Policy Review,* (153), 25–40.

Ellicott, C. (2014, 20 October). Flirty? Me? Certainly not says Nigella Lawson who maintains: 'I have nothing of the coquette about me', *Daily Mail.* Retrieved from http://www.dailymail.co.uk/tvshowbiz/article-2799489/flirty-certainly-not-says-nigella-lawson-maintains-coquette.html

Friedan, B. (1963). *The feminine mystique.* Harmondsworth, United Kingdom: Penguin Books.

Gallas, D. (2010). Padma Lakshmi, *Men's Fitness, 26*(6), 76.

Gill, R. (2008). Empowerment/sexism: Figuring female sexual agency in contemporary advertising. *Feminism and Psychology, 18*(1), 35–60.

Gill, R. (2009a). Supersexualise me! Advertising and the midriffs. In F. Attwood (Ed.), *Mainstreaming sex: The sexualisation of Western culture* (pp. 93–110). London, United Kingdom: I. B. Taurus.

Gill, R. (2009b). Beyond the 'sexualisation of culture' thesis: An intersectional analysis of 'sixpacks', 'midriffs' and 'hot lesbians' in advertising. *Sexualities, 12*(2), 137–160.

Greer, G. (1971). *The female eunuch*. London, United Kingdom: Paladin.

Grippo, K. P., & Hill, M. S. (2008). Self-objectification, habitual body-monitoring, and body dissatisfaction in older European American women: Exploring age and feminism as moderators. *Body Image, 5*, 173–182.

Haines, M. E., Erchull, M. J., Liss, M., Turner, D. L., Nelson, J. A., Ramsey, L. R., & Hurt, M. M. (2008). Predictors and effects of self-objectification in lesbians. *Psychology of Women Quarterly, 32*, 181–187.

Halliwell, E., Malson, H., & Tischner, I. (2011). Are contemporary media images which seem to display women as sexually empowered actually harmful to women? *Psychology of Women Quarterly, 35*(1), 38–45.

Hewer, P., & Brownlie, P. (2009). Culinary culture, gastrobands and identity myths: 'Nigella', an iconic brand in the baking. *Advances in Consumer Research, 36*, 482–487.

Jeffreys, S. (2005). Beauty and misogyny: Harmful cultural practices in the West. Hove, United Kingdom: Routledge.

Kleinman, S., Ezzell, M. B., & Frost, A. C. (2009). Reclaiming critical analysis: The social harms of "bitch". *Sociological Analysis, 3*(1), 47–68.

Kozee, H. B., & Tylka, T. L. (2006). A test of objectification theory with lesbian women. *Psychology of Women Quarterly, 30*, 348–357.

Lawson, N. (2001). *Nigella Bites*. London, United Kingdom: Chatto & Windus.

Lawson, N. (2010). *Kitchen: Recipes from the heart of the home*. London, United Kingdom: Chatto & Windus.

Levy, A. (2005). *Female chauvinist pigs: Women and the rise of raunch culture*. London, United Kingdom: Pocket.

Magee, R. M. (2007). Food Puritanism and food pornography: The gourmet semiotics of Martha and Nigella. *Americana: The Journal of American Popular Culture, 6*(2). Retrieved from: http://www.americanpopularculture.com/journal/articles/fall_2007/magee.htm

Malson, H., Halliwell, E., Tischner, I., & Rudolfsdottir, A. (2011). Postfeminist advertising laid bare: Young women's talk about the sexually agentic woman of 'midriff' advertising. *Feminism and Psychology, 21*(1), 74–99.

Mannur, A. (2005). Model minorities can cook: Fusion cuisine in Asian America. In S. Davé, L. Nishime, & T. G. Oren, (Eds.), *East Main Street: Asian American popular culture* (pp. 72–94). New York, NY: New York University Press.

Maxim. (2015). Padma Lakshmi. Retrieved from http://www.maxim.com/celebrity-profile/padma-lakshmi

McNally, L. (2015). Business as usual, rebranded as ethics: The whitewashing of systemic injustice. In M. Kiraly & M. Tyler, (Eds.), *Freedom fallacy: The limits of liberal feminism* (pp. 105–112). Melbourne, Australia: Connor Court.

McRobbie, A. (2009). *The aftermath of feminism: Gender, culture and social change*. Los Angeles, CA: Sage.

Mitchell, C. M. (2010). The rhetoric of celebrity cookbooks. *The Journal of Popular Culture, 43*(3), 524–539.

Montemurro, B., & Siefkin, J. M. (2014). Cougars on the prowl? New perceptions of older women's sexuality. *Journal of Aging Studies, 28*, 35–43.

Mulvey, L. (1975). Visual pleasure and narrative cinema. *Screen, 16*(3), 6–18.

Neil, D. (2009, 14 April). Seduced by a burger: Carl's Jr. advertising finds its groove. Retrieved from http://articles.latimes.com/2009/apr/14/business/fi-ct-neil14

O'Brien, S. (2014, 5 April). Carl's Jr. burgers are gross but the ads are worse. Retrieved from http://www.heraldsun.com.au/news/opinion/carls-jr-burgers-are-gross-but-the-ads-are-worse/story-fni0fhie-1226875532390

Oakley, A. (1976). *Housewife*. Harmondsworth, United Kingdom: Penguin.

Off Our Backs. (2004). United States: Hardees and Hef. *Off Our Backs, 34*(1/2), 8.

Roper, C. (2015). Sexist Carl's Jr. burger chain coming to Australia. Retrieved from http://www.collectiveshout.org/sexist_carl_s_jr_burger_chain_coming_to_australia

Said, E. W. (2003). *Orientalism*. London, United Kingdom: Penguin.
Shapiro Sanders, L. (2008). Consuming Nigella. In S. Gillis & J. Hollows (Eds.), *Feminism, domesticity and popular culture* (pp. 151–164). Hoboken, NJ: Taylor & Francis.
Shea, D. (2009). Rachael Ray defends *FHM* shoot: "I'd do it again tomorrow". Retrieved from http://www.huffingtonpost.com/2009/03/02/rachael-ray-defends-fhm-s_n_171132.html
Stylist. (2011, December). My love affair with salted caramel. Retrieved from http://www.stylist.co.uk/life/my-love-affair-with-salted-caramel
Tankard-Reist, M. (2011). Corporate sexist offenders: Cross 'em off your Xmas list. Retrieved from http://melindatankardreist.com/2011/11/cross-em-off-your-list/
Vannier, S. A., Currie, A. B., & O'Sullivan, L. F. (2014). Schoolgirls and soccer moms: A content analysis of free "teen" and "MILF" online pornography. *Journal of Sex Research*, *51*(3), 253–264.
Winch, A. (2011). 'Your new smart-mouthed girlfriends': Postfeminist conduct books. *Journal of Gender Studies*, *20*(4), 359–370.
Wirthlin, K. (2009). Fad lesbianism: Exposing media's posing. *Journal of Lesbian Studies*, *13*, 107–114.

CHAPTER EIGHT

THE AESTHETICISATION OF THE REAL BODY IN POLITICS AND PORNOGRAPHY

Tim Gregory

On 4 November 2008, election day in the United States, *Hustler* released the pornographic film *Who's Nailin' Paylin?*, which referred to the female Republican Vice Presidential candidate, Sarah Palin. Labelled a misogynistic response to women in power, or at best a weak and ineffectual parody, it was largely dismissed. However by critically examining the film, we can see that it is a celebration of the *idea* of Sarah Palin, but a critique of the reality. This critique was summarised by Presidential candidate Barack Obama's off the cuff remark during his election campaign – "you can put lipstick on a pig, but it's still a pig" (as cited in Zimmer, 2008). Obama was referring to the rapid transformation of Palin after she was nominated as Vice Presidential candidate for the Republican Party. The category "pig" that Obama was referring to is the white, working-class conservative. *Hustler*'s production was at once an attack on Palin's willingness to become a Pygmalion figure for the Republican Party and a celebration and validation of the group to which she belonged. Ultimately, *Who's Nailin' Paylin?* (2008) suggests that contemporary politics and pornography use many of the same techniques and tactics to break through the image and generate a sense of immediacy and reality.

Who's Nailin' Paylin? critiques what I describe as the traditional zero design politician: a politician who appears to effortlessly perform the ruling class in order to make a 'natural' claim to power. Zero design is a Modernist concept that treats the ornamental as deceptive (Groys, 2009). It has become a dominant ideology in Western art and architecture since the twentieth century and expanded its influence into media and politics. It is a form of euthenics where the object (or politician) is presented in its purest form allowing for a 'true' judgement to be made. *Who's Nailin' Paylin?* argues against zero design politics, suggesting that Palin's obvious political design is an asset, as her desirability should be the only qualification she requires to seek and secure power. Through the combination of pornographic and political content *Who's Nailin' Paylin?* exposes the emergence of a new type of political zero design. This new type recognises that appearing natural and sincere (a technique perfected by politicians like John F. Kennedy) is no longer sufficient to rupture systems of representation – the 'real' politician remains hidden in images of zero design sincerity. The new zero design uses moments of apparent breakdown in performance to expose the 'real' body. There are different methods politicians use to achieve this, but the most analogous to pornography is the deployment of allowable transgressions, or moments in which the performance of wife/husband, politician, father/mother is broken by an orchestrated indiscretion. These moments are designed to be within heteronormative boundaries and provide a glimpse of the 'real' person through the image. The image of this type of 'real' politician is simply an image of the perceived failure of performance – an empty image.

Who's Nailin' Paylin? makes clear that this strategy of designed transgression is not new and is in fact a fundamental trope in pornography. In pornography this design allows us to watch the actor rather than the character once the "fucking" starts (Lehman, 1999). The 'failure' of performance (the bad acting) creates a sense that something 'real' is being witnessed. While superficially, Palin's allowable transgression was her portrayal as a MILF ('Mother I'd Like to Fuck'), her actual allowable transgression was her claim to be an amateur politician. Palin's zero design as an amateur politician produced a series of failed political performances which succeeded in rupturing her representation and offering a sense of a 'real' person.

By examining politics as defined by Jacques Rancière (2015), we can see how this new zero design produces empty images that act as surfaces on to which the hopes and desires of normativity are projected. Rancière's (2015) discussion of aesthetics and politics articulates how images become visible and are distributed. The politics of visibility (and invisibility) is the organising principle of the 'public' – how it is represented, identified, called on, delineated. It produces politicians whose claim to total representation prevents the recognition of new, different or invisible discourses. This type of zero design politics reveals that political power lies in the ability to create whom it represents (or more importantly, whom it does not represent), and *success* lies in the process of aestheticisation that denies this power of creation. The empty, zero design image allows for this contradiction to exist. *Hustler*, an expert producer of professional pornography, produced a meta-structural critique of pornography and politics, laying bare the mechanism of this vapid form of representation.

The rise of Sarah Palin

For the significance of the parody to be understood, a brief examination of the politician Sarah Palin must be undertaken. Palin's image was set in the media well before her nomination for Vice President in 2008. In 1984 Palin finished third in the Miss Alaska pageant and went on to become the youngest person elected Governor of Alaska. In 2008 she was labelled "America's Hottest Governor" on the cover of Alaska's state magazine (DeVaughn, 2008). Palin deliberately engaged with this media image, for instance by winking and using catch phrases like "Drill, Baby, Drill" in the Vice Presidential debate

(Commission on Presidential Debates, 2008). She stands against the research that suggests people will only vote for women if they project masculine or gender neutral qualities (Huddy & Terkildsen, 1993; Greco Larson, 2001; Paxton & Kunovich, 2003; Herrnson, Lay, & Stokes, 2003). Anderson (2011) argues that Palin represents a broader pornification of politics which also impacted Barack Obama, who was photographed topless and benefited from the "I got a Crush on Obama…" social media campaign. The Republican Presidential candidate John McCain stated that he chose Palin because she represented "a direct counterpoint to the liberal feminist agenda for America" (as cited in Gustafson, 2011, p. 96), which Baird (2010) identified as part of a trend to sexualise conservative women in America. During the 2008 Presidential campaign, right versus left was often depicted in an image war of sexual stereotypes.

The rapid rise of Palin during the campaign was testament to the media's willingness to pick up on this narrative. Caricatures of Palin most often focussed on her beauty queen background, appearance and wardrobe (Carlin & Winfrey, 2009). Search term data reveals that 'Sarah Palin' was paired with terms like 'legs', 'Vogue' and 'sexy photos' more often than political terms (Dann, 2008). Anderson argues that these images of women politicians, generated without consent or participation, "hijack a woman politician's image or persona to serve sexist, patriarchal, or misogynist purposes" (Anderson, 2011, p. 336). Despite the criticism of Palin for fostering the media sexualisation of her image, it is important to note that Palin's own emphasis was that she was "just a hockey mom" (Beail & Longworth, 2013, p. 22). Her voter appeal was as a heteronormative middle-class, white mother, and while this image also necessitates a sexual duty (to be desirable and sexually active/productive), it was not central to her campaign strategy.

The Aestheticisation of the Real Body

The increasing visibility of Palin forced McCain to attempt to censor the very qualities for which she had chosen. Palin was left in the impossible position of trying to reverse her image during the final week of the campaign. The "just a hockey mom" image disappeared and her advisors rebranded her as an experienced politician with the necessary disposition to hold the Vice Presidency. The chaos of the McCain-Palin campaign was a result of fundamental differences between the political design of McCain and Palin. The tension between these different design strategies is exposed by *Who's Nailin' Paylin?*

Design politics

The concept of zero design is central to understanding how *Hustler* was able to produce an effective satire. In Adolf Loos's essay *Ornament and Crime* (1998), the ornamental is considered criminal because it suggests that something is being – or could be – concealed. Zero design is the opposite of the ornamental. It is an attempt to remove anything that does not directly contribute to the function of the object. The object is presented as raw, honest and total, without waste or extravagance. Zero design was the overarching concept behind Modernist maxims like "less is more" and "form follows function" (Thomas, 2002). As Groys (2009) notes, "the artistic avant-garde wanted to create design-free areas that would be perceived as areas of honesty, high morality, sincerity, and trust" (para. 7). Zero design had a significant impact on early twentieth-century social, political and cultural design and its legacy is still clearly visible in contemporary politics.

It is not that zero design is *no* design; it is a design that denies its own existence. It assumes that there is an ultimate form of an object, at which point its design becomes invisible. This principle is applied to people as well. The implication is that zero design becomes the default position of the upper classes; it is the design of 'natural' elitism. Annie Leibovitz's

1993 photograph of US President Bill Clinton is indicative of how this belief is imaged: Clinton sits on the Resolute desk in the Oval Office, one leg raised in a casual pose. He does not sit behind the desk, but rather on the symbol of power, as though the design of the desk is not important to him. He positions himself and his body as presidential – a body that does not need accoutrements of power to be powerful. The seemingly unadorned body becomes the site of zero design, the ultimate judge of form. Of course there is still design here – the design of personal trainers, dieticians and fashion consultants but it registers as 'natural'.

John McCain was a consummate zero design politician, often represented by the media as "the kind of figure whom one could effortlessly imagine being president" (Meacham, 2008, p. 45). The effortless leadership quality that McCain appeared to possess naturally was something that seemed to come very unnaturally to Palin. Palin demonstrated that the failure of zero design occurs when the *design* becomes visible. Her lack of 'class' was often translated into accusations of her being stupid. The specific use of the term stupid has class implications, as Kadi (2006) notes: "[stupid is not] a mere description of how well someone thinks, stupid has become a cultural concept with a particular code and set of signifiers that describe working-class people as the middle and upper classes perceive and construct [them]" (p. 42). The 'stupidity' of Palin was located in the obviousness of her performance, which was compounded by her gender and lack of political pedigree. While Palin is far from working class, the image she had built was as a member of the 'ordinary' working/middle class. Obama's "lipstick on a pig" comment was an attack on her inability to transcend this image and become a zero design politician. The ease with which Palin was parodied (most notably by comedian Tina Fey), suggests that Palin's performance as a politician was in contradistinction to the real Palin. *Who's Nailin' Paylin?* makes the same accusation as Obama, critiquing Palin's failed political design. The difference is that while Obama critiqued her failure to perform the ruling class, *Hustler* critiqued her for trying to present herself as anything other than her white working-class image.

The central question that Palin faced in the 2008 campaign was whether a self-described hockey mom, who proudly announced "it's time that normal Joe Six-Pack American is finally represented in the position of vice presidency", (*U.S. News*, 2008, para. 1) was qualified to be Vice President. As Meacham (2008) put it "do we want leaders who are everyday folks, or do we want leaders who understand everyday folks" (p. 44). Palin's electoral success had been achieved by convincing everyone that she was "everyday folk". Palin's "Joe Six-pack" image was not critiqued for being fake, rather the concern was that she was unable to be anything other than how she self-identified. Her adroit aestheticisation made her look like she was part of the represented group that she had in fact created. It is interesting to note that Palin had been crafting this image since 2006, when she first used the term "hockey mom" during the gubernatorial campaign (Bajaj et al., 2006). Her political success was based on recognising that to win the votes of the conservative working class she had to appear to 'be' rather than 'understand' them.

Representing class in porn

Who's Nailin' Paylin? visualises difference in class perceptions of the 'natural' location of power. This difference is the foundational, and at times antagonistic, ideological distinction between *Hustler* and *Penthouse* publications. *Penthouse*, whose target audience is the middle and upper class, locates power and money as a way to obtain the object of desire, which is usually represented as sex. The object of desire offers itself as a reward for money and power. This separation of objects of desire and power is a conventional narrative in porn and mass media, most explicitly demonstrated in advertising where the object generates power only through the act of ownership, but the desire for the object is supposedly universal. Class distinction is visualised through the display of ownership of the object to those who desire it. *Hustler* radically simplifies the equation, and in doing so challenges this construction of power. Kipnis (1992) suggests that in fact "*Hustler* works to disparage and counter identification with these sorts of class attributes on every front" (p. 383).

Hustler's position is that the object of desire is itself the source of power. The object of desire generates its own power, distinct from any external signification of power or ownership. As Penley (2006) argues:

> rather than offering the compensatory fantasy found in the more upscale *Penthouse* and *Playboy*, where the purchase of pricey consumer goods will ensure willing women and studly men, *Hustler* puts into question a male fantasy that represents power, money, and the prestige as essential to sexual success. (p. 106)

Who's Nailin' Paylin? is not opposed to Palin's attempt to gain power, but rather it criticises her attempt to become anything other than an autonomous, powerful object of desire. In other words, *Hustler* criticises her for having aspirations to be a *Penthouse* model and offer herself as a reward to the Republican Party, thereby conforming to the separation of power and objects of desire. This distinction was evident in Cimbalo's article for *Playboy* (which was subsequently removed) in which he listed ten conservative women, including Palin, that he would like to 'hate-fuck' (Breslin, 2009). Such language highlights an attitude of aggressive ownership towards conservative female politicians. During the campaign Palin was often referred to as the "trophy vice", a term that suggests she had no independent power but was merely an object for display (Perks & Johnson, 2014, p. 781). As Perks and Johnson (2014) explain,

> trophy vice refers to the depiction of McCain's gaze as the one MILF Palin sublimates herself to – that she becomes the object of his desire. McCain therefore uses his candidacy to show off his "trophy" and Palin uses her trophy status to ascend to power. (p. 781)

Hustler's pornographic version of Palin inverts this "trophy vice" stereotype and represents the values of white, conservative, working-class men through a series of radical techniques which are unusual in conventional feature-length pornography. The first difference in *Who's Nailin' Paylin?* is its narrative structure. As Williams (1999) has observed, almost all pornographic films follow predictable paths of action. Most pornographic films start with lesbianism or solo female masturbation and end with heterosexual intercourse and group sex. This structure of ordered pornographic numbers reinforces a heteronormative narrative arc, in which the woman's desire can only be properly satisfied by a man. *Who's Nailin' Paylin?* inverts this narrative, starting with a sex scene between Paylin and two Russian men and ending with a lesbian scene between Paylin, Condi and Hillary (Sarah Palin, Condoleezza Rice and Hillary Clinton respectively). This inversion is demonstrative of the collapse of the object of desire and the object of power, positioning lesbianism as the inevitable result. *Who's Nailin' Paylin?* positions lesbianism as the natural response of objects of power being attracted to each other. *Hustler* places working-class white men at the bottom of the sexual hierarchy; being neither desirable nor powerful they are relegated to sexual gratification only through voyeurism, lucky encounters or humiliation.

Pornographies

The role of Condi in the final scene is also atypical. African American female desire is not usually featured in mainstream pornography, outside of openly racialised genres. Even in racially specific pornography, targeted at a predominantly white audience, African American men are more commonly employed to represent the taboo fantasy – black men with white women. As Williams (2004) notes "black female viewing pleasure, it would seem, is the least well served by these newly racialized, noisy confessions of pleasure" (pp. 302–303). In *Who's Nailin' Paylin?* Condi is given the last orgasm and the last line: "you guys know what to do." She is presented as the alpha female throughout this scene, which aligns to the internal logic of the film – while Palin and Clinton have pretensions of power, at the time of the film's production it was only Rice who actually held power as Secretary of State.

Crucially, there is no need for contemporaneous male political figures, Bush, Cheney or Rumsfeld, to enter the scene. Lesbianism is presented as an end in itself and not a warm up act. While the gaze is still aimed at a male audience, *Who's Nailin' Paylin?* positions the audience as witnessing a narrative that excludes them. It would be hard to argue that this is an enlightened view of lesbianism; however, it suggests that women can be powerful and have sexual agency in a way that does not require validation or satisfaction from a more powerful male. As fantastical as the film is, *Hustler* offers a vision of the independent power of the object of desire. However, it is important to note that *Who's Nailin' Paylin?* does not suggest that a woman's power can be anything other than a measure of her desirability and an insatiable need for sexual activity. For the calculation of this powerful desirability to be universal it ultimately conforms to the stereotypical heteronormative image of female desirability. *Hustler*'s casting

The Aestheticisation of the Real Body

of actor Lisa Ann to play Sarah Palin does not depart from this paradigm.

While in *Who's Nailin' Paylin?* lesbianism is considered to be an acceptable and natural response to powerless white males, male homosexuality is ridiculed. There are many comments throughout the film against homosexual, effeminate and liberal men. While Paylin wants to find a 'real man', no such man ever makes an appearance. Masculinity is not portrayed as embodied by a powerful or dominant man, but rather as a female fantasy of a man whose desire and stamina could equal a woman's. The men in *Who's Nailin' Paylin?* may *act* like men, but they can never *be* men, and Paylin is expertly aware of the difference. The men who perform the role inadequately are openly admonished. The manner in which they are humiliated reveals the underlying construction of the 'natural' state of sex and power. Paylin voices this opinion in polemics such as:

> oh for criminy sake, why don't you take your nuts out of your little Gucci purse, grab your noodle, and act like a man ... It's time to drill baby! Drill hard and drill deep. Come on ya tree hugging hippie! What'ya waiting for, congressional approval?

We observe Paylin alluding to gay men and alternative men (hippies) as inadequate. The threat these men represent is to the calculation of power, as her authority is located in her assumed universal desirability. Anyone who does not naturally and immediately recognise this is at best inadequate and ultimately represented as unnatural. Paylin's rebuke of men who wait for "congressional approval" is also an illusion to this 'natural' state of power that should not need any external confirmation. Paylin is expressing her dominance and desirability, affirming her 'natural' position as a leader.

Who's Nailin' Paylin? projects a fantasy of Palin in which she uses her 'natural' disposition as a desirable, heteronormative conservative as the basis of her politics. This is evident in a scene in which Paylin plays a word association game with her aid. The aid spells out "H.M.O."(Health Maintenance Organisation), to which Paylin spells out in response "G.A.Y.". In the film 'gay' is a generic label used to generate feelings of disgust with whatever it is associated. Paylin communicates to working-class conservatives through this simple, immediate appeal to their gut reaction. One does not need to know anything more about H.M.O.s other than that they are 'gay'. Her ignorance is celebrated as an asset. She champions a power which is not political, but self-evident, a power that takes pride in existing only to affirm what everyone already knows.

Just as Paylin's desire is presented as self-evident and explicit, so too are her politics. Her political responses use the hierarchy of heteronormative desire as the 'natural' marker of good and bad politics. The politician Palin performed a version of this politics, where her gut reaction was based on reproductive futurity and the nuclear family. The connection that Palin and Paylin attempt to make with their audiences is a physiological response, achieved by using a series of triggers to play on conditioned desires, fears and prejudices. Both pornography and contemporary political design attempt to generate a connection that appears to bypass the representational frameworks necessary to establish the connection in the first place: the audience feels a connection, which transcends the image form of the connection itself. For politicians the ability to design such a message means they appear to be the direct voice of the people – unaltered, uncensored and untranslated.

The new zero design
Who's Nailin' Paylin? exposes a significant shift in contemporary politics. By using the structure and conventions of pornography to satirise Palin, *Hustler* made visible how contemporary politics uses the same process of aestheticisation as pornography. The

argument is not that there is a pornification of politics, which implies a series of negative cultural and social connotations that simplifies pornography into a universally bad signifier, but rather that the aesthetic design of pornography (independent from its content) is being adopted as a political strategy. It is this that raises *Who's Nailin' Paylin?* above a satire of women in power and towards a metastructural critique of image politics.

To reveal this critique we turn once again to the principle of zero design. US President Kennedy was the first to change the meaning of zero design in political imagery. He used candid, documentary moments to convey a sense of sincerity. These images were deployed to show himself as a zero design man, husband and father. The now iconic photographs by Stanley Tretick published in *Life* magazine in 1962 show Kennedy in the Oval Office with his children. The most popular is a photograph of John F. Kennedy Jr. playing under the Resolute desk, poking his head out as his father works above. This zero design image made Kennedy appear to be a real person and not merely a convincing politician – a man the electorate could trust, sensing they had seen a glimpse of the 'ordinary' man behind the image. Fundamental to this perception was that the 'behind the image' image form was ignored, or at least subordinate to its content. It was a very successful strategy that resulted in an industry dedicated to producing candid sincerity. However, precisely because it became an industry it ceased to function. Candid became candy – a saccharine and cynical attempt to fool voters. As Bennett (2012) maintains, media theory and critical theory have challenged these seamless performances of sincerity in which there is a "congruence between avowal and actual feeling or belief" (p. 116).

In August 2009 the official White House photographer Pete Souza took a photograph of President Obama's daughter Sasha, hiding behind a sofa in the Oval Office while her dad worked at his desk. The photograph is instantly recognisable as belonging to the lineage of Tretick's photographs of the Kennedy family, however this time very little attention was afforded to the image. The audience was either tired of these images or could see through the mediation – the design was too obvious. Commenting on Obama's book *Audacity of Hope*, Critchley (2008) states that "I was overcome by a sense of distance in reading Obama, and the more sincere the prose, the greater distance I felt" (p. 17). Despite Obama's mastery of zero design sincerity, his book and the candid photographs of his family failed to overcome their mediation. Perhaps surprisingly, the more sincere the more empty the affect. Sincerity no longer functions as a successful political strategy. The real image appears to be lost, for what is more real than sincerity? A connection to the real through the image is being re-forged in a totally different manner, borrowing strategies pioneered by the porn industry.

The connection to the real, particularly a mediated real, has been re-established through catastrophe. A world in which our fears, conspiracies and pain are manifest has a confirmation bias – something so bad must be real, because why would such a terrible reality be faked. As Groys (2009) states:

> Confronted with a world of total design, we can only accept a catastrophe, a state of emergency, a violent rupture in the designed surface, as sufficient to allow for a view of the reality that lies beneath. And of course this reality too must show itself to be a catastrophic one, because we suspect something terrible to be going on behind the design. (para. 8)

Baudrillard (2002) asserts that absolute events returned after the Al-Qaeda attacks in New York on 11 September 2001. Images were again capable of generating what he referred to earlier as a "frisson of the real" (Baudrillard, 1994, p. 28). These events were perceived to be significant enough to rupture the designed surface of mediated reality, despite the fact that the mediation was never interrupted – the broadcast never broken. Such events re-establish our trust in the image as the content's catastrophic power overrides its medium. The effect of the catastrophic real filtered into politics in a variety of forms. The form most related to pornography is what I term transgression politics. Transgression politics uses designed indiscretions, exposure and the necessitated confession to break through the strata of the image. *Who's Nailin' Paylin?* makes the connection between transgression politics and pornography explicit by collapsing the porn star and politician.

Designing the transgression in politics and porn

Politicians have learnt to how to generate a sense of realness through the image by transgressing. We are comforted not only with the fact that we were right, but that we have arrived at a truth which is ultimately easier to deal with than a secret. The new zero design politics is the politics of disclosure, the politics of designed images of the right type of transgression, failure or ignorance. As Groys (2009) states:

> Thus, to make the politicians look trustworthy, one must create a moment of disclosure. ...With this disclosure, trust in the system is restored through a ritual of symbolic sacrifice and self-sacrifice, stabilizing the celebrity system by confirming the suspicion to which it is necessarily already subjected. (para. 9)

This political strategy might have unintentionally been initiated by the Bill Clinton and Monica Lewinsky scandal. Unpredictably Clinton's approval rating as recorded by a Gallup poll (n.d.) returned to pre-impeachment levels within a year, and even during the impeachment trial his reduction in popularity was negligible and did not represent the lowest approval rating of his presidency. The incident suggested to the public that he was a real man, in both affirming his masculinity and as a real person who had broken through the fiction of his political design. Clinton's partial admission through his careful defining of 'sexual relations' confirmed to the public what they already knew – politicians lie, but Clinton's lie was one the public could accept.

For transgression politics, transgression must be allowable, which is to say within the acceptable boundaries of heteronormativity and its moral code. This is so the transgression is not read as a perversion. An illustration of this can be found in the *Starr Report* (1998), the document produced by the Independent Counsel Kenneth Starr, which led to the attempted impeachment of Clinton. Despite the final report containing hundreds of pages describing with forensic and obsessive detail each act of oral sex, the sexual practice of rimming (which the pair often engaged in) is relegated to the footnotes (St. John, 2004). Starr did not explicitly address sexual practices outside heteronormative expectations. Nelson and Curtain (2001) claim that this is one of the most obvious omissions from the public discussion. Despite the plethora of jokes concerning dresses and cigars, little attention was paid to the diversity of sexual activities (rimming, fellatio while Clinton was on the phone to male colleagues, and the presumed smoking of the dildo/cigars) that would be considered outside of straight practices. Starr's unwillingness or incapacity to confront and describe these practices, coupled with Clinton's ability to project himself as a resolutely heterosexual man, enabled the event to be classified as an allowable heteronormative transgression.

The success of the political transgression can be understood by examining pornographic transgression. A fundamental trope of pornography is the generation of realness through transgression. Pornography designs the taboo and then breaks it. Pornography is not transgressive to itself, but generates its own allowable forms of transgression within strict narrative structures. The stereotypical figures in heteronormative pornography, such as the naughty nun, the sexy schoolgirl and the MILF all highlight the rupture of performative design (virgin, girl, mother) by an allowable transgression. Unsurprisingly most of these stereotypes focus on the female body, because the transgressive agency of heteronormative porn is usually the woman who wants and finally succumbs to sex. While the narrative sets up the allowable transgression, it is not supposed to be believed by the audience. The obviousness and implausibility of the characters are used to present the zero design moment, in which, as Peter Lehman succinctly notes, "we watch the actors fuck, not their characters" (Lehman, 1999, p. 362). Hillyer (2004) further clarifies this moment stating that "the sexual act thus seems to be supposed to defeat not just characterisation but qualities of representation: while we still watch actors, it is potentially unclear that we are watching a film" (p. 65). It is not only the character but the medium that is dissolved, leaving us with the raw actor. The actor is the perceived breakthrough of the real person, despite or because of the costumes, sets and narrative. The recognition of the real pornographic actor is an important moment, for while it generates an immediacy that effaces design, it also generates the exact opposite – an emptiness or void of the actor. The real actor can be nothing other than the residue of the perceived failure of performance.

It may appear obvious that Palin's allowable transgression was her sexualisation, in particular, her association with MILF. However, her sexualised characterisation was never ruptured; unlike other politicians embroiled in sex scandals (US President Bill Clinton, Italian Prime Minister Silvio Berlusconi, Member of the US House of Representatives Anthony Weiner, Mayor of Toronto Rob Ford, Governor of South Carolina Nimrata Haley) no actual transgression occurred. Palin's ruptures occurred through her performance as a self-professed *amateur* politician. Her stringent defence of her amateur status is encapsulated in her catch phrase "I'm just a hockey mom". "Just" was her confession of an allowable transgression (that she was not a professional politician) and "hockey mom" affirmed her amateur status as entirely normative – middle class, white, suburban, heterosexual, reproductive and nuclear. This afforded her the highest possible visibility as an amateur and generated a currency she could not have achieved if she positioned herself as professional.

Amateur pornography produces the same normative hierarchies as the amateur politician. The vast majority of amateur porn has no currency and is afforded no sense of realness. These differently raced, classed, gendered bodies or different displays of desire, sexual practices and objects are ignored by mainstream amateur porn, either removed by heteronormative terms and conditions which narrowly define sex acts or simply relegated by small view counts to the lowest point of visibility. Palin's amateur status was precisely in line with what we expect from an amateur, and as such her transgression into politics attracted attention. Just as we watch the real porno actor not the character when the sex starts, Palin's failed political characterisation (in interviews, debates and policy positions) offered moments in which the 'real' Palin broke through the image.

Bennett (2012) addresses the success of these moments of failed political performance in what she terms "affective politics" (p. 124). She writes of the disjuncture between speech and gesture made visible in the failure to use language in a seamless manner. Bennett analyses George W. Bush's struggle with language and how this manifested in a series of micro-gestures and ruptures which were in themselves more compelling than the content of his speech. She argues that politicians like Bush are "not successful in spite of their stumbles, malapropisms and misadventures with language, but almost because of them" (Bennett, 2012, p. 120). Their success is due to the perceived 'realness' of these affective moments, which according to Tomkins and Demos (1995) are almost impossible to fake, unlike emotional responses. Whereas Bush's affect was unintentional and apparently unavoidable, Palin foregrounds these moments as a deliberate zero design strategy. By intentionally placing her amateur body in a highly professional context, she maximised the affective cues produced when her performed speech failed to match her gesture.

Empty images, empty politics
Rancière allocates a primary division in the world between those who do and those who do not have the luxury to play with words and images (Carnevale, 2007). Subversion or true politics begins when this division is contested. It should be clear that Palin's claim to amateur status in no way contests this division. To return to Meacham's (2008) attack against Palin in which he asked "do we want leaders who are everyday folks, or do we want leaders who understand everyday folks" (p. 44) we note that Palin could never be "everyday folk", she could only understand, interpret and manipulate. Anything actually outside this system is consigned to noise – unintelligible and non-representable and unable to enter politics (Rancière, Bowlby, & Panagia, 2001). Palin used her luxury to play with words and images to deliberately disguise that very same luxury. She achieved this by making her words and images appear closer to noise, and in doing so she was able to design herself as an amateur and appear to *be* rather than *understand*.

Pornographies

Palin is the allowable, highly visible edge of amateur politicians. The damaging assumption is that she is part of the noise in the system, rather than exemplary of the system itself. Zero design politics remains the primary method for convincing the public that they are represented; however, the method of zero design has dramatically changed. It now borrows the techniques of pornography to design moments of breakdown during which the empty actor is glimpsed. It is a politics that can only be the polemical configuration of the common. As such it operates wholly within the safe boundaries of the common. It is a politics for consensus democracy, which Rancière (1998) defines as:

> The absolute removal of the sphere of appearance of the people. In it the community is continually presented to itself. In it the people are never again uneven, uncountable, or unpresentable. They are both totally present and totally absent at once. They are entirely caught in a structure of the visible where everything is on show and where there is thus no longer any place for appearance. (p. 103)

The empty actor, who is unknown and unknowable, becomes a surface for projection in which the community sees itself through the confirmation bias of the normative politician. Political positions and policies function in the same way as the fake narrative of a porn film – they are not believed, or even recognised (Iyengar, Valentino, Ansolabehere, & Simon, 1997), they are the necessary plot to allow for the empty actor to emerge upon its breakdown. Palin, modelled on the amateur, removed the narrative as much as possible to provide more opportunities for the failure of performance to occur. The blank screen left by the empty actor is not the bland screen, it is the opposite, it has to attract the gaze and then present a vacant 'reality'. It is interesting that Obama (2006) describes his own political strategy in a similar manner: "I serve as a blank screen on which people of vastly different political stripes project their own views" (p. 11). Obama designed a more opaque persona than Palin, but Beltrán (2011) suggests that this was due to suppressed questions of race and the anxiety of white voters. It may be that Obama's allowable transgression is to be located in race politics. This did not manifest as spectacularly as Palin's transgressions, but none the less was present even in its apparent absence.

The ultimate hypocrisy of blank screen politics is that in appearing to let the people speak, in becoming their projection, politicians are doing nothing other than conserving the pre-existing constructed group.

Exposing the performance of anti-performance
Hustler's investment in pornography and politics positioned it to pick up on these emerging trends. *Hustler* revealed that the zero design of amateur pornography and transgression politics had not shifted stereotypes or hierarchies of power. *Who's Nailin' Paylin?* shows the breakdown of the character to the actor, explicitly visualising the allowable transgression of MILF and the sexy politician, but crucially it does not then offer a surface for projection. It provides the viewer with an image of the performance of anti-performance in which the actor is revealed to be another character, one as closed off to the audience as the initial character. What makes *Who's Nailin' Paylin?* different is that the sex is performed with the same opacity as the politics; neither becomes real. This is best illustrated in the production's still images, which were published on *Hustler*'s website and freely accessible. These images show behind the scenes on the set – we can see camera operators, directors and the actors. These porn set images offer the next level from "watching the actors not the characters" because we are shown a broader field of view than the intended viewer. This is highlighted in one of these photographs in which there

is a monitor displaying the limited frame for the intended viewer, contrasted to the wider actual frame of the photograph. What is most remarkable about these images is that they do not generate any "frisson of the real" (Baudrillard, 1994, p. 28). Nothing can be deduced from these images, they offer no breakdown, no opportunity to identify with the fiction of the real. We are confronted with images that make a simple but fundamental point: even if we could see the actor we would not be able to recognise them as anything other than a character. The actor can only be exactly what you already expect to see, because the mechanisms that have made the image visible have already foreclosed any other possibility. This has implications in how we understand both the pornographic and political image. *Who's Nailin' Paylin?* stands out as significant political commentary and ineffective pornography because it reveals the illusion of the pornographic real and its connection to the political real.

The world is divided between those who can afford to play with words and images and those who can only choose from existing representations. *Hustler* can afford this luxury but in producing *Who's Nailin' Paylin?* it demonstrated that it is willing to expose the processes of aestheticisation – zero design, allowable transgressions and the empty image – which attempts to disguise this division. *Hustler* also takes a polemical stance against those who further their own political ends by pretending this division does not exist. *Hustler* cannot produce equality of representation, but in *Who's Nailin' Paylin?* the narrative gives us a fantastical image of what this might look like and the structure shows why it is necessarily a fantasy.

Political success in a consensus democracy requires the deployment of zero design. Zero design politics allows decisions to be made between noise and signal and have these decisions appear to emerge 'naturally' from the citizenry. The realness effect of allowable transgression is largely successful in re-engaging a suspicious audience. By confirming our established fears through a rupture in performance, we are reassured of the reality of the actor. The mechanisms of representation (both of the image and democracy) are put aside as the perceived realness generates an intensified connection and a blank surface for projection. The medium and message of the amateur has aided this process, providing a method of aestheticisation that denies its existence and hence works to reinforce the normative claim of existing hierarchies of visibility. The democratisation of the image does not bear witness to the gaps of a consensus democracy, but functions as proof of total vision. If anything outside of this is captured it is relegated to noise, unable to enter political, social or sexual discourse.

The exposé, or documentary mode, is incapable of rupturing this system because its success is derived from exactly the same aesthetic as contemporary political success. However, modes that critique or subvert the reality effect of zero design politics do exist. *Who's Nailin' Paylin?* is successful because it exposes the *design* in transgression politics. The film doesn't allow itself to become real; it even denies the documentary voyeurism that comes with seeing the actors rather than the characters. It maintains a satirical approach without the need to offer breakthrough points of revelation or titillation. Ultimately, it demonstrates that the power of satire and self-critique, combined with the explicit and uncensored, can confront and expose structures of power.

References

Agamben, G. (2000). *Means without end: Notes on politics* (V. Binetti & C. D. Heller, Trans.). Minneapolis, MN: University of Minnesota Press.

Amann, J. M., & Breuer, T. (2007). *The brotherhood of the disappearing pants: A field guide to conservative sex scandals.* New York, NY: Nation Books.

Anderson, K. V. (2011). "Rhymes with blunt": Pornification and US political culture. *Rhetoric & Public Affairs, 14*(2), 327–368.

Baird, J. (2010, 7 February). The Palin Effect: Why we sexualize GOP women. *Newsweek.* Retrieved from http://www.newsweek.com/palin-effect-why-we-sexualize-gop-women-74365

Bajaj, V., Bosman, J., Chan, S., Dillon, S., Herszenhorn, D. M., Newman, A., Santos, F. (2006, 9 November). The 2006 Elections: State by state; west. *The New York Times.* Retrieved from http://query.nytimes.com/gst/fullpage.html?res=9504EFD71E3FF93AA35752C1A9609C8B63&st=nyt

Baudrillard, J. (1994). *Simulacra and simulation* (S. F. Glaser, Trans.). Ann Arbor, MI: University of Michigan Press.

Baudrillard, J. (2002). *The spirit of terrorism and requiem for the Twin Towers.* London, United Kingdom: Verso.

Beail, L., & Longworth, R. K. (2013). *Framing Sarah Palin: Pitbulls, Puritans, and politics.* New York, NY: Routledge.

Beltrán, C. (2011). Mestiza poetics: Walt Whitman, Barack Obama, and the question of union. In J. E. Serry (Ed.), *A political companion to Walt Whitman* (pp. 59–95). Lexington, KY: University Press of Kentucky.

Bennett, J. (2012). *Practical aesthetics: Events, affect and art after 9/11.* London, United Kingdom; New York, NY: I. B. Tauris.

Breslin, S. (2009). *When the joke's on women.* Retrieved from http://www.slate.com/blogs/xx_factor/2009/06/02/guy_cimbalo_playboy_article_generates_controversy.html

Carlin, D. B., & Winfrey, K. L. (2009). Have you come a long way, baby? Hillary Clinton, Sarah Palin, and sexism in 2008 campaign coverage. *Communication Studies, 60*(4), 326–343.

Carnevale, F. (2007). Art of the possible: Fulvia Carnevale and John Kelsey in conversation with Jacques Rancière. *Artforum, 45*(7), 256–261.

Commission on Presidential Debates. (2008, 2 October). 2008 Debate Transcript, The Biden-Palin Vice Presidential Debate. *Commission on Presidential Debates.* Retrieved from http://www.debates.org/index.php?page=2008-debate-transcript-2

Critchley, S. (2008, November). The American Void. *Harper's Magazine,* 17–20.

Dann, C. (2008, September 28). Desperately searching for Sarah. *NBCNEWS.com.* Retrieved from http://www.msnbc.msn.com/id/26903680/page/2/

DeVaughn, M. (2008, February). Palin's way. *Alaska Magazine.* Retrieved from http://www.cawp.rutgers.edu/fast_facts/elections/documents/08-AlaskaMagazinePalinProfile02-08.pdf

Gallup. (n.d.). *Presidential Approval Ratings – Bill Clinton.* Retrieved from http://www.gallup.com/poll/116584/presidential-approval-ratings-bill-clinton.aspx

Greco Larson, S. G. (2001). American women and politics in the media: A review essay. *Political Science and Politics, 34*(2), 227–230.

Groys, B. (2009). Self-design and aesthetic responsibility, *e-flux,* 7. Retrieved from http://www.e-flux.com/journal/view/68

Gustafson, M. (2011). Defining a maverick: Putting Palin in the context of western women's political history. In L. Gidlow (Ed.), *Obama, Clinton, Palin: Making history in Election 2008* (pp. 94–104). Champaign, IL: University of Illinois Press.

Herrnson, P. S., Lay, J. C., & Stokes, A. K. (2003). Women running "as women": Candidate gender, campaign issues, and voter-targeting strategies. *Journal of Politics, 65*(1), 244–255.

Hillyer, M. (2004). Sex in the suburban: Porn, home movies, and the live action performance of love in *Pam and Tommy Lee: Hardcore and Uncensored.* In L. Williams (Eds.), *Porn Studies* (pp. 50–76). Durham, NC; London, United Kingdom: Duke University Press.

Huddy, L., & Terkildsen, N. (1993). Gender stereotypes and the perception of male and female candidates. *American Journal of Political Science, 37*(1), 119–147.

Iyengar, S., Valentino, N. A., Ansolabehere, S., & Simon, A. F. (1997). Running as a woman: Gender stereotyping in political campaigns. In P. Norris. (Ed.), *Women, media, and politics* (pp. 77–98). New York, NY: Oxford University Press.

Kadi, J. (2006). Stupidity deconstructed. In E. Hackett & S. Haslanger (Eds.), *Theorizing feminisms: A reader* (pp. 529–540). Oxford, United Kingdom: Oxford University Press.

Kipnis, L. (1992). (Male) desire and (female) disgust: Reading *Hustler*. In L. Grossberg, C. Nelson, & P. Treichler (Eds.), *Culture Studies* (pp. 373–391). New York, NY: Routledge.

Larson, S. G. (2001). American women and politics in the media: A review essay. *Political Science and Politics, 34*(2), 227–230.

Lehman, P. (1999). Ed Powers and the fantasy of documenting sex. In J. Elias, V. D. Elias, V. L. Bullough, G. Brewer, J. J. Douglas, & W. Jarvis (Eds.), *Porn 101: Eroticism, pornography, and the First Amendment* (pp. 359–368). Amherst, MA: Prometheus Books.

Lehman, P., & Elias. J. (Eds.). (1999). *Porn 101: Eroticism, pornography, and the First Amendment*. Amherst, MA: Prometheus Books.

Loos, A., & Opel, A. (1998). *Ornament and crime: Selected Essays*. Riverside, CA: Ariadne Press.

Meacham, J. (2008, 3 October). Sarah Palin's 'folk' problem. *Newsweek*, 40–44. Retrieved from http://www.newsweek.com/cover-story-sarah-palins-folk-problem-91709

Nelson, D. D., & Curtain, T. (2001). The symbolics of presidentialism. *Our Monica Ourselves. The Clinton Affair and the national interest*, 34–52.

Obama, B. (2006). *The audacity of hope: Thoughts on reclaiming the American Dream*. New York, NY: Random House.

Paxton, P., & Kunovich, S. (2003). Women's political representation: The importance of ideology. *Social Forces, 82*(1), 87–113.

Penley, C. (2004). Crackers and whackers: The white trashing of porn. In L. Williams (Eds.), *Porn Studies* (pp. 309–320). Durham, NC; London, United Kingdom: Duke University Press.

Penley, C. (2006). The white trashing of Porn. In P. Lehman (Ed.), *Pornography: film and culture* (pp. 99–117). Piscataway, NJ: Rutgers University Press.

Perks, L. G., & Johnson, K. A. (2014). Electile dysfunction. *Feminist Media Studies, 14*(5), 775–790. Retrieved from http://dx.doi.org/10.1080/14680777.2013.829860

Rancière, J. (1998). *Disagreement: Politics and philosophy*. Minneapolis, MN: University of Minnesota Press.

Rancière, J. (2015). *Dissensus: On politics and aesthetics*. London, United Kingdom; New York, NY: Bloomsbury Publishing.

Rancière, J., Bowlby, R., & Panagia, D. (2001). Ten theses on politics. *Theory & Event, 5*(3), 17–34.

St. John, M. (2004). How to do things with the Starr Report: Pornography, performance, and the president's penis. In L. Williams (Eds.), *Porn Studies* (pp. 27–50). Durham, NC; London, United Kingdom: Duke University Press.

Starr, K. (1998). *The Starr Report: The Independent Counsel's complete report to Congress on the investigation of President Clinton*. Washington, DC: Pocket Books.

Tanner, J. (Director). (2008). *Who's nailin' Paylin*, United States: Hustle Video.

Thomas, D. (2002). *Architecture and the urban environment: A Vision for the New Age*. Oxford, United Kingdom: Architectural Press.

Tomkins, S., & Demos, V. E. (1995). *Exploring affect: The selected writings of Silvan S. Tomkins*. New York, NY: Cambridge University Press.

U.S. News. (2008, 1 October). Seriously? Sarah Palin Is a "Joe Six-Pack American". Palin explains what kind of American she represents. Retrieved from http://www.usnews.com/opinion/articles/2008/10/01/seriously-sarah-palin-is-a-joe-six-pack-american

Williams, L. (1999). *Hard core: Power, pleasure, and the "frenzy of the visible"*. Berkeley, CA: University of California Press.

Williams, L. (2004). Skin flicks on the racial border: Pornography, exploitation, and interracial lust. In L. Williams (Eds.), *Porn Studies* (pp. 272–304). Durham, NC; London, United Kingdom: Duke University Press.

Zimmer, B. (2008, 10 September). Who first put "lipstick on a pig"? The origins of the porcine proverb. *Slate*. Retrieved from http://www.slate.com/articles/news_and_politics/explainer/2008/09/who_first_put_lipstick_on_a_pig.html

CHAPTER NINE

GAY PORN, INK

Joseph Brennan

As far as signifiers of the ideal male physique and 'butch aesthetic' go, tattoos have become as standard in gay porn as muscle and endowment (see Morrison, 2004, pp. 172–175). However the increasing visibility of inked bodies in commercial gay porn of recent years has also resulted in these markings coming to carry other signifieds. These include: porn stardom, sexuality, violence and even disease. To illustrate the discursive role of ink in gay porn today, this chapter uses image semiotics in a Barthesian tradition of a range of gay porn inked bodies – and the meanings behind the symbols in the models' own words – so as to illustrate the potential for each of the aforementioned signifieds. I argue that the symbolism of the icons and text in the tattoos selected for analysis have meaning, not only in relation to positioning on the male gay porn body and the genre of gay porn in which the images are framed, but also in the context of the gay male porn sexed body-in-action. The chapter draws on numerous examples to examine the range of meanings associated with these markings, while also incorporating case studies of two controversial examples of ink in gay porn.

The case studies are Brice from Sean Cody and Axl from Active Duty, two performers working in 'gay-for-pay' porn – a genre featuring heterosexually identified men who turn credible homosexual performances (see Escoffier, 2003) – whose tattoos have something to contribute to understandings of the culture of fetishisation of the 'straight male' in gay porn. The chapter shows how Brice loses work as a result of a tattoo ('Born This Way') expressing his authentic gay sexuality, while Axl continues to work despite being tattooed with hate symbols (several neo-Nazi tattoos); his superior straight status within the genre enabling him to dismiss the criticisms of his gay audience. These cases and the examples throughout allow us to consider limitations of the form and the potential for ink to bring to the surface what would otherwise remain hidden, such as homophobia (both individual and systemic). The chapter also explores the prevalence and controversies of ink among certain gay porn sub-genres (biohazard symbols in pornography featuring sex without condoms, known as 'bareback', for example) and the unique insights that come from reading the marked-up male body through the gay pornographic lens.

Reading ink through the gay pornographic lens
In updating his influential late 1980s ethnographic study of tattooing, sociologist Clinton R. Sanders observes that the practice has undergone a process of "de-deviantisation" (2009, p. viii). No longer is ink exclusively meaningful to marginal social groups, where it is "produced within complex webs of collective action" (p. 21), but instead has become a recurrent feature of contemporary popular culture and an increasingly common means of self-expression. More than any other form of body modification, tattoos as "a powerful form of human expression" have become popular, and as a result, are "now considerably more open to interpretation and subject to situated definition" (Atkinson, 2003, pp. 23, 24). The situation, or 'lens', through which I will be reading tattoos is gay pornography, a field of study that has much in common with tattoos' history as a cultural stereotype and marker "of shame worn by outlaws, misfits, or those fallen from social grace" (p. 23). My analysis is influenced by Roland Barthes's image semiotics. Barthes argues that all images are polysemous, that "they imply, underlying their signifiers, a 'floating chain' of signifieds, the reader able to choose some and ignore others"

(1982, p. 39). And yet, as Barthes notes, techniques are developed in every society to combat "the terror of uncertain signs", "to *fix* the floating chain of signifieds" (1982, p. 39). Therefore, within this Barthesian tradition, I consider the underlying ideological and cultural assumptions of the signs within the images analysed, and in doing so, strategically select and present aspects of the analysed texts as evidence for my overall argument, drawing on interviews and certain performances with the models in question to inform my reading.

Certain scholars writing on gay pornography have noted, albeit briefly, the significance of tattoos in this context. In his discussion of the potential for political statement in gay porn, for example, John R. Burger argues that even where no politics are professed, "bodily presentations of the boys" in gay porn (including tattoos) may reflect certain views about activities and issues of homoerotic life (1995, p. 90). In other words, tattoo wearers textualise the surface of the body and that body becomes a surface on which various commitments are 'staged', including, for example, commitments to safer sexual practice or the refusal to accept shame for HIV infection (Brouwer, 1998, p. 115). Further, scholars have noted the agency of individual porn actors in using ink to make a statement about who they are and how they perform. Notable examples include: the late Scott O'Hara (USA), who tattooed his "HIV+" status on his bicep during the height of the HIV/AIDS crisis as an ultimate 'out of the closet' gesture (see Cohler, 2004, pp. 23–31); Raging Stallion Studios exclusive, Logan McCree (Germany), who has undertaken a full body tattoo project to give expression to his Christian spirituality (see Nynäs, 2011); and François Sagat (France) who retired from porn in 2013, known for his hyper-butch persona and scalp tattoo, two constructions the performer employs as "a conscious rejection of the stigma of effeminacy" (see Cervulle & Rees-Roberts, 2009, p. 203). The use of ink by these three performers demonstrates the breadth of meaning behind tattoos and their transnational appeal, even within a shared context, embodying three thematic symbolisms of ink, namely: disease, spirituality and masculinity. These three performers also cultivate certain 'looks' using ink, as this chapter's more wide-ranging analysis will show.

'Looks' of the inked gay porn body

Bruce W. Whitehead argues that media, gay or otherwise, "reinforces specific 'looks,' with one ideal superseding the others" (in Ellis & Whitehead, 2004, p. 208). This 'one ideal' is the dominant ideal – the hegemonic ideal or aesthetic (see Filiault & Drummond, 2007) – however, that is not to discount alternatives. Such looks are, after all, 'invented categories' (Weeks, 1991) and while it is true that gay porn may reinforce distinct masculine 'looks', such as a 'butch aesthetic', "there are several to choose from" and opportunities exist to select oppositional looks, some of which will be explored in this chapter (Whitehead in Ellis & Whitehead, 2004, p. 208). Tattoos, as expressions of personhood on the body, make clear the alternative looks and tribes available in gay porn. Master Harvey from online domination fetish site The Hard Order, for example, has tattooed the letter "W" on each of his buttocks, which – as he demonstrates in his video *Disgusting Butt Boy* – stands for "winner" and is a sign he uses to connote a desired reading, which is that Master Harvey is a "Posh gentleman with a sadistic streak" (Harvey, 2015). Harvey's tattoo is a tool of domination over his submissive, or 'slave', target audience. That it is concealable beneath underwear protects his public image as a 'posh gentleman', affording him the power to reveal his 'winning ass' only in private, whenever he chooses to play out his "sadistic streak". Harvey verifies this reading in a video in which he addresses his slaves:

> I think we have established by now that you are a fucking loser. You are a fucking loser. Me, on the other hand, I am a fucking winner. Just look … [reveals his tattoo] See, I even have it on my ass. (*Disgusting Butt Boy*, 2015)

The Harvey example is useful because it demonstrates a deliberate effort on the part of the performer to encode a preferred, "undoubtedly intentional" reading (Barthes, 1982, p. 33), on to the tattoos that appear on his posterior. This reading is intelligible within the master/slave, sadomasochistic genre in which it appears, and is further 'anchored' (pp. 38–41) through Harvey's demonstration of its function in the *Disgusting Butt Boy* video. (Sean Duran, who made his bareback debut with Lucas Entertainment in 2015, has the word "Faggot" above a cupcake tattooed under his chin, which provides an antithetical example of a performer using ink to mark himself in relation to dominant/submissive porn subjectivities.) It is worth noting, however, that tattoos continue to generate meaning based on the porn context in which they appear, regardless of whether the tattoo performs any 'function' within any of the performer's porn videos, and notwithstanding what the intentional reading may have been when the ink was first inscribed. Similar to the "intentional fallacy" idea – that emerged within literary criticism during the 1940s and 1950s (Wimsatt & Beardsley, 1946) – I acknowledge here that meaning making rests with the viewer and within the context within which the signs are viewed. Gay-for-pay performer Paul Canon's decision to tattoo a biohazard symbol down his left side is a good case in point. While Canon chose the symbol to remind himself of a turbulent period in his life that resulted in a drug overdose, the fact that it has inescapable connotations of bareback practice and HIV within the gay community has been a point of continued contention in his career, compounded by his on-screen performances of sex without condoms (see Canon, 2014).

Further, where a tattoo is positioned on the body is relevant to its signification, as the Harvey example demonstrates. Is it concealable, beneath a Speedo tan line, for example? Or is it highly visible and difficult to conceal, on the face for instance? Is it placed on the chest, over the heart, to symbolise devotion, that what is depicted is 'close to my heart'; or is it near the genitals or the buttocks, a 'tramp stamp' (on a gay male, with all the derogatory, feminine connotations associated with the term – as is testament in a scene [FX068] from hazing studio Fraternity X, when a "frat bitch" is given a makeshift "man whore" tramp stamp)? These are all questions that inform how the symbol is read and culturally interpreted. Hawaiian amateur studio Island Studs's Jarhead Jimmie, for example, has "Support Your Troops" tattooed just above his waistline. This affirms his status as an active duty marine and secures his place in the "Military Men" category on the Island Studs website. However, equally, on the unclothed male body posing in a series of photographs stored within an online, for-profit, gay porn archive, the tattoo's placement – directly above his penis – with the directive to 'support', also encodes sexual signifieds. When tattooed above a flaccid penis, this phrase seems to invite a servicing of sexual needs, particularly within the fantasy of the 'straight', gay-for-pay military performer. In this example, the "Support Your Troops" tattoo helps to situate the model within a genre of gay pornography, the military porn genre, while also promoting a particular 'look' and fantasy about military men. The models' intentions behind the tattoos in question, these symbols' placement on the body and the context in which they appear will all be considered in this chapter. First, however, it is worthwhile to examine certain symbols that are now synonymous with gay porn.

A star is born: symbols of gay porn stardom

Appropriation of symbols has played a crucial role in the homosexual community. While the merits of such appropriations are debatable (see Elman, 1996) – the reclamation of the pink triangle from a symbol used by the Nazis to mark homosexuals for annihilation during the Holocaust into a symbol of homosexual pride and liberation, for example – what is clear is the importance of context in assessing the significance of these symbols to and within the communities in which they appear. The 'Nautical Star' is a good starting point. This popular "sailors mark" (Dye, 1989, p. 522) has been traditionally used to represent sea services of the United States armed forces and most commonly appears as a five-pointed star in dark and light shades counterchanged in a manner reminiscent of a compass rose. It has been appropriated by many gay porn performers as a symbol of homosexuality and of porn stardom. Brad Star, for example, who has performed for studios such as Lucas Entertainment and Titan Media, and whose iconic appropriation of the tattoo is reflected in his name, explains in an interview:

> They are nautical stars since I was in the Navy [… R]ather than put them on my arm, chest or back, like everyone else, I put them on my lower waist line. (Gio, n.d.)

Star stays true to the naval tradition by adopting the stars, however equally reflects his porn identity by resituating the tattoos away from the chest (heart), arms or back (strength) and towards his genitals, where the stars serve as navigational tools that point to his penis. Retired performer (active 1995–2006) Will Clark has become synonymous with his film *Red Star* (Slater & Ward, 2003) and for his red shading of his tattoo that complements his appeal as a redhead. Also retired (2004–2010) Brent Corrigan famously appropriated the five-pointed star in a manner that was more Hollywood system than nautical, but is similarly noteworthy as a comment on stardom. Situated high on his right buttock, the star has a navy blue outline and a pastel blue interior. It has become an iconic marker of the dominance through the late noughties of Corrigan as a 'power bottom twink' (a twink is a young performer, aged 18–23 years, while a power bottom actively and often exclusively pursues the submissive position in penetrative sex, see Brennan, 2016), setting apart his 'bubble-butt money-maker' from lesser-known performers. Additionally, by virtue of having been tattooed on his eighteenth birthday, the tattoo has become a means by which Corrigan's of-age work can be distinguished from four films he shot with Cobra Video in 2004 while underage (now only available via illegal channels).

In addition to aspirations of porn stardom, porn performers sometimes choose to tattoo sexual preferences or affiliations with gay subcultures on to their skin. The 'Bear-Paw Print' tattoo, for example, is generally accepted as connoting an affiliation with the 'bear subculture' (see Wright, 2013). These bear tribe prints are usually positioned on the chest or buttocks, as if they were guides for where the bear should place his hands during intercourse. The bear body is denoted by hair and a larger physique. On the non-bear body, such as the youthful, smooth, toned gay male twink look of Brandon Wilde or Joey Tiger, this tattoo marks the person as sexually interested in a more hirsute male: as a 'bear chaser'. This example reminds us that, while tattoos speak to the performer and can conjure up expectations of sexual practice as seen on screen, they also speak to the person, and that person's construction of self, along with the circumstances of this construction.

"Born This Way": (no) queer identity in gay porn
In 2012, Zachary Sire of gay porn gossip blog The Sword, authored an article titled 'The 11 hottest Sean Cody models with the stupidest tattoos of all time'. The list includes examples such

as an image of Christ on a model's chest that Sire aptly describes as "Jesus making a stupid face" (Dalton, number three) and the phrase "No Means Yes" tattooed above a model's penis (Oscar, number two). Brice, who is marketed by gay-for-pay studio Sean Cody as a "complete bottom", comes in at number one on the list, with a Lady Gaga tattoo: the phrase "Born This Way" across his shoulder blades. As Sire (2012) comments:

> *Born This Way*. Even if this didn't connote the stupidest celebrity of our time who NO ONE wants to be thinking about when they're having sex, there are so many other stupid things going on here. The font, the size(!), the placement (so that when he's getting butt fucked, it's the one HUGE thing that the top is forced to see) ... just ... NO. Stupid stupid stupid. Laser removal is your friend, Brice. (Sire, 2012).

Sire argues that this example warrants first billing on his 'stupid list' for its association with Gaga, its size and its positioning, which imposes itself on the penetrative partner (and the viewer too, it would seem). Gaga is 'connoted' not only by the phrase itself – synonymous with the artist (since 2011 when it was chosen as the title for her second studio album) and her advocacy of gay rights issues (see Jang & Lee, 2014) – but also the 'font', which mimics that used on the cover art of the artist's lead single off her album of the same name (see Figure 1).

Gaga explains the significance of the phrase and the challenge she is posing through her use of it in an interview with *Metro New York*:

> 'Born This Way' is my answer to many questions over the years: Who are you? What are you about? ... [It] is me struggling to understand how I can exist as myself as someone who lives halfway between fantasy and reality all the time. (quoted in Freidson, 2011, p. 7)

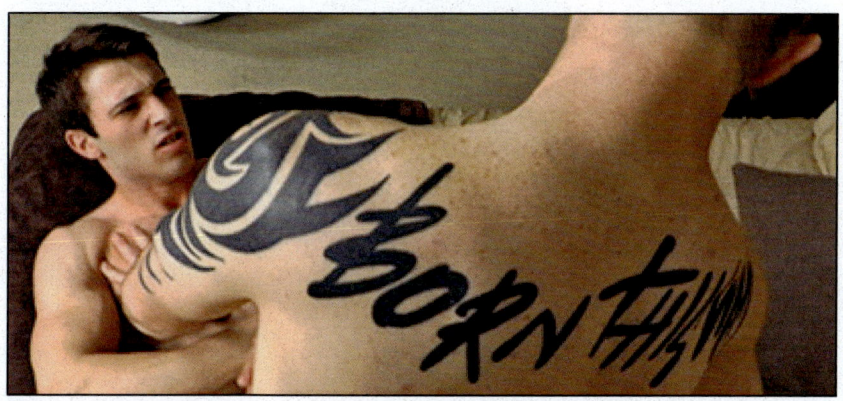

Figure 1: Born This Way tattoo (*Source:* still from *Jarek & Brice: Bareback* (Sean Cody, 2012), based on the 'Born This Way' (Lady Gaga, 2011) cover art text).

That a tattoo promoting acceptance of sexuality in a bold way outranks poorly rendered religious iconography (numbers 3, 7, 10) and connotations of sexual violence (number 2) in the stupidity stakes might seem surprising (Sire, 2012). Yet, the 'gay-for-pay' context makes it plausible that first billing is due to the performer's intrusion on the gay-for-pay suspension of disbelief: where gay porn performers "engage in sexual acts for monetary compensation that they would not otherwise choose to perform and with partners for whom they feel no desire" (Escoffier, 2003, p. 531). By forcing the heterosexual performers to witness his difference, Brice becomes encoded as somehow more 'preachy', more worthy of ridicule. The conceit of Sean Cody is that its models are gay-for-pay only (rather than gay in life), and therefore Brice's expression of his authentic gay sexuality via the tattoo disrupts the discourse of straightness (both of performers and viewers) within the genre.

As Brice concedes: "The guys aren't homophobic, they just aren't used to being around any homosexuals. ... they were ALL straight!" (Sire, 2013). Brice **is** therefore flaunting his sexuality with the tattoo, "so that when he's getting butt fucked, it's the one HUGE thing that the top is forced to see" (Sire, 2012). This 'dilemma' – of a gay-identifying performer within a particular sub-genre of gay porn that promotes gay sex among straight men (and of which Sean Cody is an industry leader) – has a more general applicability to the field. It promotes questioning of the implications of a culture of fetishisation of the 'straight male' in gay porn and of the 'butch aesthetic' as the most accepted mode of representation (see Morrison, 2004, pp. 179–181).

Sire's opinion is validated a year later when it is revealed in an interview with the model that the tattoo in question was a key factor in Brice losing work with Sean Cody: "I was in a relationship, and we decided that I should take some time off. When I wanted to come back, Sean Cody decided my tattoo was an issue" (Sire, 2013). This account makes sense given Sean Cody's identity as a bareback gay-for-pay studio, while Sire's own problem with it points to systemic, industry- and community-wide expectations that certain aspects of models' personal lives remain hidden, or at least, do not intrude on the gay porn fantasy. To return to Gaga, Brice experienced how difficult it is to be "someone who lives halfway between fantasy and reality all the time" (quoted in Freidson, 2011, p. 7), to have the identity of the person intrude on that of the performer. What this case demonstrates is the power of the tattoo in bringing to the surface (and keeping there) expressions that are not always easy to conceal and may not always be welcome in the fantasy world of porn. As Brice himself (who retired in 2014), seems to recognise: "I've thought about removing or covering it up, but it's me now" (Sire, 2013).

The 'Born This Way' case study demonstrates the role that tattoos play in marking difference and the potential implications of such a permanent gesture. As well as sexuality, tattoos that appear on the bodies of gay porn performers can mark other differences as well. John Mercer observes precisely this when he nominates tattoos as one means by which "class or social difference" is presented for sexual purposes; he points out that certain tattoos or distribution of body hair or muscular builds can function as signs that connote certain looks, such as the 'working man' (2012, p. 324).

Race is another persistent issue within gay porn that has been represented via ink. Retired Titan Media performer Dred Scott, for example, anchors his historically loaded stage name – derived from an unsuccessful 1857 African American freedom bid, commonly known as the Dred Scott Decision (see Fehrenbacher, 2001) – to race by tattooing the words "Black" and "White" across his pectoral muscles, expressing his own mixed race heritage. On the subject of Scott, Tavia A. Ochieng'Nyongó describes him as a 'subcultural figure' that represents the "spectacularly mongrel masculinities [that] proliferate in the popular imaginary" (2007, p. 459). However, the most contentious sensibility to permeate gay porn discourse is undoubtedly AIDS tattoos and those men of porn who choose to display them.

Biohazard and contagion: communicating HIV status through tattoos

In *Unlimited Intimacy*, Tim Dean describes the 'barebacking subculture' as "an arena of invention" (2009, p. 47). Using tattoos as an analogy for HIV infection, Dean writes that, in a post-AIDS era, by practising anal sex without condoms "gay men have devised a technique for tattooing the body's interior. The presence of HIV enables the act of internal ejaculation to serve as the inscription of a love relation in the face of mutability" (2009, p. 173). This analogy is particularly fitting given that the term 'barebacking' is generally attributed to gay porn star Scott O'Hara, discussed earlier, who coined the term in his memoir *Autopornography* (1997). In the memoir – published in the year before his death from AIDS – O'Hara expands on his unique relationship with the illness that is consuming him:

> I can't quite believe it's a curse. [... I]n my life, AIDS has been an undeniable blessing. It woke me up to what was important [and] gives me the freedom to behave 'irresponsibly.' I look at the HIV negative people around me, and I pity them. They must live in constant fear of infection. (1997, p. 129)

O'Hara tattooed "HIV+" on his arm to make visible to all what was already tattooed – irremovable – within. In embracing his illness and its associative stigma, to use the words of Barry D. Adam, O'Hara advocates for a "return to a sexuality no longer constrained by the fear of infection" (2005, p. 338). O'Hara chooses to embrace his sickness and adopts an emblem (the tattoo) that will make this commitment visible to all. Finding freedom in the absence of fear, O'Hara empowers himself as a sexual adventurer; marked, yet not confined by the crisis threatening those sexually active within his community. O'Hara's tattoo allows him to construct himself and those like him as "unabashed sexual rebels" (Haig, 2006, p. 862). And his position has inspired others to do the same (see Gauthier & Forsyth, 1999; Tewksbury, 2006 who discuss the phenomenon whereby men seek out sex with HIV-positive men for the express purpose of becoming infected with the virus).

What emerges from this discussion of O'Hara and his "HIV+" tattoo is a correlation between tattoos as a mode of self-expression – along with the freedom that comes with self-disclosure – and certain values of gay male sexual performance and practice. Perry N. Halkitis observes something similar in his study of the perceptions of masculinity among HIV-positive gay men (see 2001). Halkitis finds that masculinity among gay men is defined by physical appearance and sexual adventurism.

Among the appearances associated with masculinity are tattooed bodies, while adventurism includes an interest in casual sex. As the O'Hara example shows, adventurism often also involves a degree of risk, such as unprotected sex. Bareback studio Treasure Island Media, for example, shares a similar vision to O'Hara, its 'tattoo challenge' encouraging fans of the studio to tattoo the company's logo – a skull and crossed swords motif – on to their bodies in support of a bareback lifestyle (Garcia, 2013, p. 1049).

Other symbols adopted by those with HIV, or who routinely practice unprotected sex, include the universal 'biohazard' symbol, which commonly appears on the shoulder or stomach. Sam Swift, for example, who has performed with Next Door Ebony, has the biohazard symbol tattooed on his stomach with his navel at its centre, while Treasure Island Media exclusive Ethan Wolfe chose to tattoo the symbol beneath his navel. HIV/AIDS tattoos are the one domain where intentionality is clearest, where the body is branded as "potentially infected, contaminated and somehow dangerous" (Holmes & Warner, 2005, p. 15). Dan Brouwer confirms this in his reading of HIV/AIDS tattoos through the prism of visibility politics and self-stigmatisation (see 1998).

Stigma is a concept relevant to tattoos, as Erving Goffman notes in his study of the term's etymological and cultural origins (1963). To the ancient Greeks, 'stigma' referred to markings on the body, put there to connote "a blemished person, ritually polluted, to be avoided, especially in public places" (Goffman, 1963, p. 1). These 'signs' were cut or burned into the skin in much the same way that tattoos are formed today (Goffman, 1963, p. 1). Of course, what O'Hara's body project demonstrates is that there are a number of strategies at play when the body is inked with a symbol connoting HIV or other 'tainted' subject positions, among them being meanings that resist stigma and offer distinct opportunities for self-empowerment and freedom from the culture that constructs taboo. In short, by self-branding using symbols traditionally associated with 'toxic waste' and death, gay male porn stars exercise some measure of control over matters that would normally remain secret and shrouded in shame. In this case, performers such as O'Hara, Swift and Wolfe reuse these symbols in a gesture of political and cultural subversion of persistent ideologies in the dominant culture.

The appropriation of stigma symbols has played a crucial role in the homosexual community, and as has been shown, can function as a means of empowerment for men of porn, even when such appropriations promote practices that carry health risks. However, as a final case study, it is worth considering what the implications are when stigma and hate symbols that have not already been rehabilitated and absorbed into gay culture appear on gay porn bodies. A particularly memorable case in point unfolded on the forums of a gay porn message board.

Hate on display: cumming to violent messaging
In January 2012, a participant on the 'Gay Porn and Hot Guys' forum of popular website JustUsBoys authored a thread titled 'Active Duty's Axl tattoo controversy' (see CowboyBob, 2012). It sought to expose Axl, a model from Active Duty – an online studio that purportedly hosts gay sex featuring American active duty soldiers, sailors and marines – as a white supremacist based on the neo-Nazi symbolism of a number of the performer's tattoos. The author was a regular contributor to the forum and supported his accusation by aligning four of Axl's tattoos with symbols documented in the Anti-Defamation League's (adl.org) Hate Symbols Database (see CowboyBob, 2012). The thread garnered 483 responses over the course of one

Gay Porn, Ink

Figure 2: Axl's white supremacist tattoos (*Source:* Still from Active Duty with symbols documented in the Anti-Defamation League's Hate Symbols Database).

month. In the responses to the initial post, three additional tattoos are identified – by CowboyBob (2012, comment 63) and others (2012, comments 2, 4 and 6) – as carrying significance for those sympathetic to the white supremacist agenda. Figure 2 uses a photograph of Axl, as shot by Active Duty, to identify the symbols those in the community recognised as signs commonly appropriated by white supremacists.

In his discussion of societal reaction to individuals 'marked' by stigma, Goffman observes that typically the marked individual is assigned all responsibility for assuaging any social discomfort their markings cause (1963). "[T]he stigmatized individual should make an effort at sympathetic re-education of the normal," Goffman writes, "showing him, point for point, quietly, and with delicacy, that in spite of appearances the stigmatized individual is, underneath it all, a fully-human being" (1963, p. 116). In setting out the appropriate response of the stigmatised individual, Goffman establishes a normal/deviant binary:

> So complete is the individual's derivation from society, that society can rely on those who are the least accepted as normal members, the least rewarded by the pleasures of easy social

> intercourse with others, to provide a statement, clarification, and tribute to the inward being of everyman. (1963, p. 116)

It is curious, therefore, that despite the combination of these highly symbolic markings – that serve to mark this performer as so abhorrent, so countercultural as to evoke the tenets of neo-Nazism – Axl is not required to make any statement about the symbols so brazenly branded on his skin; and more curious still that the porn studio responsible for the images up for derision defends the model. In a statement published on the thread, Active Duty founder Dink Flamingo claims the model had been unaware of the tattoos' white supremacist symbolism (CowboyBob, 2012, comment 43), going so far as to 'gift' a "four way hardcore scene" featuring the model in reply to a comment from a member of the discussion who accepted this explanation (comment 12). Others, however, remained unconvinced – "1 tattoo maybe, 3-4 then you know what you're doing" (comment 29; also see 21) – and were critical both of the model and the studio for defending him, some pointing to its poor track record in representing non-white nationalities (see comment 25, 29).

As one member writes in response to Flamingo's view that the situation had been blown out of proportion: "Honestly, how DARE you? You put a model on your site who is advocating the AB [Aryan Brotherhood] on his BODY and you have the NERVE to say people are blowing it out of proportion and gravitating towards sensationalism?" Another commenter poses the following to Active Duty and the industry more broadly:

> So, I'm curious. Now that the despicable meaning behind the tattoos is out and they are clearly offensive to a great number of people, what's the upshot?
> He's "hot" so we give him a pass? He stays on the site, gets hired again and we give Active Duty a pass because he's

really a "nice guy" and he "probably" didn't know what Heil Hitler meant? We let the "market" decide whether or not AB porn is cool and MY decision to not support that is "respected" but, hey he's hot and honest he's a "really nice" maybe racist so we're still gonna have him representing the site (free market free market ya know)?
What's the answer to those customers who are offended? (LuvFindsAndyHardy quoted in CowboyBob, 2012, comment 40)

Unfortunately, no decisive answer is given. Axl has provided no comment since the controversy and has shot fifteen scenes with Active Duty to date. According to Date of Production records provided by the studio in compliance with United States Code, Section 2257 of Title 18, these scenes were shot between 16 January 2012 and 13 January 2013, with twelve of the scenes filmed after CowboyBob alerted the community to the tattoos (although the tattoos with the clearest neo-Nazi connections, the numeric symbols "14" and "88", are covered over in a temporary manner in a scene shot on 21 March 2012). Axl continued his ink project following the controversy, which has included a skull tattoo (visible in a scene shot after 19 February 2012, see Figure 2, point 7 in the key), another symbol with neo-Nazi significance.

A disturbing potential of the Axl tattoo controversy is that, within the context of gay porn, Axl, even with these symbols on his skin, is in fact the 'normal' party in Goffman's normal/deviant dichotomy. The controversy of the final case in this chapter and the polarised reactions to it that played out on the JustUsBoys forum demonstrates the arbitrary nature of ink to the performer, the studio and the audience, while the continued allowance of such symbols of hate to remain on display offers insight into the values at play in the gay-for-pay genre specifically. Axl as an active duty serviceman needs not explain himself or his tattoos to the gay men who consume the texts he creates. Connections emerge here with debates around homophobia and racism in gay porn, particularly as they relate to the valorisation of certain 'looks' – such as the butch aesthetic – and the relationship between audience, performer and producer.

Conclusion

This chapter has used a semiotic method to examine the discursive symbolism of ink within gay porn. Individual symbols performers have tattooed on their skin were analysed with respect to situated definition: on the body and within particular porn texts/genres. If tattooing is, as social anthropologist Alfred Gell defines it, a means of, "via the body, reconstructing personhood" (1993, p. 3), reading ink symbols as signs makes tangible normally elusive expressions, such as identity and belief, which are becoming increasingly exhibited within the 'fleshy' realm of gay porn. Also made explicit are divisions that arise between binaries, such as: exterior and interior, body and culture, the pole potentialities of which were demonstrated via contrasting case studies.

The ink inscribed on the bodies of Brice and Axl forced certain discourses of discrimination (homophobia in particular) to the surface. These discourses may otherwise have been concealed, and carry implications for the gay-for-pay genre that included/excluded the men. Brice's declaration of his sexuality via his tattoo resulted in him losing his job, even within a scenario where he was openly performing acts associated with that sexuality; while Axl was able to dismiss the criticisms of his gay audience due to his superior straight status. These cases expose the power of signifieds such as 'straightness' within the genre. While the appearance of ink on gay porn bodies is occurring with a permanency akin to tattooing itself, the scholarly pursuit to make sense of ink within a context as contested and at times problematic as porn is just beginning.

References

Adam, B. D. (2005). Constructing the neo-liberal sexual actor: Responsibility and care of the self in the discourse of barebackers. *Culture, Health and Sexuality, 7*(4), 333–346.

Atkinson, M. (2003). *Tattooed: The sociogenesis of a body art*. Toronto, Canada: The University of Toronto Press.

Barthes, R. (1982). The rhetoric of the image. In R. Barthes (Ed.), *Image, music, text* (pp. 32–51). London, United Kingdom: Fontana.

Brennan, J. (2016). 'Bare-backing spoils everything. He's spoiled goods': Disposal and disgust, a study of retired power bottom twink Jake Lyons. *Porn Studies, 3*(1), 20–33.

Brouwer, D. (1998). The precarious visibility politics of self-stigmatization: The case of HIV/AIDS tattoos. *Text and Performance Quarterly, 18*(2), 114–136.

Burger, J. R. (1995). *One-handed histories: The eroto-politics of gay male video pornography*. New York, NY: Harrington Park Press.

Canon, P. (2014). @ASS_DRILLER no..and ive mentioned this numerous times before..i find it insulting that it is assumed to even be associated with hiv.. March 3, 9:41am. Tweet (PaultheCanonXXX). Retrieved from https://twitter.com/paul thecanonxxx/ status/440255501540937731

Cervulle, M., & Rees-Roberts, N. (2009). Queering the Orientalist porn package: Arab men in French gay pornography. *New Cinemas, 6*(3), 197–208.

Cohler, B. J. (2004). Memoir and performance: Social change and self life-writing among men who are gay pornography producers and actors. *Journal of Homosexuality, 47*(3–4), 7–43.

CowboyBob. (2012, January 23). *Active Duty's Axl tattoo controversy*. Retrieved from http://www.justusboys.com/forum/threads/ 368091-Active-Duty-s-Axl-tattoo-controversy

Dean, T. (2009). *Unlimited intimacy: Reflections on the subculture of barebacking*. Chicago, IL: University of Chicago Press.

Dye, I. (1989). The tattoos of early American seafarers, 1796–1818. *Proceedings of the American Philosophical Society, 133*(4), 520–554.

Ellis, S. R., & Whitehead, B. W. (2004). Porn again: Some final considerations. *Journal of Homosexuality, 47*(3–4), 197–220.

Elman, R. A. (1996). Triangles and tribulations: The politics of Nazi symbols. *Journal of Homosexuality, 30*(3), 1–11.

Escoffier, J. (2003). Gay-for-pay: Straight men and the making of gay pornography. *Qualitative Sociology, 26*(4), 531–555.

Fehrenbacher, D. E. (2001). *The Dred Scott case: Its significance in American law and politics.* New York, NY: Oxford University Press.

Filiault, S. M., & Drummond, M. J. (2007). The hegemonic aesthetic. *Gay and Lesbian Issues and Psychology Review, 3*(3), 175–184.

Freidson, M. (2011, May 17). The one-on-one interview. *Metro New York,* 7.

Garcia, C. (2013). Limited intimacy: Barebacking and the imaginary. *Textual Practice, 27*(6), 1031–1051.

Gauthier, D. K., & Forsyth, C. J. (1999). Bareback sex, bug chasers, and the gift of death. *Deviant Behavior, 20*(1), 85–100.

Gell, A. (1993). *Wrapping in images: Tattooing in Polynesia.* Oxford, United Kingdom: Clarendon Press.

Gio. (n.d.). *Brad Star interview & photos.* Retrieved from http://www.jumponmarkslist.com/fan-pages/porn-stars/brad-star-gay-porn-interview.php

Goffman, E. (1963). *Stigma: Notes on a spoiled identity.* New York, NY: Simon & Schuster.

Haig, T. (2006). Bareback sex: Masculinity, silence, and the dilemmas of gay health. *Canadian Journal of Communication, 31*(4), 859–877.

Halkitis, P. N. (2001). An exploration of perceptions of masculinity among gay men living with HIV. *The Journal of Men's Studies, 9*(3), 413–429.

Harvey, Master. (Director). (2015). *Disgusting butt boy* [Video]. UK: TheHardOrder.com.

Holmes, D., & Warner, D. (2005). The anatomy of a forbidden desire: Men, penetration and semen exchange. *Nursing Inquiry, 12*(1), 10–20.

Jang, S. M., & Lee, H. (2014). When pop music meets a political issue: Examining how "Born This Way" influences attitudes toward gays and gay rights policies. *Journal of Broadcasting & Electronic Media, 58*(1), 114–130.

Mercer, J. (2012). Coming of age: Problematizing gay porn and the eroticized older man. *Journal of Gender Studies, 21*(3), 313–326.

Morrison, T. G. (2004). "He was treating me like trash, and I was loving it…" Perspectives on gay male pornography. *Journal of Homosexuality, 47*(3–4), 167–183.

Nynäs, P. (2011). Multiple bodies in the spirituality of the gay porn star McCree: Reflections on corporeality and subjectivity. *Scripta Instituti Donneriani Aboensis, 23*, 333–350.

Ochieng'Nyongó, T. A. (2007). No halvsies! [Review of the book *Hybridity, or the cultural logic of globalization*]. *American Quarterly, 59*(2), 459–466.

O'Hara, S. (1997). *Autopornography: A memoir of life in the lust lane.* Philadelphia, PA: Haworth Press.

Sanders, C. R. (2009). *Customizing the body: The art and culture of tattooing* (revised and expanded edition). Philadelphia, PA: Temple University Press.

Sire, Z. (2012, 14 September). *The 11 hottest Sean Cody models with the stupidest tattoos of all time.* Retrieved from http://thesword.com/the-11-hottest-sean-cody-models-with-the-stupidest-tattoos-of-all-time.html

Sire, Z. (2013, June 7). *Gay porn star Connor Kline's exclusive Sword interview: "My ass is natural".* Retrieved from http://thesword.com/gay-porn-star-connor-klines-exclusive-sword-interview-my-ass-is-natural.html

Slater, J. D., & Ward, C. (Directors). (2003). *Red star* [Motion Picture]. USA: Raging Stallion Studios.

Tewksbury, R. (2006). "Click here for HIV": An analysis of Internet-based bug chasers and bug givers. *Deviant Behavior, 27*(4), 379–395.

Weeks, J. (1991). *Against nature: Essays on sexuality, history, and identity.* London, United Kingdom: Rivers Oram Press.

Wimsatt Jr., W. K., & Beardsley, M. C. (1946). The intentional fallacy. *The Sewanee Review, 54*(3), 468–488.

Wright, L. (Ed.). (2013). *The bear book: Readings in the history and evolution of a gay male subculture.* New York, NY: Routledge.

CHAPTER TEN

BAREBACKING AND HISTORICAL TIME

Ricky Varghese

Is there a temporality to sex? Can sex be rendered as a historical category, given a sense of the temporal; imagined as an act or a confluence of gestures that exists both alongside and exceeds its own possible temporal limitations? In other words, what would sex taken as a historical category of how time is measured look like? Furthermore, can such a time of/for sex, or a sense of sexual temporality be mapped based on how the body experiences a sex act?

If we continue along this line of thought of regarding sex as a historical category, certain aspects of its historicity become revealed. For argument's sake, let us imagine time as moving along a linear continuum – this will be argued against soon enough. As such, we attend to a temporality that seemingly moves from the past into the present and on to the future. Such a time is often explained in how reproductive heteronormativity is imagined as functioning on an apparent linear timeline moving from sexual union to reproduction through the transmission and subsequent inheritance of biological attributes, personal histories, psychical trauma and material objects from one generation to another. Queering this time would present an opportunity to rewrite the presumed normative script of reproductive sex. This queering would problematise what appears to be reproductive sex's rigid temporality. Thinking of same-sex desire, particularly as it pertains to the AIDS crisis, my task here is to push against this rigidity. I aim to undo this linear temporality by exploring how AIDS as a rupture within it rewrote the history of sex and opened up the time of/for sex to more inventive, creative and radical ways of regarding it.

In the first section of this chapter, I describe time as a measure of historicity in philosophical and psychoanalytic terms. Here, I consider the work of philosopher Rebecca Comay (2011) on the tension between linear temporality and the time of trauma as marked by historical events, such as AIDS. I situate this exploration alongside the work of queer theorist Leo Bersani (2010) wherein he describes sex as a radical self-shattering experience by considering how we look at certain categories of analysis, namely sex, its temporality and historicity, trauma and the event of AIDS. By doing so, I set the stage for the comparative analysis I engage in later.

In the second section of the chapter, I think through the very visual nature of sexual history by attending to one of its most ubiquitous forms, pornography. My contention, in thinking specifically about 'bareback' pornography – forms of queer pornography that feature sex without condoms – is that this maintains a sort of scopic fidelity to the categories of time and historicity as it relates to queer male sex wherein we underscore the signifiers that are still present in their absence. What did AIDS do to sex and its representation? One response to this might lie in examining the very gesture of looking at pornography, searching for what remains both in and out of focus within the context of a crisis. Walter Benjamin's (1999) philosophy of history concerning catastrophe and Tim Dean's (2009) queer psychoanalytic work become useful tools in detailing what the AIDS crisis did to sex, its representation, and its possible historicity. I examine how we look at bareback pornography by accounting for how the event of AIDS in the time of/for sex caused a shift in focus with respect to what we watch.

The final part of the chapter will consider how pornography itself becomes an inventive space – a space for aesthetic pedagogy – to rethink AIDS and its impact on the time of/for sex. Queer Canadian video artist Vincent Chevalier uses bareback pornography produced by Paul Morris (2010) as the grounds for his experimental documentary *Breeden* (2014) in order to explore the gestural limits and possibilities of thinking sex as a historical category. Chevalier's (2014) single channel video is an archival repository exploring how the temporal registers associated with AIDS become situated within the history of sexuality as a rupture. Studying this rupture gives way to understanding how spatial and temporal parameters inform, confine and allow for the constitution of bareback sex as a site of/for both a constructive fecundity and destructivity implicit within erotic life. By opening up the time of/for sex to its potential as a sexual archive, I argue that Chevalier (2014) approaches the utopian possibilities within sex viewed alongside the event of AIDS. This seems particularly prudent in light of the recent changes to AIDS discourse in certain parts of the global North/West wherein it has transformed from an experience mired by the likely possibility of certain death to that of chronic illness.

Translating the rectum into a grave

In her remarkable study about the time of trauma produced as a consequence of a revolutionary event, Rebecca Comay (2011) discusses the "psychoanalytic logic of trauma – the dissolution of the event into a missed event and the hypertrophic investment in the trivial, the non-event, the negligible remainder" (p. 25). Drawing on Freud, Comay (2011) states that:

> Freud will discern in this delay the basic rhythm of human experience – a perpetual syncopation between originary inscription and subsequent transcription, translation, or re-edition. The textual metaphors are Freud's own and should

> be read as literally as possible. Translation (*Übersetzung*) implies not only a spatial relay of psychical energy (*Besetzung*) from one occupation zone to another but an economic inflation – an overinvestment or hypercathexis (*Übersetzung*) in the trifling aftermath of an intensity originally unmarked. Trauma marks a caesura in which the linear order of time is thrown out of sequence. We compound this temporal disorientation every time we try to quarantine trauma by displacing it to a buried past or a distant future. (p. 25)

Comay (2011) stages a discursive exploration of what it means to regard something as other vis-à-vis the traumatising task of translation. If the exercise I forge here is a gesture at thinking, or rather regarding, bareback sex as other in its relationship to the catastrophic event of AIDS – which could be read as an event that rewrote the normatively assumed script of reproductive linear time – then we find that this task of translation is the very one that Leo Bersani (2010) undertook when he posed the question, "is the rectum a grave?" (p. 3).

Writing in the very early days of the crisis, Bersani (2010) knew well the sorts of traumatic re-inscriptions and overinvestments being made upon the life of sex as a result of AIDS. Opening his now canonical essay, with an epigraph citing an admittedly unsettling statement made to the BBC by Dr Opendra Narayan, apparently one of the crisis's earliest specialist commentators, Bersani (2010) cuts through to the very traumatic core of this specific kind of re-inscription of queer male sexuality:

> These people have sex twenty or thirty times a night … A man comes along and goes from anus to anus and in a single night will act as a mosquito transferring infected cells on his penis. When this is practiced for a year, with a man having three thousand sexual intercourses, one can readily understand this massive epidemic that is currently upon us. (Narayan, as cited in Bersani, 2010, p. 3)

In response to such anxiety, Bersani simply asks, is the rectum a grave? By enacting a redoubling of the very term of engagement here – the rectum – he translates it into another term. Staging "a spatial relay of psychical energy from one occupation zone to another" (Comay, 2011, p. 25), Bersani offers a keen sense of regarding how AIDS would work towards over-determining the very experience of sex. Sex came to mean something else – a matter of quantity, of how it could be quantified, of how it resisted quantifiability, of how often it occurred, of how many sexual partners were involved, of how the spread of a microscopic virus and of sex itself could be contained. Through its medicalisation, the rectum became read as the very site of a grave of and for the queer male sexual subject. This subject became simultaneously responsible for, and accused of, allegedly digging his own grave, a grave marked on his own body. His search for sexual jouissance became the cause of his own demise and the dying of others (or so those like Narayan came to believe). In a sense, here, the little death of ecstatic orgasmic release became the big death implied by AIDS.

Thinking with Comay (2011), the traumatic rupture that AIDS acted as came to imply a caesura in the linear order of the time of/for sex. While the material reality of the numerous deaths during the crisis itself is an unforgettable part of the catastrophic history of both AIDS and how post-1980s sex became imagined, what I draw our attention to is the "negligible remainder" (Comay, 2011, p. 25) that AIDS itself signifies as a translated metaphor for all that it simultaneously holds and yet cannot contain. If sex became a quantifiable category, if a sexual subject was regarded as a "mosquito transferring infected cells on his penis"(Narayan, as cited in Bersani, 2010, p. 3), and if, by extension, one had to think of the rectum as the site of this subject's ultimate transfer into the realm of death, realised through his search for pleasure, we already find ourselves on a terrain where translations are enacting a series of overinvestments, accounting for a sequence of hypercathexes, excessive concentrations of desire on particular objects.

AIDS did lay the terrain of everyday life and sex in a state of ruin. However, as well, it came to over-determine sexuality itself as always already implicated in the violence it allegedly produced through this ruin, which came in the form of the many deaths incurred. HIV, the unseen virus, or rather the impossible-to-see object of idealisation of what is perceivably violent in the form of death, came to stand in for the very thing of death and dying. Because of its supposed invisibility, its status as an unseen object, it acted as a metaphor for sexual behaviour and the limits of sex's own capacity to be a gesture directed merely at the persistent and insistent quest for jouissance.

The body, signified here by the rectum as the supposed site of the traumatic event of AIDS, becomes the ground upon which all sorts of anxieties get played out in the temporal sense in the service of containing pleasure. It acts as the canvas on which historicity becomes simultaneously possible and annulled. The body as the by-product of trauma, here, marks "a caesura in which the linear order of time is thrown out of sequence" (Comay, 2011, p. 25), othered and set squarely in opposition to the time of reproductive sex. That queer male body, set in opposition to what has been considered as the normative impulses of the transmission and inheritance implied by reproductive time, searches out ways of being and desiring beyond the parameters of this rigid temporality. Rather than the queer male body submitting itself to the violence of the trauma represented by AIDS, the queer male search for jouissance attempts to think not merely against AIDS, but alongside it. Such an instance is evocatively envisioned in the conclusion of Bersani's (2010) essay. Here, he proposes a rigorous theory of ascesis, modes and forms of radical self-discipline and self-dismissal in which the queer male subject participates, as a stance founded on the mutual and tendentious co-existence of both violence, in the form of AIDS, and the ethical, in the form of sex:

> Gay men's "obsession" with sex, far from being denied, should be celebrated – not because of its communal virtues, not because of its subversive potential for parodies of machismo, not because it offers a model of genuine pluralism to a society that at once celebrates and punishes pluralism, but rather because it never stops re-presenting the internalized phallic male as an infinitely loved object of sacrifice. Male homosexuality advertises risk of the sexual itself as the risk of self-dismissal, of losing sight of the self, and in so doing it proposes and dangerously represents jouissance as a mode of ascesis. (Bersani, 2010, p. 30)

If AIDS is a rupture in linear time, a time seen to privilege the reproductive and heteronormative time of/for sex, then the ethical stance, here, is to think of this rupture and the sexual subject in terms of that subject being self-shattered vis-à-vis the experience of AIDS as crisis, a missed event, a non-event, but a historical event nonetheless. A call to ascesis demands from the subject a radical self-disciplining in relation to a fetish object. Here, the fetish object is not time alone; the desire is not to preserve reproductive time as the only time that matters within history. Rather, such an ascesis as self-discipline regards how time is fissured to accommodate new ways of thinking about sex and temporality, outside of the normative restraints historically imposed on both. Here, thinking of the time of/for sex in relation to a crisis allows the crisis itself to be produced anew. This production of something new figures centrally in how both sex and time could be regarded within the space of bareback pornography as it has been visualised over the last few decades since even before the AIDS crisis. The self-shattered subject is not so much shattered by either sex or by AIDS; rather, he shatters the very experience of time as it has been taught to us normatively.

The ontology of the look and regarding bareback porn
Let us briefly revisit the final line of Bersani's essay: "Male homosexuality advertises risk of the sexual itself as the risk of self-dismissal, of losing sight of the self, and in so doing it proposes and dangerously represents jouissance as a mode of ascesis" (Bersani, 2010, p. 30). I consider this instance of "losing sight of the self" in relation to the search for "jouissance as a mode of ascesis" as a sort of structural catastrophe experienced by the self. Here, this fidelity to the scopic, the visual, the losing sight of that which one might not want to lose sight of – the self and its jouissance – emphasises the primacy of the look, or the regard, at history. If AIDS as an event enacted a temporal rupture upon linear time, and that rupture might be deemed a "catastrophe" in how philosopher Walter Benjamin (1999) understood the term, as a moment in history in which the subject has "missed the opportunity" (p. 474), one might wonder over the question of precisely what AIDS did to sex, to the pursuit of jouissance? Put in another manner, we could consider this "missed opportunity" itself as an experience of losing sight of one's self, one's identity, as in the case of a self-dismissal that exiles one's subjectivity and its desire – queer male desire – to an elsewhere, far from a linear time assumed to be hetero-normative and reproductive.

What, then, comes after AIDS with regard to sex and time, desire and historicity? Walter Benjamin becomes instructive here, as I set the stage for thinking about sex, its visual representation, and the nature of the look we offer this representation. In *Theses on the Philosophy of History*, Benjamin (1968) describes one such regard at history and temporality vis-à-vis the conceptual figure of the angel of history, who, face turned towards the past and driven backwards towards the future, perceives history as "one single catastrophe which keeps piling wreckage upon wreckage and hurls it in front of his feet" (p. 257). The angel's look at the past as it gets inescapably propelled backwards into the future is striking because it marks a rupture in time that opens it up to thinking about a temporality beyond linearity. Unable to remove its fixed gaze at the past, we see the angel taking account not merely of the flow of time, but of the capacity of time to be annulled by the "piling wreckage". If AIDS is part of that historic wreckage, then the crisis it created serves as a traumatic fissure upon linear time and understanding this fissure helps in getting a sense of how it is positioned within the history of sexuality.

This fissure might be best explored within the space of queer male pornography and how it has evolved, specifically with respect to a shift in focus on what is being viewed and represented. An examination of this shift in focus allows us to consider how the meaning of AIDS over time has changed itself. In the case of queer male pornography, it is not so much the action unfolding before one's eyes that matters perhaps; rather, what is of significance is the very way in which the look upon this pornography – here, barebacking, which showcases sex without condoms – itself has changed over time. By thinking about this change in the look rendered upon a particular mode of sexual exchange – barebacking – we see how sex and its temporality has responded to the rupture represented by AIDS; more specifically, we see how sexual subjects themselves have responded to the catastrophe.

Here, I analyse two seemingly different genres of queer male pornography. The first, from the 1970s and early 1980s, is "pre-condom" pornography. This present-day descriptor signifies the radical shift in how sex has been, and is still being,

Barebacking and Historical Time

talked about in relation to the AIDS crisis. On the other hand, contemporary "bareback" pornography, as produced by production houses like Treasure Island Media, appears to have staked out its success precisely through an active refusal of the condom, embracing both barebacking and the virus. While I analyse the two genres to delineate differences between them, I also identify certain similarities. My contention is that in both scenarios the condom is still present in its absence and vis-à-vis how viral transmission is mobilised to think the circulation of desires both alongside and against the losses incurred by the crisis itself. Looking at both the history of bareback pornography and the past of a crisis works towards bridging the rupture produced by that crisis.

Cruisin' the Castro, produced by the production house Bijou Classics in 1981, serves as a sample case for the genre of pre-condom pornography. It is described as a classic compilation of scenes focussing on the "sexual antics of gay men in San Francisco's famed Castro area in the 1970s" (Bijou Classics, 1981, back cover). What one notices in the various scenes compiled here, apart from the hazy quality, is a nod to raw uninhibited sexuality prior to the AIDS crisis. The back cover describes these scenes as follows:

> Two young men with aching hard-ons have sex on a rooftop. Two guys in cowboy gear do it in front of a fire in a renovated farmhouse. A leather-jacketed hustler does it acrobatically, cumming in his own mouth. A three-way ends with simultaneous orgasms on to Richard Locke's hairy torso. Dick Fisk and a friend do it very conventionally in a bed. (Bijou Classics, 1981, back cover)

There is no direct mention that what is represented here is raw penetrative sex. What the viewer is offered is a series of scenes of men having sex with men and the absence of the condom is neither highlighted nor evident except in how the pornographic genre is described presently as "pre-condom". Watching these scenes, however, from the future anterior time in which the AIDS crisis has already occurred positions the viewer, like the angel of history, in a complex relationship not just with the time of film's production but with the time of/for the sex from which the production is presently being viewed; the viewer from the present acts as witness to this sexual archive of the past. The contemporary viewer watches these scenes with the knowledge of what is to come in the years following this film's production, a crisis that will wreak immeasurable havoc. The contemporary viewer becomes the holder of the knowledge that the AIDS crisis will transform the very ways in which we view sex – as that which is required to be sanitised, done cautiously. The tense and sense of the future anterior necessarily haunts this viewing. Bodies *will have learned* to guard themselves against one another. Safe sex education campaigns *will have been* implemented and *will have been* rigorously complemented by the demand on every male who participates in same-sex encounters to be regularly tested for HIV. The body and the sex it desires *will have transformed* into sites of toxicity. The present-day viewer of *Cruisin' the Castro* (1981) will have the knowledge of a historical catastrophe that renders the sexual subject altered because of how crisis fissured the presumed normative time of/for sex. This future anterior space of this viewership is one that is saturated with the ambiguity of how sex itself would be inherited as a result of the crisis.

Perhaps, in direct contradistinction, the late 1990s to the present day has seen a proliferation in the demand for what has come to be known as 'bareback' pornography. Queer theorist Tim Dean (2009) describes this proliferation as such:

> All ... changed in the late 1990s with the advent of drug therapies that sharply reduced AIDS-related mortalities in populations to which they're available. With the threat of

> death deferred, gay men's erotic practices changed again: now something called the bareback community – with its own Web sites, pornography, and subcultural codes – flourishes online and underground in the gay community. (p. 2)

Production houses such as Paul Morris's infamous Treasure Island Media (TIM) became prominent precisely because of their active withdrawal from condom use, deeming it a barrier to pleasure and intimacy. The condom has become perceived as preventing access to jouissance; seen otherwise, it might serve as a tool enacting the very self-dismissal spoken of by Bersani (2010). The condom, here, becomes understood as the object that occludes the sight of oneself *to oneself* as a subject and as a sexual subject; it is understood to cause the self to lose sight of its most intimate desires and of its own self.

The regard at the sexual subject's choice to refuse the condom, to live in immediate communion with the virus as part of sexual experience itself – Bersani's (2010) "risk of the sexual" (p. 30) – is perhaps best exemplified by the films that TIM produces. Take for instance, *Breeding Season* (2006), *Breeding Season 2* (2010) and *Breeding Season 3* (2015), a three-part series of films that explicitly articulates a desire for consanguinity with the AIDS virus. Scene after scene, the viewer finds a demand to look squarely at the very gesture of fluid transmission as signifying a desire to bind one sexual subject with another under the metonymic (what it signifies) and literal sign of the virus. Intimacy becomes experienced through condom-free sex. Furthermore, presumably redemptive language concerning life, procreation and continuation is used in connection to the practice of barebacking. The use of the term "breeding" in the films' titles creates the "analogy … of conceiving and bearing children" (Dean, 2009, p. 85) and appears to rewrite the script of linear time concerning reproductive sex by relinquishing sex from procreation and, by suggesting the breeding of the virus, allowing it to negotiate the very limits of life and death. Dean (2009) describes scenes as the ones in Morris's films as those in which "men who used to not worry about condoms because there was no danger of pregnancy in gay sex now represent their deliberate abandonment of condoms as an attempt to conceive" (Dean, 2009, p. 86). The camera explicitly focusses on the anus, on ejaculating into it, on pulling out right before ejaculation only to push the semen back in. That pleasure is derived from this signifies a shift in focus in the representational history of queer male sex and in how the experience of AIDS as a rupture has shifted. The rectum, previously imagined as a grave, under these new circumstances inspires Dean (2009) to ask quizzically, "is the rectum (now) a womb?" (p. 78).

What might be recognised in these two genres (pre-condom and bareback pornography) is a relationship between the viewer and the temporality of what he looks at to consider how it has evolved over that time. The viewer of either genre is confronted with an epistemic and ontological problem regarding the time of/for sex. In pre-condom pornography, he looks at what is playing out before him with an awareness of the crisis to come in the time after this production, while with contemporary bareback pornography, he now reorganises his very thoughts regarding AIDS, the history and memory of the crisis, viral life, and the very status of death as it relates to living in possible communion with the virus.

What we find, then, is a collusion of categories that implicitly mean destruction, as signified by AIDS as a crisis, with new ways of thinking about construction; what Benjamin referred to as a "construction that presupposes destruction" (Benjamin, 1999, p. 470) wherein life, eroticism, illness and death are seen anew, as perhaps new categories of alterity embodied in the figures of HIV-negative and HIV-positive persons. With the heightened desire for bareback pornography, what would it mean to think of seroconversion – the event of one's status changing from HIV-negative to positive – as a scene in which "destruction [becomes] ... the production of the construction of a new relation to the object" (Benjamin & Osborne, 1994, p. xi) – the "object" being the history of sex as it relates to the virus – "[or where] destruction [becomes] the condition of the possibility of experience" (Benjamin & Osborne, 1994, p. xi). It is this "experience" that the viewer's look at either of these genres of pornography, like the angel's look, might be responding to as a demand to never look away from that which unfolds before him as history. It is this "experience" of historical time as simultaneously being necessary while also impossible to contain that I examine in Vincent Chevalier's (2014) aesthetic work in the next section. Using this work, I explore the possibility for an aesthetic education mobilising bareback sex as a historical category to see if we might think in more creative ways about sex, time and historicity as experienced by the queer male sexual subject.

An aesthetic education in the time of barebacking
Connoisseurs familiar with contemporary bareback pornography will recognise the space that serves as the backdrop to Vincent Chevalier's *Breeden* (2014). Trained as a video artist and covering an extensive range of themes such as AIDS, memory, sex and queer nostalgia, *Breeden* serves as Chevalier's foray into the realm of documentary filmmaking and in particular to the genre of the staged documentary. The staging is purposeful, as purposeful perhaps as the genre of contemporary bareback pornography itself with its literal focus on the seemingly pure pleasures derived from the intensities of condomless sex. In a way, the staged documentary appears to be reminiscent of its literary counterpart, the genre of creative non-fiction, serving simultaneously as an attempt at creative storytelling and at

critically thinking of the document as one with an almost built-in expectation of being both archival and narrative.

Chevalier's project formulates a response to writer Tim Dean (2009) and Treasure Island Media (TIM) filmmaker Paul Morris (2006, 2010, 2015), particularly to the instance where the former describes the latter as "an amateur anthropologist ... [who] characterises his work as documentary porn ... and compares it to visual ethnography ... [aspiring] to represent a sexual community to and for itself, a community organised around specific erotic practices rather than around identity" (Dean, 2009, pp. 119–120). Morris takes this description further when, in an interview with Susanna Paasonen (2014) for the journal *GLQ*, he states the intentionality behind his work in more ideological terms:

> TIM is two things, basically. We're a developing and living archive of real male sexual experience. And we're a laboratory that performs experiments that the men involved in our community propose. You could say that we're a genetic laboratory exploring the vital sexual symbiosis of human and viral DNA. For the most part, gay porn pretends to represent experience without peril, experimentation without damage. Most gay porn hides behind a façade of "safeness." But in my case, the men in my work are considered and prized for being damaged, for having taken what conservative gays deem "the ultimate risk" and lost. In a world increasingly dominated by the medical gaze, to willingly live in symbiosis with a virus is seen as irrational and socially expensive. I see it as necessary and revolutionary. (Morris, as cited in Paasonen, 2014, p. 217)

Chevalier's concerns in *Breeden* (2014) are a departure, however, from producing either pornography or a straightforward archival documentary. What we notice are the tensions inherent when the two are brought together. These tensions force us to think categories like history, memory, politics, temporality and, even more specifically, sex as one such historical category mired by the event not just of sex itself which Morris privileges in his work but also the event and historicity of AIDS as a very specific rupture in the presumed linear order of the time of/for sex. Chevalier's *Breeden* (2014) troubles the living archive that Morris produces by situating sex beyond the frame of the work. His concern is not merely the realm of the sexual but the establishment of sexual subjects – both the performer and the viewer – as the ones that make the possibility of a historical archive plausible.

To consider is the point of view, quite literally understood, that forms the crux of Chevalier's (2014) attempt at locating an otherwise not-so-easily locatable figure in the history of sexuality, a history ruptured by the event of AIDS and by the more contemporary increased demand for bareback pornography. The "how" and "what" of our look, of our regard, of the point of view that Chevalier (2014) organises his video around becomes central to the analysis here.

As mentioned earlier, those familiar with bareback pornography will recognise the hotel room where Chevalier stages his project as the same backdrop for a scene produced by Morris for *Breeding Season 2* (2010). Using this room appears to be intentional on Chevalier's part. However, rather than staging a pornographic scene there, he sets the stage for staging itself. Chevalier makes his audience consider how they look at the visual nature of mediated history (of safe sex campaigns, of AIDS-related news), mediated sex (pornography), and mediated gestural spaces (of gay dating app culture, online hook-up sites, pornographic Tumblr sites). Point of view is central here – the project seems to be an exercise in thinking the very nature of the "regard", the look at history, and more specifically how a sexual archive, a repository of historical repertoires surrounding sex (particularly bareback) becomes observable. He does this by inviting a series of men to arrive at the room individually to perform in a scene in which each of them audition for the title role of a film, *Breeden*. Unlike the men in *Breeding Season 2* (2010) who go against the "façade of safeness" by participating in the "ultimate risk" (Morris, as cited in Paasonen & Morris, 2014, p. 217), the *Breeden* men perform what exceeds the archive by auditioning for a fictional film, exceeding the sex in the original.

The "regard" at the sexual archive is further complicated because *Breeden's* (2014) central figure is not any of the auditioning actors; rather, it is the cameraman who is present only as authorial and directorial voice, present as an absence in relation to the auditions happening before him. Not coincidentally, the cameraman, whose absent presence is felt throughout, is in real life named Elliot Breeden and served as the cameraman for Morris's (2010) own production.

What is Chevalier (2014) attempting to do with this complex layering process of differing temporalities, within this associative web binding this aesthetic "copy" to the pornographic "original"? What historical references become evoked and who is Chevalier's historical figure? Is it the porn star, the documentary pornographer, the auditioning actors for the fictional film *Breeden*, the cameraman who worked on both the original and the artwork, the artist himself, or the figure of the barebacker? Or, is it the room that acts, in both instances, as a metonymic conduit for the transgression of the time of/for sex and its history? If the rectum could be a grave, then the room could be an archive wherein "male homosexuality advertises risk of the sexual itself as the risk of self-dismissal, of losing sight of the self, and in so doing it proposes and dangerously represents jouissance as a mode of ascesis" (Bersani, 2010, p. 30). Chevalier (2014) underpins the risk of this capacity for self-dismissal by figuring his performers as central to the archival space itself, where thinking the virus and barebacking anew ruptures the linear time of/for sex.

Barebacking and Historical Time

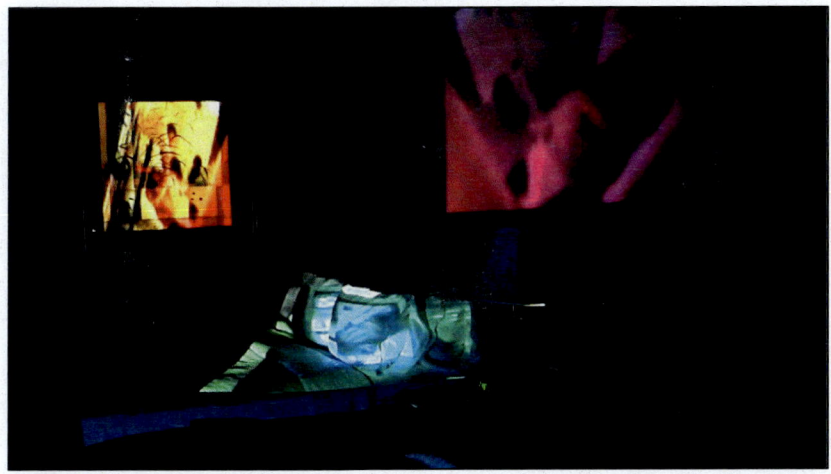

Figure 1: *Breeden* (2014). Still from video installation by Vincent Chevalier (image courtesy of the artist).

Referentiality becomes a significant marker in Chevalier's (2014) work. Immediately after the first 'actor' introduces himself and states why he is there, we are offered a collage, a visual mash-up of pornographic images, vintage news reel footage, and textures of light and dark that give the video a quality resembling the light and dark play so reminiscent of the sexually charged site of a gay club scene (Figure 1). Furthermore, we become aware of the room's location in Morris's own work through an affirmation of this relation as we notice carefully the scene each of the three actors are asked to watch – scenes from Morris's *Breeding Season 2* (2010) on the screen of the laptop they are provided with, perhaps as a way to get them in the mood to perform (Figure 2).

We are not sure what kind of film *Breeden* (2014) is – it could be narrative fiction, pornography, or a documentary about sex work and sexuality, or all at once. The move to leave the subject matter of *Breeden* (2014) elusive appears purposeful because it

Figure 2: *Breeden* (2014). Still from video installation by Vincent Chevalier (image courtesy of the artist).

is not so much a question regarding what it is that we are watching rather than how it is that we watch the space of the scene unfolding before us. A consideration about mediation is essential here. Unlike Morris's original *Breeding Season 2* (2010), a visual representation of sex, Chevalier's (2014) appropriation attends to other matters. Specific body parts as part-objects become significant as the very objects of the regard we offer the visual work. In Morris's (2010) film, whole bodies are caught in the midst of throbbing, heaving sex. Chevalier (2014), instead, hones in on the part-bodies of his actors – a tattooed thigh, a crotch, a pair of hands, a face or a pair of eyes (Figure 3, overleaf).

The video's potential is not in the sex act that is relegated to an elsewhere beyond the frame, inside that other frame where the actors watch Morris's (2010) scene on their laptops. The part-body is given an a priori attention of the look offered to it, wherein this part-object becomes the focal point on which history itself becomes partially inscribed; it exceeds representation

Barebacking and Historical Time

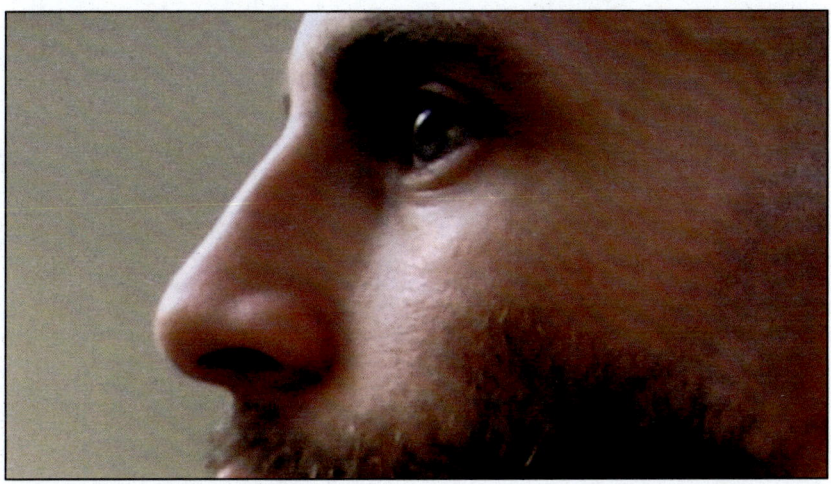

Figure 3: *Breeden* (2014). Still from video installation by Vincent Chevalier (image courtesy of the artist).

precisely because it is represented as a part-object whose placement in the video cuts across any presumption of a linear narrative that the work itself might otherwise showcase. While the room acts as the backdrop for both Morris's (2010) barebacking scene and Chevalier's (2014) video, the larger backdrop of the history of sexuality can only be measured vis-à-vis the stagnant body parts that form the narrative's rupture. The audience bears witness to the part-body as metonymically placed up against a larger history of sexuality that exists beyond the video's frame. The script for sex as a historical category traumatised by AIDS finds this rupture outside the frame. Anything within it can only be experienced from a specific point of view, as suggested by Chevalier's (2014) work – that of the cameraman, the audience, Benjamin's angel – as part-object, or part of the larger narrative of sex, wherein both barebacking as a gesture and AIDS are also mere part-objects rupturing any linear sense of historicity.

Pornographies

In our understanding of post-AIDS sex, utopia might not be possible, despite Morris's (2010) desire for one, but it behoves us to consider how sexual practice both exceeds and delimits it. The sense of such a utopia exists as both a contingency to its own relationship to the past, present, and the future and also exceeds this contingency. It is this excess that Chevalier (2014) attempts to localise. In creating an original artwork vis-à-vis an appropriated text, Chevalier (2014) unravels the aesthetic and pedagogical possibilities of pornography. Chevalier's work serves, in tandem, to reconcile and acknowledge the difficulties of representing and historicising condomless sex after AIDS, since such sex exists as a site of/for pleasure and simultaneously a site of/for both the self-becoming and the self-dissolution of queer men. The film's fragmented, intertextual narrative (the use of collage, the focus on bodily parts, the emphasis on points of view, on scopic fidelity and on referentiality) bespeaks the temporal rupture, both its capacity to, at once, disrupt and make possible an understanding of queer sex and culture in the aftermath of the AIDS crisis. Here, we recognise both the importance of, and limits to, thinking pornography as a sexual archive. Put differently, it becomes a matter of how we regard this expansive archive and its ever-changing repertoire of meanings and practices, attending to what it can and cannot contain or, rather, to what exceeds the very time of/for sex.

References
Benjamin, A., & Osborne, P. (Eds.) (1994). *Walter Benjamin's philosophy: Destruction and experience*. London, United Kingdom: Routledge.
Benjamin, W. (1968). Theses on the philosophy of history. In H. Arendt (Ed.), *Illuminations* (pp. 253–264). New York, NY: Schocken Books.
Benjamin, W. (1999). *The arcades project*. Cambridge, MA: Belknap Press of Harvard University.

Bersani, L. (2010). *Is the rectum a grave? And other essays*. Chicago, IL: University of Chicago Press.

Comay, R. (2011). *Mourning sickness: Hegel and the French Revolution*. Stanford, CA: Stanford University Press.

Chevalier, V. (2014). *Breeden* [Video file]. Retrieved from http://vincentchevalier.ca/index.php?/works/breeden/

Dean, T. (2009). *Unlimited intimacies: Reflections on the subculture of barebacking*. Chicago, IL: University of Chicago Press.

Freud, S. (2003). *The uncanny* (D. McLintock, Trans.). London, United Kingdom: Penguin Books (Original work published in 1919).

Morris, P. (Producer), & Morris. P. (Director). (2006). *Breeding season* [Video file]. Retrieved from http://www.treasureislandmedia.com/cart/BREEDING-SEASON.html

Morris, P. (Producer), & Morris. P. (Director). (2010). *Breeding season 2* [Video file]. Retrieved from http://www. treasureislandmedia.com/cart/BREEDING-SEASON-2.html

Morris, P. (Producer), & Morris. P. (Director). (2015). *Breeding season 3* [Video file]. Retrieved from http://www. treasureislandmedia.com/cart/BREEDING-SEASON-3.html

Newman, M. (Director). (1981). *Cruisin' the Castro* [DVD]. Chicago, IL: Bijou Classics.

Paasonen, S., & Morris, P. (2014). Risk and utopia: A dialogue on pornography. *GLQ: A Journal of Lesbian and Gay Studies, 20*(3), 215–239.

CHAPTER ELEVEN

PRICKED, PROBED AND POSSESSED: MEDICAL PORNOGRAPHY AND THE BIRTH OF THE FETISH CLINIC

Brenda S. Gardenour Walter

The Internet is a hyper-connected medium through which like-minded individuals from around the world might find each other and build virtual communities. One of the largest online collectives is the global pornography community, which includes those who create, distribute and consume pornographic literary and visual media (Patterson, 2004). On the surface, it would seem that engaging with online pornography would be a solitary endeavour cloaked in anonymity and secrecy. With the advent of sites such as RedTube, GayTube, Pornhub and YuVuTu, however, content creators and consumers actively and openly participate in the shaping of an online subculture. Like YouTube, upon which these sites are structured, individuals upload professional or amateur clips to their accounts, and these are shared with the community who then categorise, tag, rate and comment upon them. The participatory model of these online porn hubs has facilitated the development of a porn community that is engaged in creating its own internal modalities (Mowlabocus, 2009). Because of pornography's inherently transgressive nature, the internally set boundaries established by the porn community are of necessity in a perpetual state of flux. According to Laura Kipnis, "pornography begins at the edge of a culture's decorum", probing its most sensitive areas (2006). The transnationality of online porn communities means that a multitude of boundaries across myriad cultural layers are being pricked and penetrated through seemingly endless sexual permutations.

Against the backdrop of these variations, one narrative emerges with striking consistency and clarity – the narrative of medical pornography. As a category, medical pornography is multivalent and continually changing based on the desires of the porn community. While it has not been fully codified, online medical pornography is marked by several salient characteristics, including the power of the medical practitioner over the disempowered patient, the use of medical practices and equipment for sexual pleasure, and the use of a clinical setting to heighten anxiety and sexual anticipation. One sub-genre of online medical pornography, medical BDSM, leverages the power of the clinical environment as a sexual performative space. In what the porn community has named a "fetish clinic", doctors and nurses perform invasive and often humiliating therapies on patients who seek pleasure and pain in a highly medicalised context. While many BDSM medical fetishists are content using the Internet for virtual sexual healthcare, still others seek a physical clinical experience with a flesh-and-blood medical fetish practitioner. Several brick-and-mortar fetish clinics, including the Manchester Fetish Clinic (manchester medicalfetish.com), cater to individuals seeking medicalised sexual services such as anal gynaecology, urethral sounding, enemas, anaesthesia, intubation, sutures, and dentistry.

In both online medical pornography and the real-world medical sex industry that is shaped by it, the BDSM fetish clinic reflects the processes of medicalisation, "by which nonmedical problems become defined and treated as medical problems" (Conrad, 1992, p. 209). In this "medicalization of everyday life", individuals transfer personal responsibility for their own well-being to medical authorities, thereby adopting a submissive role, a dynamic that speaks to BDSM desires (Szasz, 2008). The medicalisation of sexual desire has in recent years been mediated by the Internet, which has become a "medium for self-help" (in this case sexual) with the power to "reorder relationships between healthcare practitioner and patient" (Webster & Brown, 2004, p. 1). Andrew Webster and Nik Brown (2004) argue that the modern patient not only has access to healthcare advice via the Internet but also exists as a medical file *within* the Internet. This high tech and disembodied approach to healthcare is efficient and profitable for the medical industry; patients not only "seek out the latest medical devices and techniques tailored to their individual needs", but also pay a premium for "high touch" in addition to high-tech care (Webster & Brown, 2004, p. 13). For the fetishist as patient, this means using the Internet to learn about cutting edge medical BDSM techniques and – for those who can afford it – to find the most advanced brick-and-mortar medical fetish clinic with the newest therapies and the best skilled practitioners to cure their medicalised sexual desire.

The kinky medical practices performed at the BDSM fetish clinic not only speak to the medicalisation of sexual pleasure but also highlight the reductive and mechanistic nature of Western biomedicine and the inequities of the physician-patient relationship, which is revealed to be one of patriarchal domination and female-coded submission. While virtual and physical fetish clinics and their pornographic narratives offer meaningful critiques of Westernised medical practice, they also offer correctives. At the fetish clinic, for example, the BDSM doctor or nurse considers not only the physical requirements of their patients, but also their emotional needs; likewise, courses of therapy are driven primarily by the patient in consultation with the fetish practitioner as expert, a true expression of patient-centred care. Perhaps most importantly, "consent and mutual respect are fundamental principles" of BDSM and are core values in the fetish clinic; unlike in the Western biomedical model, in which the patient has little voice or authority, "the consensual and egalitarian underpinnings of BDSM encounters are always present, even if they are obscure to onlookers" (Purcell, 2012, p. 196).

Online medical pornography
Medical pornography takes many forms, ranging from the relatively tame to extreme kink. The former category might include neo-Victorian gyno-pornography, a form of erotic literature in which desperate women appeal to authoritative but naive male physicians for relief from "hysteria"– the cure for which was hysterical paroxysm, or orgasm (Maines, 2001). At the other end of the spectrum are medical BDSM fetish videos featuring kinky physicians and nurses who perform invasive and humiliating procedures on restrained and powerless patients. Medical implements such as sutures, syringes, retractors, catheters, speculums and stirrups are put into service as weapon-tools for the production of pleasure and pain in a simulated clinical environment. Between these artificial extremes lie countless erotic stories and videos, professional and amateur, which feature medical personnel performing intimate acts on subjected patients in sexualised medical settings. Male physicians and nurses penetrate their female and male patients' burle, probing their secret areas and revealing what they discover there. Female physicians and nurses do the same, often using their phallic speculums as a means of asserting authority and dominance over their subordinate charges. From Japanese medical massage to Ukrainian gyno-pornography, and from Latin American naughty nurses to British and German sex hospitals, transnational online medical pornography at first appears incredibly diverse. A survey across this pornographic sub-genre, however, reveals that they share a salient feature – the role of the physician and patient, as well as the clinic in which their performance takes place, are all rooted in the Western

biomedical model. In medical pornography, it is not the local healer, the shaman or *curandera*, but the white-coated, latex-gloved and male-coded Western-style physician who dominates his patients, prescribes questionable therapies and provides pleasure through humiliation and pain (Kapsalis, 1997, p. 23).

The pervasiveness of white-coated medical authority in online pornography speaks to transnational concerns with the invasive hegemony of the Western biomedical model and its power over bodies and, by extension, cultural identities. In *Birth of the Clinic,* Michel Foucault (1994) argues that since the eighteenth century Westerners have willingly submitted autonomy over their bodies to the institutionalised and unquestionable medical authority of the learned physician. According to Foucault (1994), the power of the physician is rooted in his ability to see into the body's hidden places. That which is visible can be defined, quantified and controlled; through the medical gaze, visibility becomes equated with power. The physician penetrates the patient's body, exposing his or her most vulnerable parts for examination, and comes to possess the secrets found in those dark recesses. Despite the intimacy of the medical gaze and the invasive procedures that facilitate it, the physician is expected to remain emotionally distant from the subjectified body prone on the table. This clinical distance is particularly critical when patients present with issues that demand the narration of their past and present sexual history and the simultaneous examination of their genitalia. While the patient devolves his or her sexual experiences, the physician must not become aroused; likewise, the close examination of patient's organs of sexual pleasure must elicit no response on the part of the practitioner. In his *History of Sexuality,* Foucault (1985) argues that this (con)strained behaviour is an expression of Western *scientia sexualis,* a clinical approach to sexuality that is concerned with the moral rectitude and physical mechanics of intercourse and not its potential for pleasure. Sexual pleasure is unprofessional; controlling pleasure through denial, however, is the hallmark of Western medical professionalism.

The authoritarian construction of the Western physician makes him or her the ideal character for kinky online pornographic narratives. Likewise, the prone and submissive patient who must expose his or her darkest secrets and most private parts makes for the BDSM physician's perfect counterpart. In clinical practice, the patient is expected to obey "doctor's orders" (Veatch, 2008, p. 65). Patients are told to strip, lie down, put their feet in stirrups, spread their legs and hold still. They are pricked with needles, probed with gloved fingers, penetrated with speculums, and possessed fully by the physician who enters their hidden recesses in search of abnormalities. Naked and prone, the completely disempowered patient is subject to the authority of the fully clothed physician hovering over his or her body. Despite this humiliating dynamic, the patient must not exhibit any emotional responses – especially during medical procedures that have the potential for sexual pain, pleasure, or both. In online medical pornography involving BDSM, this patient experience of powerlessness at the hands of the all-powerful physician is magnified to an extreme. In these narratives, the physician's role is that of the master or dominatrix who forcibly strips, restrains and humiliates the subjectified patient who must submit completely to his or her authority. Whipped, clamped, sodomised and hooked to dubious machinery, the BDSM patient's body is no longer his or her own, but the property of the menacing physician who – like a colonial power on foreign soil – rules it with an iron fist, at one moment doling out punishment, the next soothing with praise and petty rewards (Bala, 2014). The patient's body likewise becomes a spectacle for the viewer-voyeur, hidden behind the camera's lens, who through the very act of seeing its deleterious suffering gains power over it and comes to possess it (Bonner, 2005), a process akin to psychoanalytic film theories such as scopophilia and the male gaze (Mulvey, 1989). In bearing witness to this bodily abjection, the viewer simultaneously identifies with the physician-tormenter and the patient-victim, the penetrator and the penetrated, in a medical theatre of pain, much like the semiotic relationship between the viewer, slasher and last-girl in horror films (Clover, 1993).

Medical pornography does not exist in a vacuum, nor does it constitute a form of "lowbrow" culture separate from a monolithic "mainstream" culture (Hall, 2009); instead, it is an integral part of the Western biomedical model, an expression of the medicalisation of everyday life, rife with hegemonic modalities and algorithmic constraints. Because it is continually engaged in a reciprocal dialogue with the biomedical culture from which it emerges, online medical pornography reflects much broader perceptions and concerns over medical practice and the patient experience. The cultural concerns about Western medicine raised in medical pornography are made manifest in the performance of BDSM medical fetishism, which exists not only in virtual venues such as online literotica and videos but also at physical BDSM conventions, clubs and other private gatherings. As such, medical fetish BDSM is a form of what Henry Jenkins calls "transmedia storytelling", in which narratives and characters are acted out in virtual and non-virtual environments that constitute a living community with its own ways of being and knowing (2003). Margot Weiss argues that the performative transmedia culture of BDSM, in which individuals engage in physical role playing, is not a fantasy realm or a distant "safe place" unaffected by lived reality, but is instead an integrated and dynamic ethos whose rules and characters are shaped by broader social and cultural forces (2011). Nowhere is this more evident than in virtual and brick-and-mortar BDSM medical fetish clinics that cater to patient populations seeking invasive, painful and humiliating medical treatments for sexual fulfilment. As a dark mirror of medical practice, fetish clinics make manifest all of the fears and desires that are otherwise sublimated in the physician-patient relationship and hidden beneath a mask of professionalism. A discursive analysis of virtual and physical fetish clinics reveals several salient critiques of modern medical practice – the horrors of the regimented clinical environment, the patriarchal and hegemonic role of the physician, and the female-coded disempowerment of patients – and offers correctives to them beyond the performance of BDSM.

At the fetish clinic

Finding a medical fetish clinic is much like shopping for any other healthcare provider. An online search yields a number of options for care, including virtual clinics such as Anna Rose's fetishclinic.com that offer medical fetish clips and photographs, and physical clinics that either send nurses and physicians on home visits (manchestermedicalfetish.com) or offer appointments at a brick-and-mortar site (fetishclinic.net). There are also community message boards such as fetishclinic-community.com that serve as referral sites for those who are looking for medical fetish practitioners and clinics, as well as those who want to discuss and rate their experiences with different providers. Like other medical institutions, fetish clinics market themselves according to their target demographics and their areas of specialisation. Both the clinic run by Lady Annisa, "Medical Mistress and Fetish Practitioner" in Scotland (fetish-clinic-scotland.co.uk) and the Manchester Fetish Clinic in England (manchestermedicalfetish.com) feature latex-clad practitioners and patients on their front pages, thereby emphasising the BDSM-kink elements of their "medical" practices. However, many other clinics, such as those in Holland (fetishclinic.net), Germany (fetish-clinic.net) and the Anna List Medical clinic in Britain (medicalmistress.co.uk), feature Western physicians clad in white coats or surgical green scrubs holding charts, examining x-rays or attentively bending over patients, thereby emphasising the "true to life" medical elements of care offered within their doors. Behind their front pages, fetish clinics offer a range of services, including but not limited to dentistry, anaesthesiology, proctology, urology and gynaecology. Some clinics, such as enemaclinic.co.uk, are hyper-specialised and offer only one type of procedure. Once individuals have found a clinic of their choice, they are required to make an appointment and wait to be seen, just like a patient at any other doctor's office.

Whether in virtual or physical establishments, the rigid procedural and structural architectures of the medical fetish clinic are critical to the experience of the patient. Like the medical facilities on which they are based, fetish clinics are realms of absolute order, regimented behaviours, and precise/excessive detail. Upon arrival, the patient is made to wait in a reception area where they must fill out paperwork including payment plans; it is perhaps worth noting that the fees at fetish clinics are comparable to those one might find at non-subsidised medical clinics, on average about 300 USD an hour. Patients are also required to sign consent forms, a particularly important component of BDSM culture (Bauer, 2008). Lady Annisa, for example, explains that she practises Risk Aware Consensual Kink (RACK) to minimise the dangers of medical BDSM, adding that she "will always explain any procedure … and the risks involved, any preparation required, as well as follow up care to be taken" (fetish-clinic-scotland.co.uk/about-medical-mistress). Once patients finish with their intake paperwork, they consult with the fetish practitioner, report any symptoms, physical or emotional, request treatment, and are admitted to an appropriate treatment room.

This mechanical intake process, familiar to anyone who has experienced Westernised medical care, is reflected in the mechanised and sterile environment of the clinic itself. The treatment rooms at the medical fetish clinic are usually whitewashed with immaculate floors, gleaming stainless steel surfaces, and humming fluorescent lights. At the centre of this hyper-sterile environment is the dental chair or treatment bed, often with stirrups, surrounded by a variety of medical devices including stomach pumps, breathing masks, intravenous bags and poles, electro-shock and electrocardiogram machines, as well as trays of probes, speculums, dental drills, picks, syringes and needles. At first glance, medical fetish treatment rooms appear no different than those found at hospitals and doctors' offices across the Western world; depressingly enough, they are better stocked than many healthcare clinics in rural and developing areas around the globe (Annis, 1981). A closer inspection of the medical environment at the fetish clinic, however, reveals interesting anomalies: interspersed with standard medical equipment are a wide selection of enemas, multiple harnesses, restraints, and mechanised devices for penetration. Also present are an array of stretchy bags, hoods, and suits for "gummi klinik" play, a form of medical BDSM that centres on the fetishistic appeal of rubber and latex, both of which have not only interesting smells and textures associated with clinical care, but also the power to restrain and punish quite effectively. The subtle placement of devices designed for BDSM sex play among very real clinical equipment speaks not only to the intimate nature of any medical treatment but also to the potential pleasure of that treatment on the part of both the patient and the practitioner, both within and beyond the walls of institutionalised medical care. For example, at both the medical fetish clinic and in films such as David Cronenberg's *Dead Ringers* (1988), the dildo and the forceps that share space on the medical tray serve as a reminder that to penetrate and be penetrated are sexual experiences and acts of desire – even in the course of therapy. As Rafael Campo writes in his memoir, *The Desire to Heal: A Doctor's Education in Empathy, Identity, and Desire*, there comes a point where a proctology patient might realise that "every lurking suspicion could be true ... The bespectacled, nerdy older man sticking his colonoscope up your ass actually *likes* it; worse yet, so might you" (1997, p. 27).

The overarching procedural and structural architecture of learned medicine as performed at the fetish clinic highlight not only the hypocrisy of concepts such as clinical detachment and *scientia sexualis*, but also the algorithmic and mechanised patient experience of Western medical care. Upon entering the clinic, the patient steps into a machine though which they progress systematically according to standardised steps. Information is extracted, histories are taken, the body is stripped, probed, hooked up to machines, and made to respond; throughout, the mechanical patient body is but one more cog in a larger machine, a product on an assembly line geared towards total submission and compliance. At the fetish clinic, this experience is guided by the patient's desire; the same cannot be said of modern medical practice.

The doctor will see you now
Medical fetish clinics offer a critique not only of Western medical structures broadly construed, but also of the practitioners who operate within them. In keeping with the medical clinics that they emulate, fetish clinics are staffed by individuals playing the roles of nurses, nurse practitioners, physician assistants and doctors, as well as specialists such as anaesthetists and dentists. Some individuals like Nurse Annisa

in Scotland and Anna List in Britain work alone in private practice, while others such as the Dutch doctors at fetishclinic.net, prefer to work as partners in a fetish-care team. Like licensed medical practitioners, clinical fetishists offer a broad range of patient experiences, from kind and compassionate to cruel and vicious. For example, Anna List changes her approach to "patient care" based on the needs and desires of her client. In some images, she wears traditional scrubs and strokes the hair of her supine patient; in others, she wears a black latex nurse uniform and glares menacingly as she applies a gas mask to her victim. This vacillation between compassionate care provider and all-powerful tormenter is an integral part of the BDSM fetish clinic experience. The person performing the authoritative "physician" role is at one minute reassuring, the next doling out painful "therapies", all of which are purportedly for the benefit of the patient who, bound and gagged, is helpless to resist.

Clinical detachment and patient submission are taken to extremes in one sub-set of clinical practices within medical fetish culture called "gummi klinik", in which patients are bound in latex bags, suits, masks, breathing restrictors and restraints while attended to by nurses and physicians completely clad in rubber. Rubber scrubs, face masks, gas masks and hoods hide the identity of the practitioner and obscure all human emotion and intent, while rubber gloves remove the possibility of warm human touch. For patients at the gummi klinik, the gummi doktor or nurse serves as a nameless, faceless, voiceless authority who performs torturous therapies upon them without warning, explanation or consent. And while this sense of powerlessness heightens the sexual experience of the submissive BDSM medical fetishist, it has a very different effect on the sick and suffering real-world patient who experiences the clinical distance, rubber-gloved palpations, mechanical interventions and hostile bedside practices of licensed medical practitioners as degrading and horrifying.

The roles played by fetish clinic practitioners highlight general concerns with the perceived aloofness and hostility of an elite medical profession. Similarly, the gendered performances of fetish practitioners reveal gender biases that persist in medical practice, particularly in the most exclusive and lucrative medical fields, including surgery, which is still dominated by men. The Dutch fetish clinic at fetish-clinic.net features a medical team comprised of a man, Dr Utah, and two women, Dr Kaat and Dr Jill. Their "Meet the Team" page features biographies for each practitioner. Dr Utah's biography states that he "holds a master degree, speaks four languages, and has a keen interest in the more technical aspects of the procedures that are carried out in the clinic". The prospective patient, now assured of Dr Utah's qualifications, then learns that he is a compassionate care provider. As a specialist in surgery, he reassures his clients that while he "does not hesitate to carry out painful treatments" when necessary, he is most definitely "not a sadist". Furthermore, Dr Utah "has experiences as a practitioner as well as a patient, which allows him to fully understand the emotions and sensations that patients might undergo during a treatment at the clinic". Well qualified, authoritative and understanding, Dr Utah is the paradigmatic medical man, the lead physician-cum-surgeon on the team. Beneath him are the women, Dr Kaat, a "tall long blonde who is spontaneous and caring" and the "redheaded" and "enthusiastic" Dr Jill, whose biographies begin not with their qualifications, but their physical descriptions. While Dr Kaat has professional experience in veterinary care, Dr Jill merely grew up in a family of doctors; emulating them, she got into "her mum's sewing box" and practised on "a handful of ignorant nephews", and now she gets to pretend to be surgeon through role playing.

Pricked, Probed and Possessed

The structure and presentation of this Dutch medical fetish team, while played for fun, reflects very real issues in the medical world. While women are entering the medical profession in increasing numbers, they often enter family practice or specialise in paediatrics, obstetrics or gynaecology, all of which are associated with domestic life and motherhood and therefore coded female. The dramatic increase in female medical practitioners does not translate to elite fields such as surgery, an area still dominated by men in the United States and the United Kingdom (Carvajal, 2011). According to the most recent report from the American College of Surgeons Health Policy Research Institute (2009), only 21.3% of surgical specialists are women, with the highest concentration of female surgeons (47%) specialising in obstetrics and gynaecology, fields long considered 'proper' to female practice. The misogynistic narrative that women are particularly unqualified to practice certain types of medicine is magnified at fetish clinics featuring female nurses, many of whom perform invasive procedures of a surgical nature. The paucity of male practitioners at these establishments is so pronounced that one commenter on a kink community message board asks if there are any fetish clinics that *don't* have female nurses: "Not that there's anything wrong with nurses, you all do a great job, but as a gay guy, I'm just not attracted to the ministrations of a female nurse. Or as an aside, are there any clinics with male nurses?" (kinkyfun81). The Manchester Fetish Clinic, for example, features a staff of nurses – Matron Buffy Brown, Nurse Sapphire, Nurse Sheba and Nurse Sarah Kane – three of whom identify as female and one who identifies as female-trans. On the clinic's "Meet the Nurses" page, the women describe themselves as "caring", "overtly nurturing", "alluring", and "seductive"; future patients are warned, however, not to "be fooled", since "once strapped down, Matron reveals her tools" and Nurse Sheba is "more than happy to push your limits". The nurses are shown in a variety of outfits, ranging from surgical scrubs to full-latex bondage suits, and performing procedures such as scrotal inflation, catheterisation, penile sounding, anaesthesia, invasive dental work, needle play and scalpel play. Many of these procedures are extreme and could be considered surgical; all of them are performed by proudly untrustworthy and unqualified female "nurses". On the website for her fetish clinic, Anna List states that "despite never having completed, or indeed even applied for, a recognised medical qualification" she is still practising "on willing patients and undertaking experimental research".

While fetish nurses are predominantly female, they practise their unorthodox nurturing on a clientele that is for the most part male. This gender dynamic intensifies the kinky potential of the practitioner-patient relationship, in part because it is an inversion of the socially constructed role of the physician-surgeon as dominant, authoritative and coded male, and the patient as submissive, compliant and coded female (Kapsalis, 1997; Lindemann, 2012). Surgeons hold the highest place in the medical hierarchy because they are licensed to slice into the human body, to look into its hidden places, to re-order its parts, and to restore it to proper working order. At no point is the patient more submissive and vulnerable than when asleep beneath the surgeon's all-powerful phallic blade. At the Manchester Fetish Clinic, male patients adopt the female-coded patient role. In many cases, male patients are treated on a gynaecological examination table, their legs strapped into stirrups and forcibly splayed. In this powerless position, they submit completely to female nurses who appear to be motherly but in reality have usurped the patriarchal authority of physicians and who penetrate their victims, pricking them with needles, probing their orifices with speculums and puncturing them with scalpels. As in "torture porn" horror films such as

American Mary (2012), the seductive-yet-dangerous medical fetish nurse highlights cultural fears of female empowerment and the submission of the "rational" adult male body to "irrational" female authority (Sipos, 2010, 45–46; Jones, 2013). In the case of medical fetishism, these fears bring with them a delightful thrill; in the broader medical milieu, however, these fears reflect an unhealthy concentration of power in the hands of male practitioners and the persistent patriarchal constructs that continue to inform the medical profession.

The kinky sick role
In virtual and physical venues, medical fetish clinics offer the ultimate patient experience for the BDSM submissive; humiliated, bound to a table, pumped full of fluids, penetrated with scalpels and needles, the patient submits fully and unquestioningly to the authority of his or her medical provider. Retractors and speculums are forced into patients' bodies, prying into their darkest places and holding them open, making of them a spectacle of submission and possession. Many of the treatments at fetish clinics are not only humiliating, but also place the patient's life in the hands of the practitioner, who regulates vital functions such as the expulsion of waste and breathing; this risk brings with it a form of intimacy (Newmahr, 2011). In submitting to treatment, patients at the fetish clinic place their unquestioning trust in the surgeon, doctor or nurse who will see into their darkest physical and mental recesses, learn their secret fantasies, witness their basest physical functions, and provide pleasure and pain beyond measure. That members of this community have chosen the Western medical clinic as a venue for the performance of BDSM and the sick role as the locus for submission, domination, suffering and delight speaks to broader cultural perceptions of the patient experience in actual medical clinics charged with providing care to the general population both locally and globally. As

performed at medical fetish clinics, elements of the kinky sick role suggest that the experience of the Western biomedical patient is not one of compassionate care, but of objectification, subjection and utter vulnerability.

In both medical kink and medical practice, the patient is treated as an object, a mechanical entity that must be probed, hooked up to machines, and repeatedly tested in order to detect malfunction (Borst, 2015). The human body is seen merely as a mechanism, a physical structure from which the soul, mind and/or Cartesian "thinking stuff" has been separated (Alanen, 2003). As such, the patient is expected to endure painful procedures, invasive testing and intimate examinations without expressing any emotion, be it horror or delight. Just as the physician is meant to be clinically detached from the patient's human experience, so too must the patient's inner being become detached from and sub-alternated to his or her physical husk. Both kinky and mainstream medicine depict the patient not only as a clinical object, but also as a powerless and female-coded subject who – laid bare beneath the physicians' medical gaze – must comply with the male-coded doctor's orders, no matter how humiliating, painful or dubious the therapy. At the fetish clinic, the patient is forced into a position of absolute compliance and utter vulnerability as part of a shared BDSM performance. In medical practice, however, powerless patients are often voiceless and vulnerable, thrown into a system dominated by medical professionals about whose true qualifications and intentions they know very little, but in whose beneficence they must place their trust.

Beneficence, one of the cherished notions of biomedical ethics, is not always practised on the part of learned physicians. The history of American medicine is replete with examples of physicians who wielded power over vulnerable populations for their own personal gain. Dr J. Marion Sims, long hailed as the "father of gynecology", used enslaved African-American women and institutionalised Irish-American women as subjects in experimental surgeries that led to the development of the duck bill speculum. Voiceless and powerless, these women had no choice but to submit to Sims's authority and suffer through his torturous experimental therapies that were ultimately designed to glorify him as a physician rather than cure their vaginal fistulae (Sartin, 2004). Dr Walter Freeman practised pre-frontal lobotomies on asylum inmates who could not advocate for themselves or effectively refuse treatment (El Hai, 2007). Doctors at the Tuskegee Institute knowingly infected African-American subjects with syphilis without full disclosure or patient consent (Brandt, 1978). Non-consensual medical experimentation continues through illicit clinical trials sponsored by Western-based pharmaceutical companies in places like India and Africa (Terwindt, 2014; Kelly, 2013). While the purported goal of such trials is to improve population health, they actually treat indigenous populations as nameless experimental subjects, objects to be manipulated for the benefit of a greedy and domineering other.

Through medical colonialism, the borders and bodies of non-Western entities continue to be penetrated, laid bare and commodified to the benefit of the West. This, too, is reflected in medical fetish pornography. One popular sub-genre of fetish clinic porn features Westernised male physicians treating virginal Japanese women in a modern clinical setting. Throughout the course of treatment, she is pricked, probed and possessed by the physician who often forces her to masturbate to orgasm as she cries; in some cases, he then rapes her, stealing her virginity while she whimpers silently or stares blankly at the wall. These narratives speak not only to the invasive and potentially rapacious nature of Western medical authority, but also to the construction of the non-Western body as a submissive object for pornographic pleasure (Capino, 2006).

Discharge: a case for patient autonomy

Virtual and physical BDSM medical fetish clinics illuminate the ways in which Western biomedical culture has pervaded everyday life and medicalised sexual desires and practices. Likewise, medical BDSM both reveals and critiques the deep structures that undergird Western biomedical culture. Through these kinky lenses, the medical clinic is shown to be a cold and disorienting environment that is filled with invasive mechanical devices. It is likewise mechanistic in its physical structure and algorithmic procedures, which move patients from room to room, processing them like products, and ultimately spitting them back out the front door. The lens of medical kink likewise reveals the Western physician as a patriarchal authority who maintains clinical distance and expects complete compliance from his or her subjectified and objectified patients, no matter how painful or intimate the prescribed therapy. Along with these critiques of Western medicine, medical pornography offers correctives. The kinky practitioner-patient relationship depicted in virtual and physical fetish clinics can be considered to be healthier and more balanced than those at many medical clinics. In the performance of medical BDSM, the dominant fetish practitioner and the submissive patient are engaged in a process of continual negotiation, one in which power moves along a gradient between them (Lindemann, 2012). In these relationships, therapy is guided by the needs and desires of the patient, who takes the lead in determining his or her own treatment. Treatment focusses not only on the physical needs of the patient but also on their desires and emotions, thereby treating and respecting the "whole person", a concept so often mobilised in cultural competence and empathy courses at medical schools.

The fetish-care provider not only plans future therapy in consultation with the patient, but makes full disclosure of the risks associated with chosen therapies. At the fetish clinic, human experimentation is performed with the complete consent of the patient before it begins. Clear lines of communication and the boundaries of the provider-patient relationship are established at the outset to prevent malpractice. Interactions at the fetish clinic, as in BDSM culture more broadly construed, are based on "negotiating consensuality, communicating, respecting"– all of which should be the hallmarks of medical practice and patient-centred care, but are in reality often lacking (Bauer, 2008, p. 233). Medical BDSM is born of institutionalised Western medical culture and emerges from within its closely circumscribed and self-important boundaries. As such, medical BDSM might serve as a mirror in which learned medicine might see itself reflected not as it wants to be seen, but through the eyes of its patient populations. There is much to be learned from the (kinky) patient's voice.

References

Alanen, L. (2003). *Descartes's concept of mind.* Cambridge, MA: Harvard University Press.

American College of Surgeons Health Policy Research Institute. (2009). The surgical workforce in the United States: Profile and recent trends. Retrieved from http://www.acshpri.org/documents/ ACSHPRI_Surgical_Workforce_in_US_apr2010.pdf

Annis, S. (1981). Physical access and utilization of health services in rural Guatemala. *Social Science and Medicine, 15*(4), 515–523.

Bala, P. (2014). *Medicine and colonialism: Historical perspectives in India and South Africa.* London, United Kingdom: Pickering and Chatto.

Bauer, R. (2008). Transgressive and transformative gendered sexual practices and white privileges: The case of the dyke / trans bdsm communities. *Women's Studies Quarterly, 26*(3), 233–253.

Bonner, F. (2005). Looking inside: Showing medical operations on ordinary television. In G. King (Ed.), *The spectacle of the real: From Hollywood to reality TV and beyond* (pp. 105–116). London, United Kingdom: Intellect Books.

Borst, C. G. (2015). From bedside to bench: The historical development of the doctor-patient relationship. In J. M. Claire & R. M. Allman, (Eds.), *Sociomedical perspectives on patient care* (pp. 60–81). Lexington, KY: University Press of Kentucky.

Brandt, A. M. (1978). Racism and research: The case of the Tuskegee Syphilis Study. *The Hastings Center Report, 8*(6), 21–29.

Campo, R. (1997). *Desire to heal.* New York, NY: Norton.

Capino, J. (2006). Reading Asian pornography. In P. Lehman (Ed.), *Pornography: Film and Culture* (pp. 206–219). Rutgers, NJ: Rutgers University Press.

Carvajal, D. (2011, 7 March). The changing face of medical care. *New York Times.* Retrieved from http://www.nytimes.com/2011/03/08/world/europe/08iht-ffdocs08.html

Clover, C. (1993). *Men, women, and chainsaws: Gender in the modern horror film.* Princeton, NJ: Princeton University Press.

Conrad, P. (1992). Medicalization and social control. *Annual Review of Sociology, 18,* 209–232.

Cronenberg, D. (Director). (1988). *Dead ringers.* Canada: Morgan Creek Productions.

El Hai, J. (2007). *The lobotomist: A maverick medical genius and his tragic quest to rid the world of mental illness.* Hoboken, NJ: Wiley.

Foucault, M. (1985). *History of sexuality: Volume 1.* New York, NY: Vintage Press.

Foucault, M. (1994). *Birth of the clinic: An archaeology of medical perception.* New York, NY: Vintage Press.

Hall, S. (2009). Notes on deconstructing the popular. In J. Storey (Ed.), *Cultural theory and popular culture: A reader* (pp. 111–141). New York, NY: Pearson Longman Books.

Jenkins, H. (2003, 15 January). Transmedia storytelling: Moving characters from books to films to video games can make them stronger and more compelling. *Technology Review: MIT.* Retrieved from http://www.technologyreview.com/news/401760/transmedia-storytelling/

Jones, S. (2013). *Torture porn: Popular horror after saw*. London, United Kingdom: Palgrave.

Kapsalis, T. (1997). *Public privates: Performing gynecology from both ends of the speculum*. Durham, NC: Duke University Press.

Kelly, S. (2013, 27 February). Testing drugs on the developing world. *The Atlantic*. Retrieved from http://www.theatlantic.com/health/archive/2013/02/testing-drugs-on-the-developing-world/273329/

Kinkyfun81. So, has anyone ever been to a fetish clinic? Message board. Retrieved from http://www.zity.biz/docs/english/medfet/stories/examination-table.html

Kipnis, L. (2006). How to look at pornography. In P. Lehman (Ed.), *Pornography: Film and culture* (pp. 118–132). Rutgers, NJ: Rutgers University Press.

Lindemann, D. J. (2012). *Dominatrix: Gender, eroticism, and control in the dungeon*. Chicago, IL: Chicago University Press.

Maines, R. P. (2001). *Technology of orgasm: "Hysteria," the vibrator, and women's sexual satisfaction*. Baltimore, MD: Johns Hopkins University Press.

Mooncarrot. Patience bared. Retrieved from https://www.literotica.com/s/patience-bared

Mowlabocus, S. (2009). Porn 2.0? Technology, social practice and the new online porn industry. In F. Attwood (Ed.), *porn.com: Making sense of online pornography* (pp. 69–87). Digital Formations, Vol. 48. New York, NY: Peter Lang Academic Publishing.

Mulvey, L. (1975). Visual pleasure and narrative cinema. *Screen*, 16(3), 6–18.

Mulvey, L. (1989). *Visual and other pleasures*. Bloomington, IN: Indiana University Press.

Newmahr, S. (2011). *Playing on the edge: Sadomasochism, risk, and intimacy*. Bloomington, IN: Indiana University Press.

Patterson, Z. (2004). Going on-line: Consuming pornography in the digital era. In L. Williams (Ed.), *Porn Studies* (pp. 104–123), Durham, NC: Duke University Press.

Purcell, N. J. (2012). *Violence and the pornographic imaginary: The politics of sex, gender, and aggression in hardcore pornography*. London, United Kingdom: Routledge.

Sartin, J. S. (2004). J. Marion Sims, the father of gynecology: Hero or villain? *Southern Medical Journal, 97*(5), 500–505.

Sipos, T. M. (2010). *Horror film aesthetics: Creating the visual language of fear*. Jefferson, NC: McFarland Publishing.

Szasz, T. (2008). *The medicalization of everyday life*. Syracuse, NY: Syracuse University Press.

Taylor, E., & Curtis, J. (Producers), & Soska, J., & Soska, S. (Directors). (2012). *American Mary*. Canada: Universal Pictures.

Terwindt, C. (2014). Health rights litigation pushes for accountability in clinical trials in India. *Health and Human Rights Journal, 16*(2). Retrieved from http://www.hhrjournal.org/2014/11/06/health-rights-litigation-pushes-for-accountability-in-clinical-trials-in-india/

Veatch, R. (2008). *Patient heal thyself: How the new medicine puts the patient in charge*. New York, NY: Oxford University Press.

Webster, A., & Brown, N. (2004). *New medical technologies and society: Reordering life*. Cambridge, United Kingdom: Polity Press.

Weiss, M. (2011). *Techniques of Pleasure: BDSM and the Circuits of Sexuality*. Durham, NC: Duke University Press.

Williams, L. (1999). *Hard core: Power, pleasure, and the "frenzy of the visible"*. Berkeley, CA: University of California Press.

CHAPTER TWELVE

"I'M GOING TO STUMP YOU":
FETISH, CONFESSION AND THE TRANSFORMATIVE
POTENTIAL OF THE EROTIC CRIP BODY

Krista K. Miranda

"My name is Long Jeanne Silver and I'm handicapped and horny. Due to a quirk of nature I was born with a bigger dick than John Holmes, and Baby, you better believe I know how to use it" (*Long Jeanne Silver*, De Renzy, 1977). A terse drumbeat, a few rising notes from a synthesiser and a high-hat punctuate the declaration. This introductory statement repeats indefinitely as one settles in to watch the DVD. Silver's confession about the unique contours of her body is enigmatic, for the menu graphic shows three differently hued stills of a blue jean-clad Jeanne Silver cropped above the knees, keeping the nature of her "dick" a secret until a few minutes into the film.

Press play and you learn that this confession, which aligns Silver with legendary porn star John C. Holmes – infamous for his giant penis which broke porn records for length and girth – is itself foreplay, for you are immediately brought into a threesome including Silver, Amber Hunt and Joey Silvera with a disorienting close-up of a vulva, hands and a woman's thighs. There is no background music. Silver is the central figure, her left leg visible at the very edge of the frame, clothed in a blue sleeve and, when the camera pans back, a lower leg prosthetic. As the threesome continues with various forms of penetration, we rarely see any body in its entirety – at the very least, a head or a couple of limbs remain out of the frame. Only when the camera shoots the reflection of the scene through a mirror does the frame encompass all of the flesh involved. When Silvera says, "Let's take this off", removing Silver's prosthetic like the final layer of encumbering clothing, it is accompanied by a bouncy, highly synthesised soundtrack. Because of the cinematic techniques of tight cropping and abrupt editing, it is impossible to determine which body part belongs to whom. There is no steady build up to penetration – Silvera inside of Silver, Silver inside of Hunt – all sex acts are democratised with the pace of the editing. After the climax the camera rests on a tight frame of a trio of 'genitals': penis, vulva and stump.

Long Jeanne Silver (1977), directed by Alex DeRenzy, is a cult classic faux-documentary in the fringe genre of amputee fetish porn. American performer Jeanne Silver, born in Tempe, Arizona in 1960, was a burlesque performer, stripper and sex worker who made a name for herself in the world of pornography until she retired in her late twenties (see http://www.imdb.com/name/nm0798709/). Because the film is centred on the sexual life of an amputee, when 'crip' was a slur devoid of its positive appropriation in critical disability discourse – and the 'crip' in question uses her stump in an erotic capacity ('stump humping') with both men and women – the film was regarded as obscene and banned by the Canadian government for its portrayal of "'gomorrahy': the insertion of a hand, a foot, or the stump of a limb (i.e., the insertion of an extremity) into an intoitus/vagina or an anus/anal canal, for a sexual purpose" (Macinnis, 2011). With a quick web search, *Long Jeanne Silver* populates numerous lists of 'censored', 'obscene' or 'extreme' cinema. Acknowledging that censorship is a disciplinary tool, we must ask, what is so threatening about Jeanne Silver's crip sex? In *Dangerous Discourses of Disability, Subjectivity and Sexuality* (2012), Margrit Shildrick explores the anxiety that disability produces, especially disability in conjunction with sexuality, for "sexuality is already a dangerous discourse that threatens always to disrupt the smooth and predictable organization of social relations" (p. 7). Shildrick (2012) explains, "[d]isabled people ... endure broad cultural discrimination and alienation ... because their form of living in the body lays bare the psycho-social imaginary that sustains modernist understandings of what it is to be a subject" (pp. 1–2). Like Shildrick, I am invested in the ways disabled bodies, specifically in the context of crip sex, reveal and then undermine psycho-social fantasies of bodily life and subjecthood that masquerade as the natural order of things. One such psycho-social fantasy is that of bodily wholeness, a normative concept of embodiment that involves specific configurations of sex, gender, sexuality and ability. For a body to be considered 'whole' it must have the 'proper' configuration of parts that perform the 'proper' functions with associated (i.e. socially coded) meanings.

My analysis builds on crip theory, a critical disability studies discourse that argues for the exposure and corruption of presumptions of bodily 'truths' that perpetuate an able-bodied perspective that, among other things, values wholeness. In Robert McRuer's *Crip Theory: Cultural Signs of Queerness and Disability*, (2006) he describes the crip perspective as a radical expansion of typical affirmative approaches by disability activists. Unlike the identity-oriented work in disability studies, crip theory neither attempts to dissolve foundations of disability identity, nor primarily engages in identity politics. This chapter employs a crip perspective to illustrate how performances of disabled sexuality – especially in the context of pornography, where the audience is implicated by virtue of the pleasure, desire and interpellation such viewing practices elicit – demonstrate the 'partial', unpredictable nature of *all* bodily life. This examination of the mutability of the erotic body not only exposes the fundamental variability of meaning-laden bodily zones, but also reveals the productive performative effects of viewing pornography that features 'crip' performers. Linda Williams (2008) addresses the intensity of the performative force of witnessing bodily expressions (which may alert us to our inherent 'partiality', among other non-normative ways of being), for "[s]ex acts ... have also become ... qualitatively significant in how we learn to live our own sexualities" (p. 6). "Screening sex", Williams explains, does more than just arouse, it exposes bodies to new social-sexual worlds (2008, p. 18). In this chapter, I argue that the threat of watching Silver's queer-crip sex is the possibility that anyone who witnesses performances of embodiment that expose the fallacy of bodily wholeness will be interpellated into notions of embodiment and sexual expressions that are not hetero- and corporo- normative. Building on Michel Foucault's (1990) theory that sexuality is created through discourse, this analysis will place Foucault's call to employ the transformative power of bodies and pleasures in conversation with Sigmund Freud's (2006) theory of polymorphous perversity, where he discusses the malleable nature of erogenous zones, to examine the queerness of crip sex and explore how bodily variation, pleasure and desire remap the body, its meanings and its taxonomies for performers and witnesses alike. From a performance studies perspective, this critical disabilities studies approach to the embodied knowledges afforded by pornography not only reveals the ways queerness and cripness coalesce in 'disability sex', but also exposes the fundamental mutability of the erogenous body, thus making room for a conceptualisation of the body, any body, as always throbbing with the potential for refiguration and transformation.

On her official website, legendary performance artist and former porn star Annie Sprinkle discusses a photo shoot with her friend Jeanne Silver as the one time she was arrested:

"I'm Going to Stump You"

> I was at the home of my friends. ... We were putting together a little, avant-gardish, one shot sex magazine, with my diary excerpts and various photos ... We needed a typesetter, so we placed a help wanted ad in the local newspaper. Little did we know, we'd hired an undercover police woman who cheerfully worked side by side with us for a month. To create something extra special for the climax of my zine, my friend, amputee centerfold, Long Jean Silver came up from New York and we did a playful photo shoot, thoroughly enjoying each others bodies, including her penetrating me with her sexy 16" stump leg ... The moment our masterpiece was completed, twenty five state police (one third of their entire department) along with our 'typesetter', entered the house, guns drawn and pointed, wielding search and arrest warrants. Seems we had been under surveillance for a month, wire taps and all. We were charged with over a hundred felony counts combined; 'conspiracy to make and distribute obscene material', 'sodomy', and my personal favorite, 'conspiracy to commit sodomy.' In Rhode Island, sodomy is defined as 'an abominable, detestable act against nature,' which is apparently what some folks consider sex with amputees. My experience with Jean felt loving and liberating, and I assure you, nature was not offended at all. (Sprinkle, n.d.)

Long Jeanne Silver and the controversy that surrounds it is exemplary for its performance of bodily parts that, in a number of ways, do not conform to the erotic mappings of heteronormative embodiment. It is this 'atypical' use of bodily parts, I argue, that marginalise the film in an already marginalised genre of fetish pornography.

Tobin Siebers (2012) argues for "the power of disability as a crucial concept to defamiliarize how we think currently about sex", and therefore, how we think about bodies (p. 38). Because of the various shapes, capacities and debilities of people who fail to conform to able-bodied norms, disabled sexuality expands our notion of what qualifies as sex (Siebers, 2012). Siebers (2008) explains how impairments that may present themselves as limitations for sexual expression to a majority of the able-bodied population are simply challenges that encourage a more creative approach to the employment of the body, which ultimately enhances the repertoire of erotic activities and pleasures. The logistics of mobilisation and variations in sensitivity due to paralysis, nerve damage, amputation and congenital 'abnormalities' foster the inclusion of zones of the body that may be neglected in able-bodied sex, for they are not typically marked as erotic in the repertoire of sexual activity. Disabled sexuality therefore presents a transgressive organisation of the body that unfixes the normative, sexual signifiers from their typical, fleshy signifieds (Siebers, 2008).

"[W]hat ... would [it] mean, ontologically and ethically", Shildrick (2012) asks, to reposition dis/ability as the common underpinning of all human becoming?" (p. 10). The forms of corporeal experimentation Siebers discusses in disability sex, performed throughout *Long Jeanne Silver* with the creative use of Silver's stump, opens up the possibilities for "a sexual culture based on different conceptions of the erotic body, new sexual temporalities, and a variety of gendered and sexed identities", that, I argue, can be shared by everybody (Siebers, 2008, p. 148). Given that the disabled body in sex is often met with a combination of fascination and disgust, as illustrated by both the iconic status and controversy behind *Long Jeanne Silver*, this chapter adopts crip theory to analyse amputee fetish porn in order to expose "the arbitrary delineation between normal and defective and the negative social ramifications of attempts to homogenize humanity" (McRuer, 2006, p. 139). In her introduction to *Freakery: Cultural Spectacles of the Extraordinary Body* (1996b), Rosemarie Garland Thomson discusses how the "extraordinary body" of the disabled individual "is fundamental to the narratives by which we make sense of ourselves and our world" (p. 1). Historically, this sense-making is performed through securing the disabled subject as "other" to create the able-bodied norm. My examination of *Long Jeanne Silver*, however, illustrates how the disabled body in sex, spectacularised through pornography, actually undermines normative fantasies of embodiment like wholeness, an unachievable ideal for *any* body, for, it is precisely the "instability of the disabled body" that "far from being peculiar to that putative category, is simply a more acute instance of the instability of all bodies" (Shildrick, 2012, p. 35).

Susan M. Schweik's *The Ugly Laws: Disability in Public* (2009) examines the literal policing of 'abnormal' bodies with a historical account of the "unsightly beggar ordinances", commonly known as the "ugly laws", in major cities across the US, which began in the late 1800s and, although primarily unenforceable, still existed in some cities until the 1970s (p. vii). She asks: "What performances generate the kind of official politics that produce, and are produced by, something like an ordinance, and how … are those performances questioned and modified?" (Schweik, 2009, p. 290). This chapter argues that the censorship of crip sex, as well as the indictment of *Long Jeanne Silver* as particularly obscene even when framed as fetish pornography, is one such expression of modern day ugly laws that seek to secure the arbitrary divide between 'abnormal' and 'normal' bodies. Acts of censorship tell us there is something threatening about performing and witnessing these bodies, these acts. The threat, I argue, stems from the interpellative nature of such work. Mikita Brottman (2005) explains that "obscene" films often challenge "traditional culture's binarism of representation and participation, shattering those ideological boundaries that separate the presentation from the partaking" (p. 3). There is no passive witnessing when the body is centralised "because the very acts they involve embrace every body and every life" (Brottman, 2005, p. 3). The 'danger' of Jeanne Silver's body is not (life-threatening) danger per se, but the possibility that anyone who witnesses these performances will be interpellated into notions of embodiment and sexual expressions that are not hetero- and corporo- normative. And when are our bodies more vulnerable, more loaded with the weight of cultural norms – regarding sex, sexuality, gender, ableism, etc. – than during sex? Williams (2008) argues that "Sex acts – both graphic, as in pornography, and simulated, as in most mainstream movies and television, have also become … qualitatively significant in how we learn to live our own sexualities" (p. 6). Simply watching sex, therefore, has pedagogic possibilities. In other words, pornography is pedagogy.

Foucault (1990) argues that the history of sexuality should be depicted as a history of discourses, for "the essential features of … sexuality … correspond to the functional requirements of a discourse that must produce its truth" (p. 68). The discursive formulations that constitute sexuality involve the intersection of discursive examinations of the self through truth-telling, or confession, and scientific or medical investigations of the bourgeoisie subject (Foucault, 1990). Sexuality is the linchpin of various strategies of power-knowledge to articulate bourgeois identity (Foucault, 1990). While sexuality is centralised (but not essentialised), we must keep in mind the breadth of this discursive formation of the subject; attending to one's body and pleasures will affect more than just one's sexuality. Ladelle McWhorter (1999), building on Foucault, explains that sexuality is "the foundation of our subjectivity … [and as] such, sexuality must be seen as our most fundamental truth, and this in turn means that sexuality, as truth, both marks and occupies an epistemic field" (p. 11). With this in mind, exploring one's sexuality can be understood as experimenting with subjectivity itself. This is not to suggest that the self can simply be distilled to one's body or sexuality; McWhorter (1999), like Foucault, is a genealogist, not an essentialist – bodies, and the body's pleasures, have their own genealogies.

While *The History of Sexuality, Volume 1* (Foucault, 1990) does not lay out a specific set of practices to undermine various normalising regimes, Foucault does name the body as a "potential rallying point for radical politics" (p. 148), explaining the exploration of new forms of pleasure can open up our subjectivities to new possibilities, and therefore, new worldviews. The book's final gesture speaks to the transformative power of bodies and pleasures, which McWhorter terms Foucault's "*askeses* of pleasure" (1999, p. 177). McWhorter explains that pleasure for Foucault, "is not just a state of the body and/or mind that occurs following some particular accomplishment or stimulus. Pleasure is not just an outcome. Pleasure, like power, is creative" (1999, p. 177). Simply watching pleasure can be just as creative. This analysis of *Long Jeanne Silver* takes the creative power of pleasure seriously by looking at the performative force of pleasure in a variety of ways. Williams's discussion of the performative effects of "screening sex", the ways it "habituates" and "opens up" bodies to new social-sexual worlds, thus builds on Foucault's affirmation of pleasure's creative power (2008, p. 18). The "discipline" of sex and sexuality, Williams (2008) explains, does not have to be considered as workaday as the word implies, for we may also discipline ourselves to "play at sex" through both participation and the "mimetic faculty" of spectatorship (p. 18). Sex play as a viewer, then, "is a kind of tactile training that habituates viewers to adapt to changing environments" (Williams, 2008, p. 18).

Placing Foucault in conversation with Freud allows us to contemplate how attending to bodies and pleasures, playing with sex and watching others play at sex, can affect radical transformation both corporeally and ideologically. While Foucault's work on the discursive body (1990), at its surface, seems incongruent with psychoanalysis, this chapter illustrates how Foucault's notion of a body shaped through discourse speaks to both polymorphous perversity and fetish when the latter concepts are stripped of their developmental, ideological weight. After all, psychoanalytic concepts, like fetish and trauma, are part of a cultural understanding of oft-used vernacular that circulates as yet another discourse that shapes the erogenous body.

Freud's (2006) discussion of childhood sexuality and fetish in his "Three Essays" exposes the mutability of bodily signification, thus allowing for a conceptualisation of the body as unfixed and composed of movable, substitutable parts. Freud's promiscuous characterisation of erogenous zones, defined as locations "on the skin or mucous membrane where stimuli of a particular kind cause a sensation of pleasure of a particular quality" places depictions of fixed bodily mappings and meanings into question (2006, p. 160). Although Freud makes an argument for erogenous zones that are predetermined in some way, exemplified by the infantile predilection for thumb-sucking, he explains that the erogenous zone can attach itself, ostensibly, to other parts of the body. Since specific erogenous zones become preferred out of 'habit', the status of the genitals as the arbiters of sexual differentiation holds little sway. In a discussion of polymorphous perversity in children, Freud, attempting to explain the how and why of erogenous migration, argues that the relocation of value to different parts of the body can occur from environmental factors like seduction (2006). While the bodily mappings of childhood sexuality provide a perspective on one's experience of one's own body, Freud's discussion of fetish examines the mutability of how one values the body, or bodily parts, of another. Fetishisation, Freud admits, is a universal element of sexual life and involves "anatomical transgressions" where the individual is supplanted by a part of the body (foot, stump) or an inanimate object (shoe) closely associated with the sexual object (2006, p. 131). Since parts can be substituted for wholes, and associated objects are exchanged for 'the real thing', the bodily contours of the sexual object contract and expand through the libidinous interest of another. The erogenous body is transformational, but such transformations, although performed by and on the flesh, are not simply expressions of biological change.

Silver's sexuality is contoured by the conversations that reference both the history of her body in sex as well as her bodily history with medical and anatomical precision (*Long Jeanne Silver*, De Renzy, 1977):

> You were born with this?
>
> Yeah, I was born with a deformity. I have a missing fibula, and a pinky toe. And my left leg was shorter than the rest of the amputated one. I was about two and a half, so I've had it pretty much all my life.

Not only does the film's confessional format exemplify Foucault's emphasis on the function of truth-telling in the discursive formation of sexuality, but the "fetish" genre also allows us to witness how Freud's theory of parts and (w)holes plays out in practice. The way these parts play, in and out, allows us to put Tobin Siebers's discussions (2008, 2012) of 'disability sex' in conversation with Freud's theory of polymorphous perversity.

Publicised for *Long Jeanne Silver*'s 'freak show' appeal, the content on the back of the DVD (1977) boasts a day-in-the-life style exposé of the "exotic" sexual habits of a "pretty amputee" in a "documentary" format. Jeanne Silver's sexuality, because of the unique shape of her body, is framed as exceptional not because she has sex with both men and women; in the context of pornography driven by a female protagonist this performance of queerness is by no means unusual. Her body, specifically her stump used in a variety of creative yet unsurprising ways, shapes her queerness and the queerness of those with whom she has sex. After we are introduced to Silver's fleshy contours cinematically as a sum of her erotic parts, the film jumps to an aside with Silver speaking directly to us, incorporating the viewers into her erotic world as if sharing a video diary. Silver stands outdoors with teased hair, a rust-coloured, faux fur, waist-length jacket and skin-tight jeans: "School is a great place to find any kind of sexual adventure", she says, directly to camera:

> For instance, I have one boy who was in my art class ... He kind of turned me on a little bit ... So one day I just decided to ask him to come over to my house and grab a little snack and maybe talk a little bit and try to fool around a little bit before my mother would come home. (*Long Jeanne Silver*, De Renzy, 1977)

This dialogue combines three key concepts – schooling, sex and adventure – regarding the ways in which the erotic body is both understood and approached by the film: there is something experimental and pedagogical with the sex work and play of Jeanne Silver and her exceptional body as it is framed within the film's dialogue and press materials.

Before each sex scene, except for the first described above, Silver tells a story about her sexual exploits in an aside while fully dressed and outdoors. This narrative device strings together disparate sex scenes and serves as a truth-telling strategy to inform viewers about the (sexual) life of Jeanne Silver. The asides provide a confessional, matter of fact framework for Silver's character. She reveals nothing remarkable about the day-to-day manner in which she meets her sexual partners; however, the sex scenes offer a portrayal of the distinctive qualities of Silver's erotic life. Foucault (1990) discusses the important role of confession in the discursive formation of sexuality:

> What if sex in our society, on a scale of several centuries, was something that was placed within an unrelenting system of confession? The transformation of sex into discourse ... the dissemination and reinforcement of heterogeneous sexualities, are perhaps two elements of the same deployment: they are linked together with the help of the central element of a confession that compels individuals to articulate their sexual peculiarity – no matter how extreme. (p. 61)

The secret of Silver's erogenous body is treated like a gift, wrapped in the unassuming package of a pretty young thing in stylish, casual clothes, and a lower leg prosthetic that is not removed until everybody is sufficiently naked.

"I decided I wanted to get into these two little foxes that were in my sex education class. They were really naive though. They've hardly had any kind of sexual experiences" (*Long Jeanne Silver*, De Renzy, 1977). The following threesome between Silver and the two naive schoolgirls follows this pedagogical theme, for Silver "wanted to show them what it was like to be a woman". In the next scene Silver chats up the two young women, talking about a (real life) photo shoot she did for *Cheri*, a national sex magazine. Flipping through *Cheri*'s glossy pages, Silver talks them through the shoot, then pauses – "this is my centrefold" – at the picture of herself that serves as the cover of the DVD. "I've been told people freak out when people see it." She says she wants *Cheri* to send her the letters about the centrefold to find out people's reactions to it. She heard some people really liked it, "it was one of the best things they could have done. They have a certain type of fetish for it."

She pauses at another photo, narrating, "my friend Alda. She's going to give it a blow job there." Sex education indeed.

"Wow, like, is this the same size as a cock?"

"No it, uh, a little bit bigger." They laugh. "Yeah, slightly, I've been told I'm bigger than Johnny Holmes." Although these girls are purportedly naive, they laugh knowingly, as if familiar with Holmes and his sizeable penis. The young women press Silver to further expound on Silver's "dick"/"stump" conflation. She explains the advantages of stump fucking: because it doesn't ejaculate, no one needs to worry about "diseases" or pregnancy (*Long Jeanne Silver*, De Renzy, 1977).

To show them "what it's like to be a woman", Silver, seemingly unproblematically for her pupils, shows them her phallus. In "The Lesbian Phallus", Judith Butler (1993) uses Freud's 1914 essay "On Narcissism: An Introduction" to argue that "the ambivalence at the center of any construction of the phallus belongs to no body part, but is fundamentally transferable" (p. 62). This ambivalence, much like the transferable nature of erogenous zones, allows for the possibility that the phallus can be represented by other parts of the anatomy aside from the penis (Butler, 1993). Since the phallus can be symbolised by any bodily part, including a limb or a stump, then one must reconsider who anatomically 'has' possession of the phallus and its emblematic power, for the difference between the male 'having' and the female "lacking" predicates the symbolic order of sexual differentiation (Butler, 1993). Importantly, in the cultural imagination, this having/lacking dichotomy is also mapped on to an (albeit false) able-bodied/disabled binary, where people with disabilities, regardless of sex or gender, are constantly marked as lacking and therefore feminised (and infantilised) by this association. McRuer (2006) describes how this symbolic association of lack with sex, gender, sexuality, and ability are enmeshed with his assertion that "[c]ompulsory heterosexuality is intertwined with compulsory able-bodiedness; both systems work to (re)produce the able body and heterosexuality" (p. 31). The converse is also true, Shildrick (2012) explains: "Disability quite fundamentally performs a queering of normative paradigms" (p. 5). In other words, crip bodies, simply by virtue of their cripness, have queer sex.

The displacement of "having", Butler (1993) argues, is a theoretical move that would open "up anatomy – and sexual difference itself – as a site of proliferative resignifications" (p. 89). Not only would this anatomical displacement of the phallus allow for the lesbian 'having', but it also opens up the possibility for a reframing of 'lacking' in general. While Butler (1993) employs this argument for the conceptualisation of the lesbian phallus, I extend this symbolic capacity to include any body, regardless of sex, gender, sexuality or classification as able-bodied or disabled. As an amputee, in the cultural imagination of disability, Jeanne Silver's body is partial, lacking. As an anatomical female who has a vulva, her body is partial, lacking (a penis). However, if the phallus can be mapped on to other parts of the body, such as a fist or a stump, then the 'lack' that accompanies the body of an amputee, if understood in an erotic context and employed in a variety of creative ways, enables the phallic 'having'. Accordingly, Jeanne Silver's crip 'lack' redefines her gender/sex 'lack' into a form of 'having'. The capacity to both have and lack the phallus undermines not only the sex and gender binaries, but also thrusts the entire fantasy of bodily 'wholeness', emblematic of neoliberal ideologies that centralise the importance of autonomy and individuality, into a crisis of perpetual partiality, a partiality that is both part and whole, both has and lacks.

"Does it hurt?"

Pornographies

"Uh, I've heard, well, some people say it hurts but I'm usually really easy with it, you know, I don't want to hurt anybody" (*Long Jeanne Silver,* De Renzy, 1977). She explains the slow care she takes with "listening" to her partner's bodies, a capacity derived from her cripness because of the sensitivity of her stump.

Freud (2006) identified the phenomenon exhibited by Silver's sensitive and versatile phallus as polymorphous perversity. For a body part to be elevated to the heights of an erogenous zone, the nature of the body part itself (as genital or limb) is irrelevant; pleasure, and the repetition of this pleasure, makes it so (Freud, 2006). It should not come as a surprise that Silver has mapped her erogenous body through playing with sex to take into account the unique shape it acquired with the amputation of her lower leg as a child. Not only does she use her stump as a phallus, but she also derives pleasure from its muscles and nerves: "if someone tickles the end … it jumps" (*Long Jeanne Silver,* De Renzy, 1977). During the sex scenes when the central stimulative action involves Silver's stump, she too moans with pleasure.

After Silver explains that, yes, she even penetrates guys with her stump and after a series of giggles and back and forth about whether or not to go for it, Silver makes a claim for the value of experimentation: "It's always good to do new things right?" (*Long Jeanne Silver,* De Renzy, 1977). The scene abruptly cuts to the three woman already naked, "[giving] it a try" and ends with them giggling, feeling each other up, and jumping up and down on the bed, "playing at sex".

It is important to consider the reception of Silver's sexuality in terms of its portrayal in *Long Jeanne Silver* alongside viewer accounts of the film and its history of censorship on sites like *The Cultural Gutter* and *Alienated in Vancouver,* which focus on the 'extreme' of the 'obscene'. It is Silver's cripness and not her

"I'm Going to Stump You"

performed bisexuality that makes her queer (in the sense that her sexuality is beyond the pale) according to every review I have read of the film.

Consider this 'mainstream' eight out of ten star review on the Internet Movie Database:

> Long Jeanne has a phallic birth defect ... Meaning: A stump in the shape of a huge wang! Jeanne's stump is pretty repulsive, and yet kind of erotic at the same time. She waves it around throughout the film like a plucked chicken wing, but when she actually penetrates some poor miserable co-star, you have to fight your eyes to keep them from poppin' out of your head. (http://www.imdb.com/title/tt0178711/reviews)

In fact, the only one-on-one sex scene she has with a man, referenced in this review, which one would assume to be the most heteronormative of the bunch, pushes *Long Jeanne Silver*, albeit a work of fetish pornography, into the realm of what many at the time deemed to be downright unwatchable. During the sex scene that follows Silver's seduction of this somewhat hesitant red-headed gay boy (his gayness a noteworthy element of their casual, pre-sex chat), Silver unsurprisingly anally penetrates the young man with her stump. For some time this scene was deleted from the film altogether to facilitate its circulation in North America. Self-proclaimed "obscene" cinema connoisseur Robin Bougie (2006), posted the following regarding this particular scene online in *The Cultural Gutter*, "a website dedicated to thoughtful writing about disreputable art":

> According to exploitation film historian Johnny Legend, we're damn lucky to even see this scene. It seems [director] Mike Weldon ... had purchased the rights for the film from DeRenzy and couldn't figure out why when he tried to resell it, every potential buyer was balking at the halfway point during the screenings. Legend himself was put in charge of

editing out whatever it was that was scaring off potential customers.

At a time when male-on-male pornography did indeed exist, the elements that coalesced within this scene to make the film "unwatchable" is quite telling: anal penetration between a woman and a gay man by a portion of the (woman's) body not typically deemed part of the body's sexual geography. The use of her stump shapes her sexuality in a way that was, and perhaps still is, illegible to audiences in 1979 and the 1980s. That she is without a lower left leg and uses her stump, a body part not shared by the able-bodied majority, to give and receive pleasure is what, according to the discourse about the sex acts within and without the film, makes her sex particularly queer. It is not with *whom* she sleeps that makes her queer, it is *how* her crip body is eroticised and comes into contact with other bodies.

Returning to Silver's conversation with the young women about how she uses her stump on men (the men's queerness implied by their experience with anal penetration), Silver aligns fist fucking with stump fucking, which is critical when a term like "gomorrahy" circulates in legal and online "obscene" cinemaphile discourses. To censor and legislate (i.e. Annie Sprinkle's arrest in Rhode Island) on the basis of penetration with a body part that is not a genital illustrates a static understanding of the erotic body. In the "perverse" and therefore potentially divisive context of fringe pornography, what is so threatening about consensual stump fucking between a man and a woman? The press materials on the back of the DVD state: "Long regarded as one of the more bizarre films of the 1970's [sic] *Long Jeanne Silver* fulfills all expectations for those seeking a 'freak show' event!" (*Long Jeanne Silver*, De Renzy, 1977). According to Garland Thomson (1996a), freak shows "choreographed human variation into a spectacle of bodily otherness … [uniting] audiences in opposition to the freaks' aberrance ... [to] assure the onlookers that they were indeed 'normal'" (p. 17). The repetition of Silver's quote about her "quirk of nature" as a veritable soundtrack for the DVD's menu page immediately frames Silver's erotic body as otherly, as freakish. But does Silver's "monstrous body" truly "demarcate the borders of the generic"? (Garland Thomson, 1996a, p. 20).

Williams (2008) brings together the notions of interpellation, Foucauldian theory, and, I add, polymorphous perversity, stating, "through screening sex, our bodies are not simply shocked into states of arousal but habituated and opened up to this changing environment in newly socialized ways" (p. 18). Williams (2008) explains that this communal habituation, this slackening of normative rules of sexuality, is a social form of disciplining the body into fresh modes of arousal. Sex as an active participant, and "screening sex" as an always-active viewer, allows us to envision the transformative potential of the body when we consider its erotic capacities and the limitations culture attempts to adhere to it. If the queer-crip sex performed by Jeanne Silver's queer-crip body can open up the bodies of the viewers to a myriad of erogenous configurations and pleasures, then the function of the freak show, which secures the aberrant "other" at a safe distance from the onlooker, is dismantled; and "without the pathological to give form to the normal", Garland Thomson (1996a) states, "the taxonomies of bodily value that underlie political, social, and economic arrangements would collapse" (p. 20). *Long Jeanne Silver*, then, simultaneously participates in and undermines the freak show tradition. By virtue of the mimetic aspects of screening sex, her queerness and cripness, which are mutually implicated, are not safely cordoned off as "other" for the viewing subject. Sexing the body – regarding both the "making" of the sexual body (generally denoted via the male/female binary) and active sex-having and sex-watching – is indeed threatening if the fantasy of the body as fixed and autonomous is to be maintained. Jeanne Silver's erotic body and erotic life, therefore, are threats to normative taxonomies of bodily wholeness that underpin intelligible categories of sex, gender, sexuality and compulsory able-bodiedness. Sex education indeed.

References

Bérubé, M. (2006). Foreword. In R. McRuer's *Crip theory: Cultural Signs of Queerness and Disability* (pp. viii–xii). New York, NY: New York University Press.

Bougie, R. (2006). Long Jeanne Silver. *The Cultural Gutter*. Retrieved from http://theculturalgutter.com/movies-2/long_jeanne_silver.html

Brottman, M. (2005). *Offensive films*. Nashville, TN: Vanderbilt University Press.

Butler, J. (1993). The lesbian phallus and the morphological imaginary. In J. Butler, *Bodies that matter: On the discursive limits of "sex"* (pp. 57-91). New York, NY: Routledge.

De Renzy, A. (Director). (1977). *Long Jeanne Silver*. [DVD]. Oakland, United States: Alpha Blue Archives.

Foucault, M. (1990). *The history of sexuality, Volume 1: An introduction* (R. Hurley, Trans.). New York, NY: Vintage Books.

Freud, S. (2006). Three essays on the theory of sexuality. (S. Whiteside, Trans.). In *The Psychology of Love* (pp. 111–220). New York, NY: Penguin Books.

Garland Thomson, R. (1996a). *Extraordinary bodies*. New York, NY: Columbia University Press.

Garland Thomson, R. (1996b). Introduction: From wonder to error – a genealogy of freak discourse in modernity. In R. Garland Thomson (Ed.), *Freakery: Cultural spectacles of the extraordinary body* (pp. 1–19). New York, NY: New York University Press.

Macinnis, A. (2011). Extreme and censored cinema, plus a word I learned tonight: "Gomorrahy." *Alienated in Vancouver*. Retrieved from http://alienatedinvancouver.blogspot.com/search?q=long +jeanne+silver

McRuer, R. (2006). *Crip theory: Cultural signs of queerness and disability*. M. Bérubé, Forward. New York, NY: New York University Press.

McWhorter, L. (1999). *Bodies & pleasures: And the politics of sexual normalization*. Bloomington, IN: Indiana University Press.

Schweik, S. M. (2009). *The ugly laws: Disability in public*. New York, NY: New York University Press.

Shildrick, M. (2012). *Dangerous discourses of disability, subjectivity and sexuality*. London, United Kingdom: Palgrave Macmillan.

Siebers, T. (2008). *Disability theory*. Ann Arbor: University of Michigan Press.

Siebers, T. (2012). A sexual culture for disabled people. In R. McRuer & A. Mollow (Eds.), *Sex and disability* (pp. 37–53). Durham, NC: Duke University Press.

Sprinkle, A. (n.d.). My brushes and crushes with the law *Anniesprinkle.org(asm)*. Retrieved from http://anniesprinkle.org/my-brushes-and-crushes-with-the-law

Williams, L. (2008). *Screening sex*. Durham, NC: Duke University Press.

INDEX

A

ableism, 294
Active Duty, 16, 220, 234–237
addiction, 1, 55, 76
advertising 14–15, 91, 144, 147, 148, 167–173, 178, 180, 183, 186–188, 200
agony aunts (see sexperts)
AIDS (see also HIV), 17–18, 222, 231–233, 242–255, 257, 261–262
amateur, 7, 50, 51, 52, 56, 131, 194–195, 210–215, 225, 256, 264, 267
amputee pornography, 3, 19, 288, 291, 292, 297, 301
anti-anti debate, 7
anus (see rectum)
audiences, 1, 3, 16, 18, 121, 143, 153, 160, 170, 180, 181, 183, 184, 204, 304
authenticity, 15–16, 49–50, 54, 59–63, 126, 131, 133–134

B

barebacking, 3, 17–18, 221, 224, 230, 231, 233, 243–245, 249–255, 257, 258, 261
Barnard Conference, 25–26, 32
Barthes, Roland, 220–222, 224
Baudrillard, Jean, 18, 206, 214
Benjamin, Walter, 18, 243, 249, 254–255, 261

Bersani, Leo, 18, 243, 245–249, 253, 258
BDSM
    bondage and discipline, 18, 52, 88, 145, 150, 278
    dominance and submission, 128, 266, 274–275, 279
    sadomasochism, 29–31, 224
biomedical discourse, 18, 38, 41, 266, 268–270, 280, 282, 304
bisexuality, 23, 38, 41, 303
Black and Minority Ethnic, 41, 177, 179–180, 202, 231
body art (see also tattoos), 16
Breeden, 17, 244, 255–261
Breeding Season (and sequels), 253, 257–261
Bright, Susie, 53–54
burlesque, 73, 288
Butler, Judith, 42, 60, 300–301

C

Canadian case law, 117, 128
capitalism, 6, 87
Carl's Jr., 14, 167, 171–175, 177–179, 187–188
celebrity, 116, 119, 123, 134, 167, 181, 183, 188, 207, 228
censorship, 7, 10, 23, 25, 26, 28, 29, 30–31, 32, 37–38, 40, 42–43, 146, 148, 288, 293, 302

Index

Chevalier, Vincent, 3, 17, 244, 255–262
Christianity, 29, 222
Cody, Sean, 16, 220, 227–230
Comay, Rebecca, 18, 243, 244–247
comics (see also manga), 51–52, 63, 145, 147, 149
condomless sex (see barebacking)
costumes, 11, 89, 209
cougar, 14, 174–177
crip sex, 288–290, 293, 305
crip theory, 289, 292
Cruisin' the Castro, 17, 251–252
culinary culture, 14–15, 168, 170, 180, 187–188

D

Daily Mail, 105, 111, 112
deviancy, 147
dirty food (see also junk food), 167, 170–171, 175, 182
disabled sexuality (see also crip sex and crip theory), 289, 291–292
doctor-patient roles, 18
documentary, 3, 17, 205, 215, 244, 255–256, 259, 288, 297
DVD, 56, 122, 153, 287, 297, 299, 304, 305
Dworkin, Andrea, 1, 4–5, 9, 27–29, 30, 34, 36, 39, 39–40, 169, 178

E

empowerment, 2, 6, 9, 13, 15, 72, 97, 104, 117, 156, 169, 170, 172, 173, 174, 179, 185, 186, 188, 234, 271, 279
eromanga (see manga)
erotica (see also *Fifty Shades of Grey*), 50–51, 53, 60, 61, 63, 143, 149, 153, 270
explicit art, 3, 100

F

family, 126, 154–155, 204, 206, 276
female pornographers, 5, 12–13, 61, 117, 122–123, 125
feminism
    anti-censorship feminism, 7, 10, 23, 25, 26, 32, 40, 42, 43, 148
    anti-porn feminism, 5, 24–28, 29–31, 32, 35, 36–37, 38, 40, 41, 42–43
    lesbian feminism, 23, 30, 31, 32, 33
    postfeminism, 6, 11, 12, 70–73, 77–78, 80, 82, 86, 91, 92, 116–119, 123, 126–127, 129–131, 133–134, 167–168, 169, 171, 172, 177–179, 180–188

radical feminism, 23, 31, 32–33, 39, 141, 155, 157, 186
sex-positive feminism, 9, 23, 24
feminist art, 12, 30, 106
feminist pornography, 5, 49, 53–54, 59–60, 62, 112, 116–117
Feminist Porn Awards, 54
fetish clinic, 18, 265–266, 271–283
fetish cultures, 3, 8, 275
fiction 50, 51, 56, 60, 62, 258, 259
Fifty Shades of Grey, 49, 63, 88
First Amendment, 29
Fluxus movement, 101
Foucault, Michel, 74, 119–120, 268, 290, 294–297, 299, 305
freak (see also crip theory), 19, 292, 297, 299, 304–305

G

Garland Thomson, Rosemarie, 292, 304–305
gay for pay, 3, 16–17
gay porn (see also queer pornographies), 220–223, 225–226, 227, 229–234, 237–238, 256
gender
    bias, 276
    differences, 79
    division, 10
    ideology, 154, 156, 159
    inequality, 77, 96, 102
    intimacy, 74, 92
    norms, 2, 13, 155, 180
    queer, 61
    reinforcement, 39
    relations, 33, 92
    representation, 64
    roles, 109, 133, 157, 159
    sexuality, 11, 13, 19, 33–35, 42–43, 148, 289, 292, 294, 300
Gill, Rosalind, 6, 12, 72–73, 77, 83, 86–89, 92, 118, 126, 128, 129, 133, 135, 167, 169, 172–173, 179, 188
girl boss films, 144, 156–157
gomorrahy, 288, 304
gustatory pleasure, 14, 167, 172–174, 177, 183–185, 187

H

hard-core pornography, 5, 8, 14, 15, 16, 19, 60, 74, 236
health, 1, 3, 5, 40, 107, 124, 204, 234, 265–266, 271, 273, 277, 281
heteronormative, 1, 3, 6, 10, 13, 16, 18, 24, 38, 77, 78, 134, 173–174, 180, 184, 187, 194, 196, 201–204, 208–210, 248, 291, 303
heteronormativity, 208
historical understandings of porn, 10, 17–18, 27–30, 149, 159
HIV (see also AIDS), 222, 224, 231–233, 247, 252, 254–255
Holmes, John C., 287, 300

Index

homophobia, 17, 41, 221, 229, 238
'hot lesbians' (see lesbian stereotypes)
Hustler, 193, 195, 197, 199–202, 204, 213–214
Hustler Video, 15

I

identity, 5, 6, 15, 17, 33, 35, 51, 59, 97, 176, 226, 227, 230, 238, 249, 256, 275, 289, 294
ideology, 28, 34, 35, 42, 117–118, 154, 159, 193
Internet (see also online forums), 43, 56, 75, 96, 98, 106, 122, 130, 152, 264–266
interviews, 12–13, 210
   with participants, 57, 74,
   with porn stars, 117, 120–125, 127, 130–133, 222

J

Japanese pornographies, 14, 51–52, 63, 141–144, 145–148
Jenkins, Casey, 3, 11–12, 96–97, 99–100, 103–104, 105–113
junk food, 170

K

Kardashian, Kim, 171
kink (see fetish cultures), 64, 88, 266–267, 269, 272, 277–280, 282, 283

L

Lady Snowblood, 143, 145, 153
Lakshmi, Padma, 15, 177–180, 181, 183–184, 188
Lawson, Nigella, 14, 167, 181–182, 184–185, 188
lesbian feminism (see feminism)
lesbian stereotypes, 14, 171–174, 175, 177, 200
libertarianism, 23–26, 29, 36, 38, 40, 41, 44
Long Jeanne Silver, 19, 287–306

M

MacKinnon, Catherine, 4, 28, 30, 33
mainstream pornography, 2, 12, 14, 176, 202
male gaze, 13, 38, 39, 168–169, 172–174, 176–178, 180, 184, 187–188, 270
male partners' use of porn, 11, 70, 74, 85
manga, 51–52, 63, 145, 147, 149
masculinity, 16, 61, 80, 203, 208, 223, 232–233
medical pornography, 3, 18, 264–265, 267–270, 282
Meese Commission, 29
MILF, 16, 174, 194, 201, 209, 213
Minneapolis Ordinance, 27–29
misogyny, 133–134, 193, 196, 277

N

neoliberalism, 6, 12, 13, 70–73, 77, 79, 83–84, 86–88, 92, 117–118, 130, 301
neo-Nazism (see also white supremacy), 17, 221, 234, 236–237
New Explicit, 12, 96–104, 108, 111–113
Nigella (see Lawson, Nigella)
Nikkatsu film company, 142, 143, 144, 151

O

obscenity, 28, 104, 128, 146
online forums, 11, 74–76, 78–91, 104, 122, 234, 236
Orientalism, 14, 148, 179, 184

P

Palin, Sarah, 15–16, 193–197, 198–204, 209–213
paratext 117, 120–121, 133, 134
pedagogy, 7–8, 18, 244, 262, 294, 298, 299
penis, 225, 226, 228, 245, 246, 287, 288, 300, 301
performance artists, 3, 11–12, 99, 101–104, 290–291
pinky violence, 13–14, 141–153, 156, 157, 159–160
Playboy, 171–172, 182, 200
politicians, 15, 29, 157, 193–213
pornification, 3, 43, 70, 71, 116, 149, 196, 205

pornonormativity, 2
pornosphere, 2, 14, 15
pornresearch.org, 56–57
porn stars, 12, 61, 72, 116–135, 226–227, 231, 234, 258, 287–288, 290
porn studies, 2, 3–4, 7–9, 14, 49, 55, 59–64, 148
Porn Studies (journal), 7
postfeminism (see also sexual subjectification), 6, 11, 12, 70–73, 77–78, 80, 82, 86, 91, 92, 116–119, 123, 126–127, 129–131, 133–134, 167–168, 169, 171, 172, 177–179, 180–188
pre-condom pornography (see also barebacking), 17, 250–252, 254
public health, 5

Q

queer pornographies, 3, 6, 16, 17, 50, 59, 61, 243

R

race (see also Black and Minority Ethnic and white), 59, 210, 213, 231
Rancière, Jacques, 195, 211–212
rape, 28, 29, 36, 39, 43, 52, 81, 142, 146, 148, 281
rectum, 244–247, 254, 258
revenge porn, 1–2, 142, 156

Index

S

sadomasochism (see BDSM)
Sean Cody (see Cody, Sean)
second-wave feminism, 4, 155, 186–187
Second World War, 149, 151
self-esteem/self-confidence, 11, 83–86
semiotics, 220, 221, 238, 270
sex industry, 1, 35, 39–40, 72, 92, 124, 265
sex-positive feminism (see feminism)
sexperts, 11, 54, 87
sexual behaviour, 5, 247
sexualisation of culture (see pornification)
sexual objectification, 12, 13, 33–34, 72–73, 118, 146, 148, 168, 178, 184
sexual subjectification, 6, 12, 13, 17–18, 81, 118, 168–171, 177–181, 184, 187–188
sexual violence, 14, 27, 30, 33, 34, 49, 147, 229
sex wars, 9, 23–26, 32–33, 36, 41–43
sex work, 13, 23, 40–41, 72, 259, 288, 298
Shildrick, Margrit, 288–289, 292–293, 301
soft-core pornography (see also erotica), 13–14, 142–144, 168, 169, 174, 185, 186, 186, 187–188
spicy other, 14
Sprinkle, Annie, 11, 12, 54, 61, 99, 102–103, 108, 111, 112, 113, 290–291, 304
study of porn (see porn studies)
subculture, 227, 231, 264
surgery, 276–277

T

tattoos (see also body art), 16–17, 220–227, 230–238
teaching of porn (see pedagogy)
The Feminist Porn Book, 5, 59
Tōei film company, 143–145, 152
trauma, 18, 242–247, 296

U

Upton, Kate, 167, 171

V

vagina, 11–12, 97, 100–105, 281, 288
vaginal knitting, 11–12, 100, 103, 105
video art, 17, 244, 255
violence against women (see sexual violence)
voices, 2, 5, 12, 13, 43, 117, 122, 128, 131, 132

W

webcams, 131
white, 17, 41, 60, 103, 134, 193, 196, 199, 201, 202, 203, 205, 210, 213, 231, 234–236
    white supremacy (see also neo-Nazism), 17, 234–236
Who's Nailin' Paylin?, 15–16, 193–194, 197, 199, 200–205, 207, 213–215
Williams, Linda, 7–9, 60, 98, 133, 142, 201, 202, 290
women
    as consumers of pornography 5, 13, 49, 50–52, 55, 56, 59, 62–64, 99
    and domesticity, 13, 49–51, 63, 154, 159, 160, 167, 170, 181, 183–188
    as producers of pornography, 6, 13, 49, 54, 61, 74, 111
Women Against Pornography (WAP), 26
women's magazines, 11, 71, 74, 78, 79, 84, 91, 92

Y

yaoi (see manga)

Z

zero design, 15–16, 193–195, 197–198, 204–206, 207, 209, 211–215